EPISTEMIC JUSTIFICATION

Epistemic Justification

RICHARD SWINBURNE

CLARENDON PRESS · OXFORD
2001

OXFORD
UNIVERSITY PRESS
Great Clarendon Street, Oxford OX2 6DP

Oxford University Press is a department of the University of Oxford.
It furthers the University's objective of excellence in research, scholarship,
and education by publishing worldwide in

Oxford New York
Athens Auckland Bangkok Bogotá Buenos Aires Cape Town
Chennai Dar es Salaam Delhi Florence Hong Kong Istanbul Karachi
Kolkata Kuala Lumpur Madrid Melbourne Mexico City Mumbai
Nairobi Paris São Paulo Shanghai Singapore Taipei Tokyo Toronto Warsaw

and associated companies in Berlin Ibadan

Oxford is a registered trade mark of Oxford University Press
in the UK and in certain other countries

Published in the United States
by Oxford University Press Inc., New York

First published 2001

British Library Cataloguing in Publication Data
Data available

Library of Congress Cataloging in Publication Data
Swinburne, Richard.
Epistemic justification/Richard Swinburne.
p. cm.
Includes bibliographical references and index.
1. Justification (Theory of knowledge) I. Title.
BD212.S95 2001 121—dc21 2001016291

ISBN 0–19–924378–6
ISBN 0–19–924379–4 (pbk)

1 3 5 7 9 10 8 6 4 2

Typeset by Hope Services (Abingdon) Ltd.
Printed in Great Britain
on acid-free paper by
T.J. International Ltd.
Padstow, Cornwall

PREFACE

This book is intended to serve as a guide to the different accounts of epistemic justification (that is the justification of belief) and knowledge current in the philosophical literature, as well as primarily to provide an answer to the somewhat neglected but all-important question of which kinds of epistemic justification are worth having. I distinguish (as most writers do not) between synchronic justification (justification at a time) and diachronic justification (synchronic justification based on adequate investigation). I argue that most kinds of justification that have been advocated are worth having because beliefs justified in most of these various ways are probably true, although only justification of an 'internalist' kind can be of any use to a person in deciding how to act. The probability calculus is useful in elucidating what makes beliefs probably true, but it requires every proposition to have an intrinsic probability (an a priori probability independent of empirical evidence) before it can be used to elucidate the force of empirical evidence in increasing or decreasing that probability. I claim that every proposition does indeed have an intrinsic probability.

As philosophical discussion of these issues can get very complicated (in my view quite unnecessarily complicated), I have relegated all discussions of the finer points of current theories and of objections to my own views, as well as all very technical points involving the probability calculus, to an Appendix and a series of Additional Notes. This will, I hope, enable the main text to be readily comprehensible by the average undergraduate taking a course on epistemology, while providing in the notes and appendix the fuller discussion of the issues rightly required by more expert readers.

A few of the ideas contained here were originally put forward in somewhat different and less satisfactory ways in parts of my *An Introduction to Confirmation Theory* (Methuen, 1973) and in the first two chapters of my *Faith and Reason* (Clarendon Press, 1981). I have used in the present book also in a substantial way material from three more recent publications: *Simplicity as Evidence of Truth* (Marquette University Press, 1997—my Aquinas Lecture at Marquette University), 'Predictivism' (in *Trames*, 1 (1997), 99–108), and 'Many Kinds of Rational Theistic Belief' (in G. Brüntrup and R. K. Tacelli (eds.), *The Rationality of Theism* (Kluwer Academic Publishers, 1999)). I am grateful to the publishers of these items for permission to reuse the material. I have given lectures and classes on this topic several times in recent years, and many thanks to those who heard me for many useful comments (especially to Elizabeth Fricker, with whom I gave a class on epistemic justification at Oxford in 1998). I am very grateful to various other people who have also provided comments on individual points or general comments—Paul Davies, Deborah Mayo, Timothy Williamson, and Sarah Coakley. I am especially grateful to William Alston and Michael Sudduth, who provided detailed comments on many chapters, and above all to Robert Audi, who provided large numbers of comments on more than one draft of the book. And very many thanks to those who typed draft after draft of the book—Mrs Lan Nguyen and Mrs Chio Gladstone.

CONTENTS

Introduction

My beliefs are true if (and only if) things are as I believe them to be. My belief that the earth revolves annually round the sun is true if (and only if) the earth does revolve annually around the sun. But my beliefs are ones that I am justified in holding if in some sense they are well grounded; if in some sense I have reason for believing that they are true. My belief that Brutus killed Caesar is one that I am justified in holding if I read in a history book commended to me by someone who is or who I believe to be a Professor of Ancient History that Brutus killed Caesar. Not all justified beliefs are true—the evidence (even the evidence available to a Professor of Ancient History) may indicate that Brutus killed Caesar, although in fact he did not. This book has as its major concern, what it is for a belief to be justified. More precisely, it is concerned with what it is for someone to be 'justified' at a certain time in holding some belief—which I shall take as equivalent to their belief (at that time) being 'justified'. Beliefs that are true often amount to knowledge—especially if they are justified beliefs, but not always then and perhaps not only then. This book has as its other concern, what is the difference between my believing truly that Brutus killed Caesar, and my knowing it.

'Justification' is a central notion in contemporary epistemology in the analytic tradition. Epistemologists are concerned with the kind of justification that is indicative of truth. There is a sense in which one is justified in believing one's husband to be faithful, even when the evidence suggests that he is not—because of the instrumental value of having that belief (quite independently of whether or not it is true) in helping one to continue to live happily or to love one's children. But justification of that kind is not my concern. My concern is with the kind of justification a belief has, when in some way or other that is indicative of its truth.

Twentieth-century philosophers have spent a lot of time trying to analyse what it is for a belief to be justified, and they have given some very different accounts, the great divide being between internalist and externalist accounts. An internalist theory of justification is one that analyses a person's belief being 'justified' in terms of factors accessible by introspection to that person—for example, it being supported by that person's other beliefs. An externalist theory of justification is one that analyses a person's being 'justified' in terms of factors of which the subject may be unavoidably ignorant—for example, in terms of whether the belief is produced by a reliable process, that is, one that usually produces true beliefs. Some of these philosophical accounts of justification are extremely complicated, and yet very different from each other. Analysing what it is for a belief to be 'justified' typically consists in reflection on many (actual or imaginary) cases of beliefs that we (almost) all agree to be 'justified', and on many cases of beliefs in many ways similar to the former but that we (almost) all agree not to be 'justified', and producing a general formula analysing what it is for a belief to be justified, which yields and plausibly explains the result that the former are all justified and the latter all not justified. Such a formula would enable us to resolve many disputed cases of whether certain beliefs were justified.

The trouble is that there is rather a large range of kinds of actual and possible beliefs about which the intuitions of philosophers and ordinary speakers of the language differ as to whether or not they are 'justified', and the various internalist and extremalist accounts give different answers as to whether those beliefs are justified. This will be illustrated abundantly in the first eight chapters of the book. There are great differences between these accounts, and they have become equally complex in the attempt to make them yield even the answers about which we agree as to whether some particular belief is 'justified'. What all this suggests is that there is no good reason to suppose that the various internalist and externalist accounts are in general rival accounts, one at most of which is the true account, of a univocal concept.[1] The notion of a belief being 'justified' is far too unclear, and the intuitions of philosophers and more generally speakers of ordinary language about when a belief is 'justified' are far too diverse for it to be plausible to suppose that they are analysing one concept that we all share, and that adding even more details to some proposed analysis will eventually yield the true analysis of this concept of 'justification'. Rather, these philosophers are giving accounts of different kinds of justification. My aim is to distinguish these kinds, to show how they are related to each other, how a belief being 'justified' in these different ways is for different reasons indicative of its truth, and then to proceed to the deeper issue of which of these kinds of justification is worth having.

[1] As Alston has urged recently. See W. P. Alston, 'Epistemic Desiderata', *Philosophy and Phenomenological Research*, 53 (1993), 527–51.

It should not be surprising that the notion of a belief being 'justified' is ambiguous, for the notion of an action being morally 'justified' is ambiguous and in a respect paralleled in the case of belief. Suppose abortion is wrong but that Jane does not believe that it is wrong. Is she justified in having an abortion? No, in an objective sense, for (we have supposed) abortion is wrong. But yes, in the subjective sense that she is not blameworthy for having an abortion, for she did not believe it wrong. We shall see that there are objective and subjective senses of the justification of belief—but in this case more than one objective and more than one subjective sense.

Most contemporary theories of justification are theories of what it is for a belief to constitute a justified response to the situation in which the believer finds herself at a given time. I shall call such theories theories of synchronic justification. I contrast these with theories of diachronic justification, which are theories of what it is for a belief to constitute a justified response to adequate investigation over time.

My concern with knowledge is a concern with knowledge-that (as opposed to knowledge-how—for example, knowledge how to ride a bicycle; and to knowledge of persons and things—for example, knowing John. It may be that these can be analysed in part in terms of knowledge-that.) We know that 7+5=12 and that William the Conqueror invaded England in 1066. Almost all writers assume that an analysis of ordinary-language uses of the word 'know' shows it to involve true belief. If we know something, we believe it and that belief is true. Granted, there are odd uses of the English word 'know' where this assumption does not seem to hold. We might speak of ancient peoples 'knowing' that the earth is the centre of the universe (when of course it is not). But it is natural to enclose the word 'knowing' in this context in quotation marks, to indicate that we are talking, not about what they knew, but about what they claimed to know. Really, it is natural to say, they did not know that the earth was the centre of the universe, although they claimed to do so. Slightly more naturally, we may speak of someone knowing something, although they did not believe it. We may speak of the unconfident examinee as knowing the answer to a question since he wrote it down, yet not really believing that that was the answer. But we feel that there is something paradoxical about this claim—either the examinee did not know the answer, he was merely guessing (and so lucky to guess correctly); or he did know it and so believe it—although he wrote it down with such hesitation that it did not look as if he believed it. Because suggested counter-examples to the assumption that knowledge involves true belief, seem to use English in odd ways that we can understand only by analysing them in ways that involve the assumption, I shall go along with that assumption. The issue is whether conceptual analysis of ordinary language can take us much further. For the extra needed to turn true belief into knowledge I shall use the technical term of 'warrant'.[2] Knowledge is warranted true belief. Warrant is not, we shall see, the same as justification, although there was a time when philosophers supposed that it is (that knowledge is simply justified true belief), and although justification may be involved in warrant. But the issue is whether our concept of knowledge is a clear enough one for analysis of ordinary language to provide a clear account of warrant.

The prospects for providing a clear account of warrant might certainly seem brighter than the prospects for a clear account of justification. There is a very large range of (actual and imaginary) examples of people who have in certain circumstances a true belief that such-and-such who, we (almost) all agree, know that such-and-such; and of examples of people who are in circumstances not greatly different who have a true belief that such-and-such but who, we (almost) all agree, do not know that such-and-such. And the range of disputed cases—actual and possible cases of true beliefs about which the intuitions of philosophers and ordinary speakers of the language differ as to whether they are cases of knowledge—is, I believe, much smaller than it is in the case of justification. So the prospects for a satisfactory analysis seem good.[3] It then becomes puzzling why philosophers have given as many very different and equally complicated accounts of warrant as they have of justification (some of them totally externalist, some of them largely internalist), which leads to a similar suspicion that there is no one univocal concept of knowledge involved. The different accounts arise because there is still a range of disputed cases (as I shall illustrate in Chapter 8), and the accounts provide formulae of very different kinds that all yield the answers that we give as to whether someone knows such-and-such in the agreed cases, but disagree in their verdicts about the answers for the cases about which we differ in our intuitive judgements. The formulae extrapolate from paradigm examples of knowing and not knowing in different directions. There are in consequence different kinds of warrant, and so of knowledge; and what needs to be explained is why these very different

[2] This definition of 'warrant' is that given on p. 3 of Alvin Plantinga, *Warrant: The Current Debate* (Oxford University Press, 1993). On the following page he introduced a slightly more complicated definition. 'Warrant' is defined there as a 'quantity that comes in degrees, enough of which is what distinguishes knowledge from mere true belief'. I shall not adopt this more complicated definition.

[3] Thus Alston: 'I think there is a much stronger case for a more or less determinate pre-theoretic conception of knowledge that we can use to locate our subject matter, than is the case with justification, or rationality' ('Epistemic Desiderata', 538 n. 15).

formulae in general yield the same results as to whether or not some true belief constitutes knowledge, why the range of disputed cases is as small as it is. I shall seek to explain why this is in Chapter 8 in the course of tracing the relations between these kinds of warrant, and considering which of them are worth having.

My concern is with analyses of the contemporary use of 'justified' belief and 'knowledge'—and not of course just with the use of the English words, but since—I believe—most other languages have words with similar roles, with the concepts picked out in different languages by words that translate the English words. But I need to make the point that these concepts have not always been the ones in which philosophers of the past have been interested. Philosophers have always been interested in a concept of 'knowledge', or in a concept delineated in their language by a word translated—perhaps unavoidably—as 'knowledge'. They have always been interested in what 'knowledge' is and what kinds of thing we can 'know'. But that interest seems often to have been an interest in a concept far narrower in one or both of two ways than our modern ordinary language concept.

Philosophers of the ancient and medieval West held that you only had ἐπιστήμη or *scientia* that something was so if not merely in our sense did you know it, but you understood why it was so. In *Meno* Plato tells us through the mouth of Socrates that true opinion plus αἰτίας λογισμός—the working-out of an explanation—is what constitutes ἐπιστήμη.[4] ἐπιστήμη is perhaps just as naturally translated 'understanding' as it is translated 'knowledge'. But it was translated into Latin as *scientia* and the most natural translation for that is certainly 'knowledge'. So translated, the typical objects of knowledge are theorems of mathematics or some event whose explanation in terms of the principles of science we have grasped—according to philsophers of the ancient and medieval West. Mere observed contingent facts (for example, 'that today it is sunny here') were not objects of knowledge, but only of true belief.

Philosophers of the modern West, from Descartes until very recent years, have tended to confine 'knowledge' in a different way. You could only 'know' that something was so if your knowledge (in our ordinary sense) was infallible or at any rate (in some sense) not too far off that, let us say, almost certain. 'All [*scientia*] is certain and evident cognition',[5] wrote Descartes in discussion of his Second Rule for the Direction of the Mind. Hence the empiricist philosophers of the eighteenth century tended to

[4] *Meno* 98a.

[5] *The Philosophical Writings of Descartes*, trans. J. Cottingham, R. Stoothof, and D. Murdoch, i (Cambridge University Press, 1985), 10.

confine knowledge to the evident principles of logic or the immediate deliverances of sense—either our sensory states ('I am now in pain', 'there is such-and-such a pattern of colour in my visual field') or immediately observable physical objects and their states, and to propositions evidently deducible from these. Locke claimed that we had knowledge of our 'ideas' and their logical relations to each other, and as regards 'the real actual existence of things', 'we have an intuitive knowledge of our own existence, and a demonstrative knowledge of the existence of God; of the existence of anything else, we have no other but a sensitive knowledge, which extends not beyond the objects present to our senses'.[6] And even early in the twentieth century Prichard claimed that 'it seems impossible to distinguish the meaning of knowing and being certain'.[7]

Ordinarily, however, we do not confine the scope of knowledge to what we think we can explain or to what we think certain in the sense of that of which we have an almost infallible awareness. We claim to know what we did years ago, or what happened in ancient history. I shall be concerned to see what is meant by our ordinary claims to know such things.

Ancient, medieval, and early modern philosophers considered that, if we could not have knowledge, all we could have was δόξα (*opinio*), belief, and they were not on the whole very interested in that. Knowledge was what they wanted.[8] They did, of course, allow that in some sense various opinions that did not amount to knowledge were better supported than others. They argued in particular cases that this scientific theory was to be preferred to that one, and this witness was to be preferred to that one. But they had no general theory as to what made one theory or witness preferable to another. Nor did they have a general concept for the kind of support that witnesses or authorities or physical events gave to some theory—the concept of making it probable.[9] And, hence, they had no measure for that kind of support. So any notion of a 'justified' belief was of the vaguest of kinds. But with the empiricist tradition of philosophy in the seventeenth and eighteenth centuries, it suddenly became a commonplace that very few of our beliefs were not open to some possibility of error, and the important

[6] John Locke, *Essay Concerning Human Understanding*, IV. 3. 21.

[7] H. A. Prichard, *Knowledge and Perception* (Clarendon Press, 1950), 97.

[8] Indeed some thinkers had such a high view of knowledge and such a low view of belief that they claimed (though sometimes not consistently with other things they claimed) that knowledge and belief were distinct faculties (so that presumably knowing something did not include believing it). Thus Locke: 'The mind has two faculties conversant about truth and falsehood. First, knowledge . . . Secondly, judgement [i.e. belief]' (*Essay*, IV. 14. 4).

[9] This thesis is developed at length and convincingly by Ian Hacking in his *The Emergence of Probability* (Cambridge University Press, 1975).

issue was which ones were (in some sense) much less liable to error than others, and by how much. Hence the notions of justified belief and—closely connected therewith, as we shall see—the notion of a hypothesis being probable became important, requiring analysis and measure. Bishop Butler made the famous remark 'to us, probability is the very guide of life'.[10] But these connected notions—justification and probability—were each developed in different but connected ways, to the differences and connections between which philosophers (and mathematicians) have been insufficiently sensitive. Again, once we are clear about the kinds of justification, we can proceed to investigate their value.

Contemporary accounts of justification are largely accounts of synchronic justification, of what it is for a belief to constitute a justified response to the situation in which the believer finds herself at a given time. Chapter 1 distinguishes the various internalist theories of this (theories claiming that justification depends on how the belief is related to factors mentally accessible to the believer, such as other beliefs of hers) from externalist theories (claiming that it may depend on factors inaccessible to the believer). Chapter 2 analyses the concept of a belief. A belief being justified is often spelled out as it being probable. Chapter 3 analyses the different senses of 'probability' required by internalist and externalist theories. One crucial sense is the sense in which a belief is rendered probable by evidence. I call this 'logical probability'. Chapter 4 analyses the criteria for one proposition making another one logically probable. To be justified a belief has to be, not merely rendered probable by, but based on its evidence. Chapter 5 analyses the different ways in which being 'based' and 'evidence' can be understood. The various theories of synchronic justification differ in the ways they understand probability, basing and evidence. Having clarified their different structures, Chapter 6 argues that beliefs justified by the standards of most of these theories are worth having, because a belief having such justification makes it (logically) probable that it is true. Chapter 7 then analyses different kinds of diachronic justification, the different ways in which a synchronically justified belief can be based on adequate investigation; and argues similarily that most of them are worth having because investigation of most kinds makes for the resultant beliefs being more probably true. However, it is only in so far as the justification of a belief is internally accessible that it can guide a person in deciding what to do. Chapter 8 analyses the different senses in which a belief can amount to knowledge, and explains how far different kinds of knowledge are worth

[10] Joseph Butler, *The Analogy of Religion*, Introduction.

having. The Appendix argues a crucial point arising from Chapter 4, that it is irrelevant to the support that evidence gives to a hypothesis whether the evidence is known before the hypothesis is formulated, or whether it is discovered in the process of testing the hypothesis.

1

Theories of Synchronic Justification

Synchronic and Diachronic; Internalist and Externalist

I proceed to set out the different theories of what it is for a belief to be 'justified' and to show how they differ from each other. Theories of justification that analyse what it is for a belief to constitute a justified response to the situation in which the believer finds herself at a given time, I shall call theories of synchronic justification. I contrast them with theories that I shall discuss later in the book that are theories of what it is for a synchronically justified belief to be based on adequate investigation over time, which I shall call theories of diachronic justification. Writers who advocate a theory of justification often do not say of which kind their theory is, and one needs to read their detailed exposition in order to see what is intended, and sometimes there is some doubt. But I think that it is right to construe most proposed theories as theories of synchronic justification.

It is usual to distinguish epistemic theories into internalist and externalist theories; and into foundationalist and coherentist theories. All of these terms can be understood in various ways, but some kind of distinction along these lines is useful for mapping theories. The basic idea of an internalist theory is that what makes for the justification of a belief is necessarily internal to the believer; and of an externalist theory that it is not necessarily internal to the believer. What counts as 'internal' depends, therefore, on what one regards as the boundaries of the believer. And obviously there is a sense in which the boundaries of the believer are the boundaries of his or her body. But to think of internal factors as those within the subject's body does not provide the basis of a very useful classification of theories of justification. For what the writers normally called 'internalist' have claimed is that what makes for justification is accessible through 'introspection'. Factors of two distinct kinds are thus accessible. The first are mental states (or events—I shall use these words interchangeably) such as beliefs, sensations, desires, purposes, and occurrent thoughts to which the subject has privileged access in the sense that he can know better than anyone else what he is thinking about, what sensations he is having, and so on, because he has a special means of access to them—by experiencing them. (That we have privileged access to our beliefs is a point that will be developed more fully in the next chapter).

But we have access by introspection also to those necessary truths that are a priori[1] in the sense that we can discover them by mere reflection—we do not need to make observations of the public world or do experiments in it to discover them—or at least we would not if we had sufficient logical ability. The a priori truths include very elementary truths of arithmetic (for example, '2+3=5'), and of deductive syllogistic logic (for example, 'if all *A*s are *B*s and all *B*s are *C*, then all *A*s are *C*'), and the general and more subtle relations between concepts that constitute philosophical truths. These latter range from the obvious (for example, the law of non-contradiction: 'for any proposition *p*, not both *p* and not-*p*'), through the fairly obvious (for example, 'no surface can be totally red and totally green all over'), to the much disputed (for example, 'no cause can be later than its effect'). They also include—I shall be arguing in a later chapter—truths about what is evidence for what. In claiming that these are a priori truths, I am not claiming that all of us know all of them—indeed most of us have never heard of most of them. I am simply claiming that we can, or if we had greater logical abilities than we do, we could, come to know them. Nor am I claiming that we cannot make a mistake when we claim that some proposition is a necessary a priori truth. We can make mistakes in philosophy and mathematics, as in almost all other areas of enquiry; but it is sometimes fairly obvious that we are not mistaken.

Mental states and necessary a priori truths I count as introspectible and so internally or mentally accessible. Of course no internalist wishes to deny that how things are outside his mind is often accessible to the subject. But that accessibility to the subject of things outside the mind (his ability to learn about them) arises from their causing the subject to have certain patterns of sensation rather than others and to have beliefs about their presence; and so the accessibility of the external arises from the mental accessibility of the internal.

[1] Many writers, since Kripke (S. Kripke, 'Naming and Necessity', originally published in D. Davidson and G. Harman (eds.), *Semantics of Natural Language* (D. Reidel, 1972)), have held that there are necessary propositions—necessary in as hard a sense as the more obviously necessary of the examples given in the text above—that are, however, a posteriori, only to be discovered empirically. They include 'Nixon is a person' ('Nixon' picked out by pointing) or (though this example is not Kripke's) 'Water is H_2O'. Such truths are apt to be called metaphysically necessary in contrast to those whose necessity is discoverable a priori, which are apt to be called logically necessary. My concern here is only with the latter.

Theories of synchronic justification often claim that a belief is justified if (and only if) it is based on adequate grounds. Justification is a matter of degree and the more adequate (the better) the grounds, the more justified is the belief. On some theories, however, some beliefs do not require grounds, and I will come to those in due course. Theories usually include a provision that the justification of a belief is normally only prima facie; and so, in order to remain, must not be overridden or undermined—that is, there must not be 'available' other grounds that are adequate for the falsity of belief (or adequate for making the previous grounds inadequate). I will ignore the issue of overriders and underminers (together called 'defeaters') for the present and return to it at the end of the chapter. For now I will concentrate on the main structure. We can then classify theories according to whether they are internalist or externalist in each of the three elements—grounds, their basing, and their adequacy.[2]

Externalist Theories of Prima Facie Justification

The basic idea of an externalist theory of justification is that what makes for the justification of a belief are states of affairs that need not be mentally accessible; and this is normally spelled out in terms of its justification consisting in a belief being produced by a process of the right kind, whose rightness is something to which the believer has no necessary privileged access. A simple theory of justification externalist in all its main respects is Goldman's 1979 theory.[3] For Goldman the 'input'—in our terminology, the grounds—of our belief-forming processes have to be 'events within the organism's nervous system',[4] but it does not seem to be required that they be the events of which the subject is or can become aware. The belief being based on those grounds is, for Goldman, it being caused by those grounds—and clearly, if the subject does not need to be aware of the grounds, she need not be aware that they cause the belief. Finally, the adequacy of the grounds of a particular belief for Goldman, as for many externalists, is a matter of it being produced by a reliable process—that is,

[2] This three fold classification of theories of epistemic justification used in this chapter is due to Kihyeon Kim, 'Internalism and Externalism in Epistemology', *American Philosophical Quarterly*, 30 (1993), 303–16. In other respects too this chapter is much indebted to that article.

[3] Alvin Goldman, 'What is Justified Belief?', in G. Pappas (ed.), *Justification and Knowledge* (D. Reidel, 1979). Reprinted in his *Liaisons* (MIT Press, 1992). My references are to the latter.

[4] *Liaisons*, 116.

one that which produces mostly true beliefs. Where a belief *B* is produced by two processes in succession, the later process producing *B* from an earlier belief *A* produced by the earlier process, it is natural to require that the total process constituted by the joint operation of the two successive subprocesses be reliable.[5] For Goldman the process must be reliable, but it is not in the least relevant whether the subject believes that the process is reliable. A belief satisfying these requirements is prima facie justified. Thus my belief that there is a desk in front of me is caused by some event in my optic nerve. This process of optic nerve events causing beliefs (accompanied by characteristic patterns of colour in the subject's visual field) may be considered as an example of a process of apparent visual perception—that is, a process that leads to a subject's beliefs about what she is seeing outside her body. This process is a normally reliable process—most beliefs so caused are true. So my particular belief about the desk is prima facie justified. In Goldman's theory, as in all other theories, there are provisions for prima facie justification to be overridden or undermined, and we will come to those in due course.

Externalist theories may understand the three different elements in different ways from Goldman. They may construe the *grounds*, more generally, as any public event involved in the causal process of producing the belief—including events outside the body. They may, for example, include the desk that so affects my optic nerve as to produce the belief that there is a desk in front of me. As we shall see shortly, how generally the grounds are construed can make a great difference to the adequacy of grounds, and so to the justification of belief.

Being-based-on is almost always understood by externalists as entailing being-caused-by. But even so, there remains an issue whether any sort of causing is good enough; or whether we need to rule out 'deviant causal chains'. The problem of 'deviant causal chains' is one that arises with attempts to give causal analyses of various mental concepts. Remembering

[5] What Goldman formally requires in his 1979 theory is only (p. 117) that the earlier sub-process be reliable and that the later sub-process be conditionally reliable (i.e. such as to produce mostly true beliefs from true beliefs). Yet he claims (p. 125 n. 8) that his theory was merely 'intended to capture our ordinary notion of justifiedness'. But he acknowledges that this ordinary notion could count a belief as justified, even though the total process of its production was unreliable (e.g. because the earlier sub-process is 60% reliable and the later sub-process is 60% reliable and so the total process together may be only $60/100 \times 60/100 = 36\%$ reliable). He writes that 'if we want a theory to do more than capture the ordinary conception', we could strengthen it. I have done that in the text, in order to provide an account of this kind of justification that (even if Goldman were right that his account described the 'ordinary conception') would make it more plausible to suppose that it is worth having.

doing such-and-such plausibly involves believing truly that one did such-and-such when that belief is caused by one's previous awareness of doing such-and-such. But the issue then arises whether it is still remembering if the causal chain is not the normal one (through intermediate brain states). If I write down my experience in my diary, and then come to hold a belief about it again through reading my diary, surely that does not constitute memory. The same problem arises with respect to the basing of beliefs. What if my belief that there is a desk in front of me is caused by the desk all right, but by an odd route. Suppose the desk triggers off some camera that sends a signal to my brain that disturbs my reasoning processes in such a way as to make me temporarily mad; and, whenever I am temporarily mad, I imagine that there is a desk in front of me. Is my belief that there is a desk in front of me 'based' on the presence of the desk? Is the existence of such a causal chain, given that the other conditions for justification are satisfied, enough to make my belief that there is a table in front of me prima facie justified? I shall return to this issue in Chapter 6.

Reliabilism

Most externalist theories of the *adequacy* of grounds can be represented as reliabilist theories of various kinds, the central idea of which (to put it now more carefully) is that grounds of a particular belief are adequate if (and only if) the particular (token, to use the philosophers' term) process of belief formation belongs to a reliable kind (type, to use the philosophers' term). A process is more reliable, the greater the proportion of true beliefs it produces; and so the greater the justification of a token belief produced by that process. The particular belief of mine acquired at noon on Thursday, 28 August 1998, in bad light (when, let us suppose, I have recently taken LSD) that there is a desk in front of me was caused by an event in my optic nerve, and the latter was caused by (light rays coming from) a desk. This token process is a token of many different types. It is a token of object-in-world to belief-about-world transitions (that is, perception as such). It is a token of optic-nerve to belief-about-world transitions (that is, apparent visual perception as such). It is a token of object-in-world to belief-about-world-when-the-light-is-bad transitions. It is a token of belief acquisitions by me on a Thursday. And so on. These types differ in what I shall call depth and what I shall call width.

The depth of a type of a process is a matter of the length of the process terminating in the acquisition of the relevant belief. Thus optic-nerve to belief transitions are the later stages of processes of belief acquisition. Whereas object-in-world to belief-about-world-when-the-light-is-bad transitions involve more stages in the process of belief acquisition. They trace the process back beyond the optic nerve to the object in the world (for example, a desk), light rays from which caused a disturbance in the optic nerve. Whereas the type 'belief acquired on a Thursday' has no depth at all; the type is not individuated by the process leading to the acquisition of the belief. The width of a type is a matter of how detailed are the factors by which it is individuated. Thus 'optic-nerve to belief transitions in me' is a much narrower type than the type 'optic-nerve to belief transitions' generally; and the latter is much wider than 'optic-nerve to belief transitions on Thursday, 28 August 1998'. The token process of production of the belief mentioned in the last paragraph belongs to all the types of different depth and width mentioned. As stated earlier, for Goldman, only events within the organism should be considered as the grounds of a token belief; and also as defining the type to which the process of belief production belongs. As regards width, he commented that 'our ordinary thought about process types slices them broadly',[6] but he did not put forward any very detailed doctrine as to how they should be individuated. However, the different types to which the token process of belief production belongs will differ greatly in their reliability. Some of these types are very reliable indeed—perhaps 99 per cent of perception beliefs are true. Others are less reliable. And maybe most beliefs produced by optic nerve-to-belief transitions in subjects who have recently taken a large dose of LSD are unreliable. We cannot determine whether the adequacy condition is satisfied unless we have some rule for determining to which type we are to refer tokens.[7] This problem is often called the 'generality problem'.

Two recent authors—Linda Zagzebski and William Alston—have claimed that there are non-arbitrary ways to select the relevant type. Both of them reasonably urge that the type should be picked out only in terms of causal factors that influenced on the occasion in question whether the subject acquired the belief. If a token process led to the acquisition of a belief on a Thursday, but the fact that the day was a Thursday had no causal influence on whether the belief was acquired, then the description of the type to which the token process belongs should not include the operation

[6] *Liaisons*, 115.

[7] Richard Feldman has developed at a little length this difficulty for reliabilism of specifying the type to which a token process should be assigned in 'Reliability and Justification', *Monist*, 68 (1995), 159–74. He concludes (p. 172) that there seems to be no satisfactory way of specifying the type.

of the process on a Thursday. But these writers seem in effect to think that limiting description of the type in this way will solve the problem. It will not.

The issues remain—over how long a stage of the causal process terminating in the production of the belief should we take the causal factors into account? That is, how 'deep' should be the type of causal process? Do we take into account only causal factors within the body (the presence of LSD) or within the immediate environment (the objects in the room, the state of the lighting)? And how many of those causal factors should we take into account? All of them? Or—put slightly differently—how narrow should the description of the causal factors be? The state of the lighting in a room affects which perceptual beliefs are held. But do we define the type to which a token perceptual process belongs as perception in a room with such-and-such lighting (described in precise detail) or simply as perception in a room with bad lighting? Confining the factors by which the type is to be individuated to causally influential factors may reduce the number of possible types to which a token process of belief acquisition belongs, but it leaves a vast number of possible types, differing enormously in their reliability.

For example, Linda Zagzebski[8] argues that 'the process by which beliefs are formed soon become habits', and that the type whose reliability is crucial for epistemic assessment is that of the habit involved. She discusses the example of Oblonsky (as described in Tolstoy's *Anna Karenina*), who always unreflectively accepted the opinions of others. But this habit may be the habit of accepting the opinions of whatever circle he happens to be in, or the habit of accepting the opinions of his present circle when they are available to him. Empirical investigation should reveal the answer.

> Does Oblonsky tend to conform his beliefs only to the opinions of his present circle of friends and his present newspaper? Or does he go on to believe whatever his friends and newspaper believe even when his newspaper and circle of friends gradually change? I suspect that it is the latter, in which case, Oblonsky's belief-forming process is less likely to be reliable. So even if conformity with Oblonsky's small circle of friends is reliable, conformity will probably lead him to believe in an unreliable fashion in the future. The unreliability of his future belief formation therefore infects the reliability of his present process.[9]

[8] See pp. 305–11 of Linda Zagzebski, *Virtues of the Mind* (Cambridge University Press, 1996). In these pages she discusses reliabilism in connection with reliabilist theories of knowledge rather than reliabilist theories of justification. But, since she regards her discussion as a response to Feldman, who is concerned with reliabilist theories of justification, she clearly sees it as applicable to these as well and I shall construe her discussion as applying to these.

[9] Ibid. 310

A particular belief then results from a reliable process if the habit that generated it yields mostly true beliefs.

Now, as presented by Zagzebski, this is a very simple example, because Oblonsky's beliefs are affected directly by just one causal factor—the habit of believing others is the sole determinant of which beliefs Oblonsky acquires. Let us suppose that Oblonsky believes whomever he comes into contact with. Then which beliefs result and whether they are true will depend on who these others are. One could treat the token process as beginning at Oblonsky's ears, or with his informant, or with their sources of information; and the token process will belong to types of different depths accordingly. But let us understand it as the process beginning with the informant. The more substantial problem is that this process can be regarded as belonging to types of very different widths. Suppose that in 1860 in St Petersburg this habit yields generally true beliefs in Oblonsky. But in 1861 and 1862 he lives in Moscow, when the habit yields in him generally false beliefs. Is the adequacy of Oblonsky's grounds for a certain token belief in St Petersburg in 1860 to be assessed by the reliability of the type 'belief acquired by Oblonsky believing others in St Petersburg in 1860'? In that case he will have adequate grounds. Or are we to refer his belief to the wider type 'belief acquired by Oblonsky believing others'? In that case the reliability will be a matter of whether his believing others in the different environments in which he is situated yields generally true beliefs. In my story, his token belief in 1860 will not then have adequate grounds. If one habit alone really determines Oblonsky's beliefs, Oblonsky is unlikely to be the only person who has this habit of believing others. Is the type, by which the reliability of the token belief is to be assessed, 'belief acquired by Oblonsky believing others' or 'belief acquired by believing others'? But, maybe in others who have the habit it yields generally false beliefs in St Petersburg in 1860, but generally true beliefs in Moscow in 1861 and 1862, and so again there will be very different answers to the question whether Oblonsky has adequate grounds for his belief. So generally, even if we refer the token process of the formation of a given belief in Oblonsky to a type of one fixed depth, and assume that the habit of believing others is the only factor that influences his beliefs, there will be very different answers to the question whether he has adequate grounds for this belief that vary with the width of the type to which we refer the token process.

Most people's processes of belief acquisition are not nearly as simple as in this artificial example. Most token processes of belief acquisition involve many different causal factors (including what other people say) with varying degrees of influence and counter-influence. A particular belief *B* will be caused by the combined influences and counter-influences of factors *C*, *D*, *E*, *F*, and so on. And so the further issue affecting the width of the type is—how many of these are to be included in the description of the type, additional to the issues of how long a period of time and how many similar believers are to be taken into account, and to the issue of depth of the type, for the purpose of assessing its reliability. All these difficulties arise also in connection with Alston's discussion, which I consider in an Additional Note.[10]

And the final aspect of the generality problem for reliabilism is—given the type, defined by a certain kind of width and depth of the causal factors involved on the token occasion—whether it is the operation of those factors in that kind of environment in the actual world or in some wider class of possible worlds by which their reliability should be judged? Is reliability to be calculated by the proportion of true beliefs actually produced in our world (that is, in the past, present, and future), by the proportion of true beliefs that would actually be produced in the world in which the belief occurs, or by the proportion of true beliefs that would be produced in our world if the world was different in various ways but the same physical laws held, or by the proportion of true beliefs that would be produced if the world was the way we believe it to be in its most general respects (for example, in the laws of nature by which it is governed)? The difference between the first and second suggestions arises when you consider a belief produced in some world different from ours, whose belief-forming processes have different degrees of reliability from those processes in our world. For example, memory may be only 40 per cent reliable in that world, whereas in our world—let us suppose—it is 70 per cent reliable. Then on the second view a memory belief in the other world would be unjustified because memory processes in that world are only 40 per cent reliable; whereas on the first view the belief would be justified because memory processes in our world are 70 per cent reliable.

The trouble with calculating reliability by actual proportions in the actual world (or in some particular imagined world) is that there may (if you take a narrow type) be very few instances of the type—in an extreme case only one, and the results obtained then yield an implausible account of justification. If I am the only person who has taken a large dose of LSD, I acquire a belief that there is a desk in front of me and then fall asleep until the effects of LSD have worn off, then the proportion of true beliefs produced by perception by LSD subjects is 100 per cent if there is a desk in

[10] See Additional Note A.

front of me and 0 per cent if there is not. My belief is justified if and only if it is true!

So it becomes natural to suggest that the proportion required is the proportion of true beliefs that would be produced if the type process were operative frequently, while physical laws remained the same. The trouble is that, if we are to assess whether I am justified in holding some perceptual belief that I acquire after taking LSD by the proportion of true perceptual beliefs that would be produced in those who take LSD, if physical laws remain the same, everything depends on how other things are allowed to vary. Do we consider the proportion that would be produced in those who have good sight, or who are over 20 years old, or have never read any books or articles about the effects of LSD? One needs to say something like—other things being allowed to vary to the extent to which they do in the actual world—that is, for example, if the proportion of people in the actual world among those who take LSD who have good sight is 50 per cent then when we measure the proportion of occasions in which the type process yields true beliefs in LSD-takers, 50 per cent of those occasions must include ones in which the subjects have good sight.

One of the factors determining the width of the type is the spatio-temporal region involved. Our type to which the token process is referred may be the type of perceptual beliefs produced in those who take LSD in Britain this year, or in Europe over the past century, or whatever. 'Other things being allowed to vary to the extent to which they do in the actual world' is then to be read as 'other things being allowed to vary to the extent to which they do in the actual world in the spatio-temporal region involved'. The proportion among people this year in Britain of those who take LSD who have good sight may be very different from the proportion among Europeans over the past century. As we vary the range of conditions under which we suppose physical laws to operate in producing perceptual beliefs in those who take LSD, so the proportion of true beliefs produced will vary and so therefore—on this account of justification—will the justification of any individual perceptual belief in someone who takes LSD.

However, maybe we live in a world as to whose character we are greatly mistaken—maybe the physical laws are quite other than we suppose, or—more extremely—maybe we live in a world controlled by an evil demon in which there are no physical laws but the demon makes it such that, within a very narrow spatio-temporal region of which each of us has experience, the world behaves as if there were certain physical laws. In that case, on the latter reliabilist theories virtually none of our beliefs would be justified—for there are no such reliable processes as we suppose. But intuitively it might seem, even if the evil demon deceives us, we are still justified in holding the beliefs to which he leads us. So that suggests that the reliability of belief-forming processes should be assessed relative to a 'normal world'—that is, a world in which our general beliefs (about physical laws, and frequency of initial conditions, and so on) are true. A belief is then justified if it would be produced by a reliable process in a normal world.

Alvin Goldman has moved among many of these versions of reliabilism. I write 'among', because he has not always spelled out his various versions of reliabilism precisely enough, and often ends his presentation of the alternatives by leaving it to the reader to choose between them. He always insists (as he did in 1979) that the grounds of a belief must be internal in his sense (that is, within the skin of the believer), and that the process is the process of moving from such grounds to the belief. The type (thus limited in the causes we can take into account) will, of course, differ, according to how narrowly we describe that process. In 1986, in considering the similar issues involved with knowledge, in apparent contrast to 1979, he suggested that it should be 'the narrowest type that is causally operative in producing the belief token in question'.[11] This process may be virtually deterministic, but whether it ends up with a true belief or a false belief will depend on what holds when such processes operate, outside the believer—the proportion of occasions on which the belief produced is true. In his 1979 version he offers us a choice between the first two alternatives described in my paragraph beginning 'And the final aspect'—proportions in our present world, even though that is not the world in which the belief is being formed; and proportions in whatever world the process is operating—though he does not state how things in that world are to be allowed to vary. So, on the first alternative, if different processes operate in another world, what would make a belief held there justified is whether the process that produced it would reliably produce a true belief in our world.

Goldman's most sophisticated theory (1986) distinguished between basic processes (perception, memory, inductive inference) and more detailed methods of belief acquisition that they license. But—just to concentrate on the basic 'processes'—it was proportions in 'normal worlds' which were crucial there.[12] Goldman (1988)[13] commented that Goldman (1986) left various matters unresolved, such as which 'general beliefs' had

[11] Alvin Goldman, *Epistemology and Cognition* (Harvard University Press, 1986), 50.

[12] Ibid. 107

[13] Alvin Goldman, 'Strong and Weak Justification', in James E. Tomberlin (ed.), *Philosophical Perspectives 2—Epistemology* (Ridgeview Publishing Company, 1988). Reprinted in his *Liaisons*. My references are to the latter.

to be the ones by which 'normal worlds' were picked out.[14] Instead he introduced us to two kinds of epistemic justification—an externalist kind determining when a belief was 'strongly justified', and an internalist kind that determined when a belief was 'weakly justified'. For his crucial 'strong justification' Goldman recommended that a belief is strongly justified if it is produced by a process that is reliable in 'near possible worlds'—that is, in worlds where the same general laws hold, but other things are allowed to vary.[15] He does not tell us how they are allowed to vary, but I suppose that it is in the way they do vary in the actual world over some spatio-temporal region that includes the actual process; and so we have again actual-world reliabilism—the justification of a belief (in any world) is a matter of whether the process that produced it is reliable in the actual world. A 1992 article confirms that as his most recent view.[16] Goldman, like many other theorists, often uses the word 'probability' to spell out his view, but this is a word that can be highly ambiguous, and we shall be attending to its ambiguities in Chapter 3.

It is tempting for the reliabilist to go for a very precise type—a deep type, a narrow type individuated by all the causal factors spelled out very fully, and for proportions in totally similar circumstances in the actual world. But such a precise type of belief-forming process will have only one member—the token process in question. For there will no other process occurring in totally similar circumstances in which exactly those causal factors operated. In that case, as illustrated above, if the token belief is true, the type to which it belongs is 100 per cent reliable; and, if it is false, it is 0 per cent reliable. But an account of justification in which all true beliefs are justified, and all justified beliefs are true, is implausible as an account of any ordinary-language concept of justification. Only if types are individuated in a less precise way will we begin to get an account of justification that has any plausibility as an account of any ordinary-language concept of justification. And there seems no very obvious reason for individuating types in any one less precise way rather than any other.

Theories More and More Internalist

If one is seeking to analyse what one thinks of as a clear ordinary-language concept of justification, it is natural to think that, for his belief to be justi-

[14] *Liaisons*, 136. [15] Ibid. 137.
[16] *Liaisons*, ch. 9, 'Epistemic Folkways and Scientific Epistemology'. See p. 163.

fied, its grounds must be ones of which the subject is aware. If I believe that John robbed the safe, and you ask me why I think that, and I cannot tell you why, it is open to question whether my belief is justified. Of course, there may be some public phenomenon that in some sense constitutes grounds for that belief—John's fingerprints were on the safe. But the internalist reasonably claims that I can claim that as a justification only if I believe that John's fingerprints were on the safe; and then suggests that the justification for my belief that John robbed the safe remains even if my belief that his fingerprints were on the safe is false. Really, he says, it is my belief that John's fingerprints were on the safe that provide the grounds for my belief that John robbed the safe. While externalist in other respects, William Alston held (in 1989) that, for a belief to be justified (though not necessarily for it to amount to knowledge), its ground must be 'a psychological state of the subject'[17]—namely, some other belief or sensory state. We shall be noting in due course that internalists differ among themselves as to whether the only permissible grounds are other beliefs or whether other mental states can also serve as grounds. Among the beliefs that may form a subject's grounds for some other belief *B* are beliefs that the process by which *B* came to be formed was a token of a reliable process. I may believe my apparent memory of what I did on my sixth birthday because I believe that my apparent memories of what I did when I was young are reliable (and I may have further beliefs that support the latter belief). But the internalist insists that it is only the subject's beliefs about whether a process is or is not reliable that are relevant to the justification of a resulting belief, whereas for the externalist it is only the fact that the process is or is not reliable—whether or not the subject believes that—that is relevant.

But it is natural then for the internalist to go on to claim that the subject is justified in holding a belief having mental grounds only if the fact that those grounds support or apparently support that belief is also something accessible to the subject; and that the justification is greater, the greater the support or apparent support. If I believe that Jones robbed the safe and the grounds of belief are my belief that his fingerprints are on it, surely, in order for the latter belief to provide adequate grounds for the former, I have to believe that Jones's fingerprints being on the safe is evidence that he has touched it. The mere existence of an empirical correlation between fingerprints on a surface and people touching that surface is not enough for justification. If I think that 'fingerprints' are mere patterns of lines that occur

[17] William P. Alston, 'An Externalist Internalism', in his *Epistemic Justification* (Cornell University Press, 1989), 233.

spontaneously and have no connection with their owner having put his fingers on a surface (in the way that people used to think that animal fossils were chance rock formations having no connection with the previous presence of animals of similar shape), then it does not look as if my belief that Jones robbed the safe is well justified. On the other hand, perhaps it is enough for my belief to be justified that it is a fact a priori accessible to me (no mere empirically discernible connection) that its grounds support the belief. This would be so if I had, as well as the belief that Jones's fingerprints are on the safe, the belief that it was once discovered in a large sample of fingerprints that there was a one-to-one correlation between someone's fingerprints on a surface and their having touched it—even if I do not believe that these evidential beliefs support the belief that Jones robbed the safe. There are thus alternative ways in which internalists may spell out the requirement that the adequacy of their grounds for a belief should be mentally accessible—either that it be supported (by objective a priori criteria) by those grounds; or alternatively that the subject believes that (in some way or other) the grounds support the beliefs. (The objective a priori character of support relations will be defended in Chapter 3.) These are both internalist accounts, for both the a priori and the mental are accessible by introspection. Chisholm seems to understand adequacy in terms of objective a priori support. He endorses the view of the internalist that

> merely by reflecting upon his own conscious state, he can formulate a set of epistemic principles that will enable him to find out, with respect to any possible belief that he has, whether he is *justified* in having that belief. The epistemic principles that he formulates are principles that one may come upon and apply merely by sitting in one's armchair, so to speak, and without calling for any outside assistance. In a word, one need consider only one's own state of mind.[18]

And he goes on to claim that the principles that *we* judge to be correct are the principles by which we should assess whether other people are justified in their beliefs; that is, we must assume that we have access to correct principles, whether or not they are shared by other believers. But, one might say whether or not I have the correct criteria for what is evidence for what, surely if I believe *p* and believe *q* and believe that *q* is evidence for *p*, then I am justified in believing *p*. These different ways in which the 'adequacy' of grounds can be understood will be explored more fully in Chapter 3.

But, even if *q* is evidence for *p* and I believe this and I believe *q*, plausibly I am still not justified unless it is because I believe that *q* is evidence for *p* that I believe *p*. This is the 'basing' requirement. The belief must be based

[18] Roderick M. Chisholm, *Theory of Knowledge*, 3rd edn. (Prentice Hall, 1989), 76.

on its grounds. And the natural interpretation of 'based' is the causal one—the belief must be caused by its grounds (via a non-deviant causal chain), and that looks like an externalist requirement. Some thinkers would claim that I have no privileged access to what causes my beliefs—that is a matter for investigation for psychologists who study under what circumstances I acquire or lose beliefs. The internalist can, however, spell out the 'basing' requirement in a way other than that the belief should be caused by its grounds. He can say simply that the subject needs to believe that the belief is caused by its grounds, these being picked out as that mental state that is in fact adequate for his belief. Or he can say that a belief being based on its grounds is simply the subject believing that those grounds are adequate for the belief. I shall examine these accounts more fully in Chapter 5.

Someone can be an internalist solely about the grounds, like Alston (1989), or an internalist about both grounds and their adequacy or about grounds and their basing, or finally about all three factors.

I have spelled out the internalist's position in terms of his holding that for a belief to be justified at a time a certain relation must hold between it and other states (and, if he is fully internalist, these are mental states). A subject's being justified is not a matter of his doing anything; it is a matter of his being in a certain state. Past philosophers such as Descartes and Locke,[19] who are often cited as classical internalists, stressing that the justification of belief is something internal to the subject, have often explicated justification in terms of 'epistemic obligation'. A subject's belief is justified if (and only if), in holding it, he is not flouting his epistemic obligations. And what is an 'epistemic obligation'? Presumably 'an obligation with respect to truth-seeking'. But, since such obligations are sometimes quite unimportant (there are some issues about which it does not matter much what we believe), epistemic obligations can be regarded only as hypothetical, not categorical obligations. An epistemic obligation to believe such-and-such must have some such form as 'if you want a true belief, you ought to believe such-and-such'. So epistemic 'obligations' are to be regarded as recipes for getting at truth, fulfilling them being the best one can do towards getting the truth. It is, however, odd to talk of 'obligations' with respect to synchronic justification. For obligations are obligations to perform actions, and plausibly exist only where there is some action available to the subject. So since (as I shall argue more fully in Chapter 2) we

[19] In the opening chapter of *Warrant: The Current Debate* (Oxford University Press, 1993), Alvin Plantinga brings out with many citations how, for these authors, 'the notion of duty or obligation plays a central role in the whole doxastic enterprise' (p. 12).

cannot at a given moment choose which beliefs to hold, we cannot have any obligation at that moment to hold one belief rather than another. One could perhaps construe the epistemic obligation as the hypothetical obligation one would have if (*per impossibile*) one were able to choose one's beliefs—you are epistemically justified in holding a belief if and only if you hold one, which, if you had a choice about it and wanted a true belief, you would not be obliged not to have. But to analyse a notion in terms of an obligation one would have if some logical impossibility were not a logical impossibility is not very illuminating. It is better not to bring in the notion of 'obligation', when our concern is with synchronic justification. As we shall see in due course, while we cannot help which beliefs we have at a given time, we can choose whether or not to investigate our beliefs over time, and we are diachronically justified in our beliefs in so far as they result from adequate investigation. We can have obligations to pursue such investigation. Philosophers sometimes confuse synchronic justification and diachronic justification, and I shall argue later that Locke's concern with obligation (even if not that of Descartes) was a concern with the obligation involved in diachronic justification.

Basic Beliefs

For an internalist, a belief's grounds must be mentally accessible. They will, therefore, be some other belief or beliefs or some other mental state or states (normally sensory states—patterns of colour in the subject's visual field, noises he seems to hear, and so on). If the grounds of a belief *B* are another belief *C*, we need to add an extra clause to the internalist's account. A belief *B* whose grounds are another belief *C* (*B* being based on *C* and *C* being adequate grounds) will be justified only if the belief *C* is itself justified; and if *C* is justified by being based on another belief *D* that constitutes adequate grounds for it, *D* must be sufficiently strong to provide adequate grounds not merely for *C* but for what *C* supports—*B*. And so on. But, while *B* may be justified by *C*, and *C* by *D*, and so on, plausibly we cannot go on forever—for we do not have an infinite number of beliefs.

That leaves three possibilities for the internalist. The first is that the chain of support always ends in mental states other than beliefs—for example, sensory states. This is a species of foundationalism, the view that there are justificatory foundations for our belief-systems; but it is non-doxastic fundationalism, the view that these foundations are mental states other than beliefs. My belief that you have gone to London today is grounded on my belief that you told me yesterday that you were planning to go to London today and this belief is grounded on my having auditory images of the noises 'I am planning to go to London tomorrow' correlated with visual sensory images of the kind that would be produced by a photograph of you. But, many an internalist will be inclined to say, the having of such images will not justify any belief, unless I have a belief about what they are images of—I have to believe that the images are of what happened yesterday, that the noises are of a kind typical of your voice, that the visual images are typical of your appearance. And these beliefs will need justification. So it is not plausible to suppose that sensations by themselves could provide any adequate grounding for beliefs. We need other beliefs as well. And in any case many of our memory beliefs have no sensations at all to back them up. I may remember that I have been told by someone or read somewhere that there is no greatest prime number without having any images of the page on which I read it or of the sound of someone's voice saying so.

The second possibility is justification in a circle. My belief that *B* is justified by my belief that *C*, my belief that *C* by my belief that *D*... and so on, until we come back to my belief that *B*. This view is often dismissed far too quickly on the grounds that it would justify equally well a contrary belief—for example, the belief not-*B* (which is the negation of *B*) could be justified by a belief that not-*C*... until we come back to not-*B*. It will not, however, automatically be the case that the second circle of justification (if it were to exist; that is, if I were to have these beliefs) would provide as strong a justification as does the first circle. (Not-*C* might not support not-*B* as well as *C* supports *B*.) But, even if the circles of justification (if they were to exist) would give just as much support to not-*B* as to *B*, that fact would not provide a good objection to the possibility of justification in a circle, given the involuntary character of beliefs. I cannot help having which belief I do, *B* or not-*B*. The only issue is, when I do have whatever belief I do have, is it justified? The answer given by this view is yes—if my belief is justified by my other beliefs, even if their justification ultimately depends on being justified by the original belief. This view is epistemic coherentism—the justification of a belief consists in its 'cohering' with the subject's other beliefs. 'Cohering' with other beliefs is more than just being consistent with them—it is a matter of it being adequately supported by them. (The coherence theory of epistemic justification is not to be confused with the coherence theory of truth. The latter holds that there is nothing more to a belief's being true than its cohering with other beliefs—of the subject or community. That is far less plausible than the coherence theory that is our concern, the theory of epistemic justification).

But, if we are spelling out the normal understanding of what is evidence for what, coherentism suffers from the deficiency that some beliefs seem to have privileged status, and this leads to the third possibility for the internalist—(full or partial) doxastic foundationalism. (Foundationalism is doxastic to the extent that it claims that all the justificatory foundations for a belief-system consist only of beliefs.) To have adequate grounds for believing that you have gone to London today, I need a belief such as that you said to me yesterday that you were going to go to London today. But to believe the latter does not require support from any other belief. It can, of course, be undermined by other beliefs—for example, by a belief that I never hear what you say correctly. But in the absence of undermining or other defeating beliefs, my mere having the belief that you said to me that you were going to London today is, on our normal view of the matter, adequate grounds for believing it to be true. Some beliefs are basic—that is, not grounded on any other beliefs; and some beliefs are what I shall call 'rightly basic'[20]—that is, ones that we are justified in holding without their needing other beliefs or other mental states as grounds, in the sense that, intrinsically or merely in virtue of our having them, they are probably true. Plausibly memory beliefs and perceptual beliefs are in this category. The former sometimes and the latter normally[21] are accompanied by sensory experiences. And an internalist whose foundationalism is only partially doxastic will hold that—at any rate for most perceptual beliefs—we need the sensory experiences to accompany the belief in order for us to be justified in having the basic belief; and so these sensory experiences form some of the foundations of our belief-systems.[22] (I need to hear certain sounds

[20] I use the term 'rightly basic' instead of Plantinga's term 'properly basic' (see his essay 'Reason and Belief in God', in A. Plantinga and N. Wolterstorff (eds.), *Faith and Rationality* (University of Notre Dame Press, 1983), 46). For Plantinga a properly basic belief is one that the subject is justified in holding without that justification being provided by other beliefs; in order to be properly basic the belief might still need grounding in other mental or non-mental states. See his p. 48. (Whereas to be rightly basic a belief needs no grounding in anything else.)

[21] Blindsight (where subjects can identify the location of a spot on a screen while not having any visual sensations of it), and a case when a blind man can identify the location of a wall without being aware of any sensory input, seem cases of perceptual beliefs not involving sensory experiences. See L. Weiskrantz, 'Varieties of Residual Experience', *Quarterly Journal of Experimental Psychology*, 32 (1980), 365–86; and J. J. Gibson, *The Senses Considered as Perceptual Systems* (Houghton, 1966), 2.

[22] There is an ambiguity here in the literature. Some writers write of 'doxastic foundationalism' as the view that (some or all) basic beliefs form the justificatory foundations of our belief-systems, while allowing that what gives them that status might be the 'conditions' or 'circumstances' in which they occur. (As was the view of Plantinga in 'Reason and Belief in God', pp. 76–7. Not that he called this view 'doxastic foundationalism'.) If these

in order justifiably to believe that you are now telling me that you are going to go to London. But I also need the belief that the sounds have that meaning, and the belief that it is you who are uttering them). But an internalist whose foundationalism is fully doxastic will deny the need for any sensory experiences to accompany beliefs about what we are perceiving or what we remember or indeed anything at all, in order for those beliefs to be properly basic. My mere having the belief justifies my having it.

Either way, we reach 'foundations'; and these consist either totally or in part of beliefs that require no grounds in order justifiably to be believed. In a very simple picture some beliefs are rightly basic; other beliefs get their justification by being adequately grounded in the former and each other. I shall explore how this view can be most satisfactorily developed in Chapter 5. Foundationalism in the internalist sense that our belief-systems do have mentally accessible foundations (and, in a simple form of the theory, these will be merely beliefs) is opposed to coherentism, as I set it out, in the sense that for all beliefs their sole justification consists in their cohering with other beliefs. But clearly there can be a modified internalist foundationalism that holds that all beliefs require some coherence with other beliefs, but that there are foundational beliefs whose justification does not consist solely in their cohering with other beliefs.[23]

I have written in the last paragraph about 'foundationalism in the internalist sense', because many writers hold that there are foundations for our belief systems in a subset of our beliefs, but that all of these themselves require grounding in external states other than beliefs. Someone who is largely externalist can hold this—he does, however (if he is to make a distinction between foundational beliefs and other beliefs), need the minimum view that some beliefs need other beliefs as their grounds (even though he will spell out this grounding in an externalist way). And someone externalist as regards adequacy can be coherentist in holding that to be justified all beliefs must be grounded in other beliefs while still holding that the adequacy of grounds is to be analysed in reliabilist terms. 'Foundationalism' and 'coherentism' are positions that can be held in extreme or more moderate forms, and in forms largely externalist as well

conditions are public phenomena, then we have a species of externalism and one less naturally called 'foundationalist'. But, if the conditions are other mental states of the subject such as her sensory experiences, then it seems to me misleading to call this view 'doxastic' foundationism, since it is those other mental states on which the justification of belief depends.

[23] Thus Susan Haack describes her position as 'Foundherentism'—justified beliefs need foundations, and also need to cohere with one's other beliefs. See her *Evidence and Inquiry* (Blackwell, 1993).

as in internalist forms. But they are terms that seem most naturally fitted for describing internalist epistemologies.

Defeaters

Grounds that are adequate to justify a belief under normal circumstances may not be adequate under abnormal circumstances. Normal justification may be either undermined ('undercut') or overridden ('rebutted'). It is undermined if there are new circumstances in which the original grounds no longer provide adequate grounds for the truth of the belief; but they provide no grounds for the falsity of the belief. The belief is overridden if the new circumstances constitute grounds that taken by themselves favour the falsity of the belief, and that in consequence make the old grounds inadequate for its truth. *A* tells me that *B* has gone to London today. Plausibly (on virtually any internalist or externalist theory of justification, in the absence of counter-considerations) that makes my belief that *B* has gone to London justified. But then someone else *C* tells me that *A* only said that because he did not want me to talk to *B*. That undermines the adequacy of my original grounds; it means that they are no longer good enough for me justifiably to believe that *B* has gone to London. It gives me no grounds for supposing that he has not gone to London, only makes me no longer justified in believing that he has. On the other hand, suppose I actually seem to see *B*, not in London but still in Oxford. That overrides my original belief. It provides grounds in favour of the falsity of the original belief and, in consequence of that, makes the original grounds in favour of its truth inadequate.

These points will be expressed differently by the internalist and the externalist.[24] For both, the old grounds occur in new circumstances, and the belief is no longer justified if the grounds are not adequate for the belief in the new circumstances. But for the internalist, for whom a belief is justified if and only if it is supported on objective a priori criteria by his evidence, these 'circumstances' are just new evidence; both undermining and overriding involve the believer acquiring new evidence that together with the old evidence no longer gives enough support to the original belief to

[24] For some of the various ways in which internalist and externalist writers have expounded the role of 'defeaters', see Chisholm, *Theory of Knowledge*, 55; John L. Pollock, *Contemporary Theories of Knowledge* (Hutchinson, 1987), 38–9; and Alvin Plantinga, *Warrant and Proper Function* (Oxford University Press, New York, 1993), 40–2.

make it justified.[25] For such an internalist no new process is involved—the justification of a belief is relative to the evidence; more evidence may render a belief originally justified no longer justified, or conversely. An undermining defeater will leave the belief as likely to be true as it had been without the original positive evidence in its support. An overriding defeater makes it likely that the original belief was false.

For a reliabilist, the new circumstances mean that the token process of belief production is occurring in a different environment from the one in which it was occurring earlier or would otherwise have been occurring. This may have the consequence that the type to which the token belongs, though reliable (producing mostly true beliefs) in the original environment, is no longer reliable in the new environment. In that case, the new circumstances will be undermining. My belief that *B* has gone to London was produced by *A*'s testimony, a token of the reliable process of testimony. But counter-testimony is now added to the environment—*C* tells me that *A* did not say what he did because he believed it true. The proportion of true beliefs produced by testimony when the hearer is told by someone else that the testifier was not seeking to say what he believed true is presumably a lot lower than the proportion produced by testimony as such. So the belief that *B* has gone to London would not be as well justified as before, probably not justified at all.

An overriding defeater will also, for a reliabilist, undermine. The belief that *B* has gone to London produced by *A*'s testimony, sustained in an environment where I seem to see *B* in Oxford, belongs to a type—belief formed by testimony when the believer seems to observe its falsity—which is clearly unreliable. But its overriding character would seem to be a matter of there being adequate grounds for a belief in the negation of the original belief, even if those grounds did not operate to produce such a belief. In the example there were grounds adequate for believing that *A* did not go to London (namely, that it seemed to me that I saw him in Oxford), even if I persuade myself that really I did not see him.

However, an externalist who expounds the overriding character of a defeater in terms of a contrary belief that was not produced but in some sense ought to have been produced by a process that was 'available' is in danger of compromising his pure externalism with an internalist strand. Consider the final definition in Goldman's (1979) article of when a belief is justified: 'If S's belief at *t* results from a reliable cognitive process, and there

[25] Or evidence that, when the old evidence was not certain, makes it less certain. For how the probability of uncertain evidence can be altered by new experience, see Additional Note M.

is no reliable or conditionally reliable process available to S which, had it been used by S in addition to the process actually used, would have resulted in S's not believing *p* at *t*, then S's belief in *p* at *t* is justified.'[26] But what is it for a process to be 'available'? Is it something public—people in my community use this process? If the definition of availability is of this kind, externalism is preserved. But there is the obvious objection—why should the existence of such a process make my belief unjustified if I am not aware of the process? Goldman is aware of this problem, and it forces him into a distinctively internalist account of availability: 'What I think we should have in mind here are such additional processes as calling previously acquired evidence to mind, assessing the implications of that evidence etc.'[27] 'Previously acquired evidence' is presumably evidence of which the subject is aware.

This last point brings to our attention the fact that many apparently hard-line externalist theories tend to be mixed, to contain internalist elements.[28] The range of theories of epistemic justification involving mixtures of all the elements discussed in this chapter is indeed considerable. This chapter has merely outlined the elements involved in most theories, and exhibited how they fit together in the formation of fairly simple theories. But the very great diversity of different theories allegedly elucidating a simple concept of ordinary language—epistemic 'justification'—and the many kinds of case considered in this chapter about which the different theories yield different answers as to whether some belief is 'justified', answers that will seem right to some people but wrong to others, should begin to warn us that something is amiss. It looks as if there is no one concept

[26] *Liaisons*, 123. ('A process is conditionally reliable when a sufficient proportion of its output-beliefs are true, *given that its input-beliefs are true*' (*Liaisons*, 117).)

[27] Ibid. 123.

[28] One kind of internalist requirement common to these prominent largely externalist theories of justification or warrant (of a belief that *p*) is that 'the believer does not believe that her belief that *p* is defeated'—that is, a belief that the belief that *p* is defeated for other reasons is itself a defeater. Michael Bergmann finds this requirement in Goldman's account of justification (in *Epistemology and Cognition*, 62), in Nozick's account of warrant (not under that name, in his *Philosophical Explanations* (Clarendon Press, 1981), 196) and in Plantinga's account of warrant (in *Warrant and Proper Function*, 40–2). See Michael Bergmann, 'Internalism, Externalism, and the No-Defeater Condition', *Synthese*, 110 (1997), 399–417 (especially for his justification for finding this requirement in Plantinga.) On how Plantinga's epistemology can usefully take internalist requirements on board, see Michael Sudduth, 'The Internalist Character and Evidentialist Implications of Plantingian Defeaters', *International Journal for Philosophy of Religion*, 45 (1999), 167–87, and 'Proper Basicality and the Evidential Significance of Internalist Defeat: A Proposal for Revising Classical Evidentialism' in G. Brüntrup and R. K. Tacelli (eds.), *The Rationality of Theism* (Kluwer Academic Publishers, 1999).

in ordinary use; and the crucial question will be—which of these various concepts that different writers have elucidated is worth having?

However, some of the various constituent elements of the different theories need fuller elucidation, and subsequent chapters will elucidate the concepts of belief, probability, being based-on, evidence, and basic belief, before we return to the issue of comparing the theories. I begin with the concept of belief itself.

2

Belief

Narrow Content Belief

A person's beliefs are his or her 'view' of the world, what they 'hold' to be true about it, what they 'accept' as true. When one believes something, one has a relation (of believing) to what is believed, the content of belief, which I shall call a proposition. But the proposition may be such that the believer could still have that belief even if the world outside his mental life were different from how it is in any way at all; or, alternatively, it may be such that the believer could not have that belief if the world were different in a certain way. Thus I could not have a belief that that lake in front of me is beautiful if there is no lake in front of me—if, for example, I am dreaming. For the belief (if it exists) is a belief about a certain lake, and if there is no such lake there can be no belief about it. But whatever the world is like outside my mental life, I can still have a belief that there is a lake in front of me that is beautiful. I could still have that belief, whether or not there is really a lake in front of me. Beliefs that depend for their existence on how the world is beyond the subject's mental life are called wide content beliefs; beliefs that do not so depend are called narrow content beliefs.[1]

All *de re* beliefs,[2] which are the beliefs they are partly in virtue of the objects that they are about, are clearly wide content beliefs. The belief that Tony Blair is Prime Minister could not exist if there was no Tony Blair (although the belief that there is a Prime Minister called 'Tony Blair' could still exist). But there are other beliefs whose wide content status is not so obvious. There are, in particular, some predicates (which are not names or descriptions of individuals) that purport to designate properties but will

[1] This distinction derives from Putnam's distinction between psychological states 'in the narrow sense' and 'in the wide sense'. See 'The Meaning of "Meaning"', in his *Mind, Language and Reality, Philosophical Papers*, ii (Cambridge University Press, 1975), 220.

[2] With the sole exception of *de se* beliefs, beliefs about oneself, e.g. 'I am tired' or 'I am old'. These beliefs do not depend for their existence on anything beyond one's own mental life.

do so only if the world is a certain way—otherwise there will be no such property that could be a constituent of someone's belief. Thus, plausibly, in the eighteenth century 'water' meant 'made of the same stuff (whatever it is) as the actual stuff in our rivers and lakes.' (I write 'in the eighteenth century' because plausibly now 'water' means simply 'H_2O'.) So *S*'s belief in the eighteenth century that there is water in a glass in front of her is also a wide content belief[3]—for if there are no rivers and lakes and so no stuff in them, she could not have the belief that there is water in the glass—because there is nothing that would constitute being water and so no content to her belief. But *S*'s belief that there is in a glass in front of her something made of stuff also to be found in rivers and lakes around her is a narrow content belief—it can still exist even if there are no rivers and lakes.

Now I suggest that wide content beliefs always involve narrow content beliefs and something else. To believe that the lake in front of me is beautiful is to believe that there is a lake in front of me that is beautiful, and for there to be a lake in front of me. Or—to take a more complicated example—to believe that Tony Blair is the Prime Minister is to believe that there is someone about whom I have certain other beliefs (for example, that he is forty-something, has four children, has a degree in law, is addressed as 'Tony', and so on; or is the person about whom others are talking when they use the name 'Tony Blair') who is the Prime Minister; *and* for those other beliefs to be true of the actual Tony Blair. There are detailed disputes into which we need not enter about just which other beliefs I need to have about some person in order for them to be beliefs about Tony Blair.[4] But clearly, if there is no Tony Blair, I cannot have a belief about him, and certain things have to be true of an individual in order for that individual to be Tony Blair. Yet I can have a belief that there is someone who has four children and is addressed as 'Tony' who is Prime Minister without there being any Tony Blair. And so on generally. It follows that there is not really belief with wide content as well as belief with narrow content. There is really just belief with narrow content, which may be described either as it is in itself or in terms that locate it by its relation to a wider context.[5] An

[3] As argued in Tyler Burge, 'Other Bodies', in A. Woodfield (ed.), *Thought and Object* (Clarendon Press, 1982).

[4] For the dispute between the two main views about what has to be true of an object for some name to refer to that object, the so-called descriptivist and causal theories of reference, see the papers of Gareth Evans and J. E. J. Altham, in *The Causal Theory of Names*, *Proceedings of the Aristotelian Society*, supp. vol., 47 (1973), 187–225.

[5] Thus Tyler Burge: 'Mistakes about the *res* in *de re* judgments are not counterexamples to the claim that basic cogito-like judgments are self-verifying (hence infallible). Suppose I judge: I am thinking that my aunt is charming; and suppose that the person that I am

ontology that seeks to describe the basic constituents of world will, therefore, confine itself to beliefs with narrow content.[6] Hence, for simplicity's sake, my concern with the rationality of belief will be a concern with the rationality of belief with narrow content. However, having made that point, I shall often consider beliefs that do have wide content, when nothing turns on the narrow/wide distinction—simply because they can often be expressed in shorter sentences than beliefs with narrow content. But such consideration is meant only as consideration of the narrow content beliefs that are involved in the wide content beliefs.

Strength of Belief

Beliefs may be strong or weak. My belief that the Second World War ended in AD 1945 is a strong one; I am strongly convinced of it. My belief that the War of the Roses ended in AD 1485 is considerably less strong; I do believe it but I could easily have got the date wrong. Can strength of belief be analysed further? I think that it can be and must be if a certain vagueness of ordinary language in our use of the term 'believe' is to be removed, and the concept of belief tightened up in such a way that the question of the justification of belief becomes clearer.

Belief, I suggest, is a contrastive notion; one believes this proposition as against that alternative proposition. The normal alternative with which a belief is contrasted is its negation. The negation of a proposition *p* is the proposition not-*p* or 'it is not the case that *p*'. The negation of 'today is Monday' is 'it is not the case that today is Monday' or 'today is not Monday'. This contrast can be explicated and made more precise with the aid of the

judging to be charming is not my aunt (I have some particular person in mind). It is true that I am making a mistake about the identity of the person thought about; I have no particular authority about that, or even about her existence. But I am not making a mistake about what I am thinking about that person; there is no mistake about the intentional act and intentional content of the act. Authority concerns those aspects of the thought which have intentional (aboutness) properties. For me, those arc the only aspects of the content of a thought.' ('Individualism and Self-Knowledge', *Journal of Philosophy*, 85 (1988), 649–63; see his n. 8 on p. 658).

[6] It does not follow that all psychological theories must be individualistic (i.e. in terms of narrow content)—see the controversy sparked by Tyler Burge, 'Individualism and Psychology', *Philosophical Review*, 95 (1986), 3–45. I endorse the conclusion of Frances Egan ('Must Psychology be Individualistic?', *Philosophical Review*, 100 (1991), 179- 203): 'Psychology does not have to be individualistic. Sometimes it is, sometimes it isn't' (pp. 202–3). But, even if wide content belief is what is required to explain behaviour, the point remains that a belief with a wide content consists of a belief with a narrow content and something else.

concept of probability.[7] When humans become sophisticated enough to have this concept, they will acknowledge—I suggest—logical connections between their believing a proposition *p* and their believing that *p* is probable. (For *p* to be probable is for it to have a probability of greater than $\frac{1}{2}$; and so not-*p* to have a probability of less than $\frac{1}{2}$. I understand *p* being certain as an extreme case of *p* being probable; it is *p* having a probability of 1.) To start with, they will acknowledge that, if I believe that *p* is not probable, I cannot believe that *p*—that is, that *p* is true. If I believe that it is more probable that not-*p* than that *p*, I cannot believe that *p*. If I believe that it is not probable that Liverpool will win the FA Cup, then (barring considerations to be discussed below, arising from the existence of a number of alternatives) I cannot believe that they will win. But what about the other way round? Suppose that I do believe that *p* is probable. Must I believe that *p*? Clearly, if either I am to believe that *p* or I am to believe that not-*p*, I must believe the former. But might I not believe that *p* is probable without believing that *p* or believing that not-*p*? If I believe that *p* is very, very probable, surely I believe that *p*. Cases where we would say the former are always cases where we would say the latter. If I believe that it is very, very probable that Liverpool will win the FA Cup , then I believe that Liverpool will win . The only difficulty arises when I believe that *p* is marginally more probable than not. Here we might be hesitant about whether to say that I believe that *p*. The hesitation arises, not from ignorance about any unobserved matters, but because the rules for the application of the concept of belief are not sufficiently precise. Maybe some people do use 'believe' so that (given that *S* has some belief about the probability of *p*) *S* has to believe that *p* is significantly more probable than not if *S* is to believe that *p*. But certainly others are prepared to allow that *S* believes that *p* if *S* believes merely that *p* is marginally more probable than not. It seems tidier to follow this latter usage. For, if we do not follow this usage, there would have to be some value of probability θ between $\frac{1}{2}$ and 1, such that only if *S* (having a belief about *p*'s probability) had the belief that *p* had a probability greater than θ would he believe that *p*. But any value chosen for θ would be extremely arbitrary. I conclude that, although our ordinary rules for the use of words *may* not be

[7] In writing in the remainder of this chapter about subjects' beliefs about probability, I am writing about what I shall call in the next chapter their beliefs about subjective probability—that is, probability by their own criteria and given their own limited abilities, of what is evidence for what. To believe that one's beliefs are probable is to believe that they are probable on the total evidence available to one. Evidence is, I suggest, to be understood in the sense of one's basic beliefs, as delineated in Chapter 5. These will include (see later in this chapter) strong beliefs about the public behaviour of others, which make very probable beliefs about their beliefs and purposes.

sufficiently precise for my suggestion to be clearly logically necessary (that is, to bring out what is involved in our current concept of belief), there is a strong case, if we are to have a clear concept of 'believe', for tightening up usage so that to believe that *p* is probable entails to believe that *p*, and to believe that *p* is not probable entails not to believe *p*. (And so to believe that the probability of *p* is $\frac{1}{2}$ entails to believe neither *p* nor not-*p*.)[8]

Although normally the sole alternative to a belief that *p* is its negation, sometimes there will be other alternatives. This will be the case where *p* is one of a number of alternatives being considered in a certain context. Thus 'Liverpool will win the Cup' may be being contrasted only with 'Liverpool will not win the Cup'. That is the normal contrast. But it may be being contrasted with a range of alternatives of the form 'Arsenal will win the Cup', 'Aston Villa will win the Cup', and so on; the belief that Liverpool will win the Cup is contrasted with each of these alternatives, but not with their disjunction. In this case similar considerations to those stated above indicate that we should explicate '*S* believes that *p*' so that only '*S* believes that *p* is more probable than *q*' and '*S* believes that *p* is more probable than *r*' and '*S* believes that *p* is more probable than *s*', and so on, for all the alternatives *q*, *r*, *s*, etc. together entail '*S* believes that *p*'; whereas for any one alternative *q*, '*S* believes that *p* is not more probable than *q*' entails '*S* does not believe *p*'. But, the normal alternative to a proposition being its negation, I shall assume (unless I state otherwise) that belief that *p* is governed by the logical relations stated in the previous paragraph.

For those who have beliefs of a very rough comparative kind about the probability of our simple beliefs (that is, beliefs that do not themselves involve the concept of probability), and they—I think—include most of us humans, strength of belief is then explicable as belief about how much

[8] In 'Swinburne on Faith and Belief', in Alan G. Padgett (ed.), *Reason and the Christian Religion* (Clarendon Press, 1994) (see pp. 25–9), William Alston criticized an earlier version of my account of the connection between believing and believing probable (as stated in my *Faith and Reason* (Clarendon Press, 1981), 4–8). There I wrote that to believe *p* is to believe *p* more probable than not. Alston made two objections to this account, both of which I now acknowledge as valid. The first was that a child could have a simple belief without having the concept of probability and so without having a belief about the former belief being probable. The second objection was that my account led to a vicious infinite regress. For, if to believe that *p* is always to believe that *p* is more probable than not -*p*, to believe that *p* is more probable than not-*p* will be to believe that (*p* is more probable than not-*p*) is more probable than not-(*p* is more probable than not-*p*), and so ad infinitum. Alston reasonably argued that this regress is a vicious regress, because it entails that each of us has beliefs of infinite complexity—which is absurd. The claim in the text above avoids these problems. It claims only that beliefs about *p*'s probability entail beliefs about *p*, but not vice versa. It constrains which beliefs about *p*'s probability can be held by a believer that *p*, but is compatible with her not having any such beliefs.

more probable a belief is than its negation. I believe *p* strongly if I believe that it is a lot more probable than its negation, weakly if I believe that it is only a little bit more probable than its negation. With this explication, we shall see—in a subsequent section—why it is not belief as such, but relative strength of belief that affects action (leads to our doing this rather than that). Since the effect of strong beliefs on action is the same in young children and others who do not have beliefs about the probability of other beliefs, as in adults who do have such beliefs, we can treat young children as if they had such beliefs, for the purpose of analysing the effect of belief on action. Their belief, like all beliefs, is a contrastive attitude—it consists in believing this as against that—that involves a vague and primitive form of a belief about relative probability. Strength of belief consists in having a strong contrastive attitude.

It follows from this that there is a sharp contrast to be made, often obscured in ordinary talk, between believing a conjunction and believing each of the conjuncts (where the contrasting alternative in all cases is the negation). I can believe that *p* and believe that *q* without believing that (*p* and *q*). For to believe that *p* is to believe *p* to be more probable than not-*p*; to believe that *q* is to believe *q* to be more probable than not-*q*; and to believe (*p* and *q*) is to believe (*p* and *q*) to be more probable than not-(*p* and *q*). I can believe that it is more probable that Liverpool will win the Football Cup than that it will not, and more probable that Arsenal will win the Football League than that it will not, without believing that it is more probable that (both Liverpool will win the cup and Arsenal will win the League) than that at least one of these things will not happen. I can believe that there is a probability of $\frac{3}{5}$ that Liverpool will win the Cup (and $\frac{2}{5}$ that it will not), and a probability of $\frac{3}{5}$ that Arsenal will win the League (and $\frac{2}{5}$ that it will not), and believe that there is a probability of $\frac{9}{25}$ that both of these things will happen (and so $\frac{16}{25}$ that at least one of them will not happen). So I can believe that Liverpool will win the Cup and also believe that Arsenal will win the League without believing that both Liverpool will win the Cup and Arsenal will win the League. Failure to note this point leads to such paradoxes as the 'Lottery Paradox'. Clearly I can believe of each of a million tickets in a lottery that it will not win (and on normal evidence it is rational to believe this), without believing the conjunction of these million propositions—that no ticket will win. The solution to the paradox is that each of the conjuncts is being contrasted with its negation (that one of the other tickets will win), whereas the conjunction is being contrasted with its negation (that some ticket will win). The possibility and rationality of each of the former beliefs does not entail the possibility or rationality of the latter belief. (Having made this important contrast between {believing *p* and believing *q*} and {believing *p* and *q*}, I shall in future—when nothing turns on it—gloss over it, in order to make the text more readable).

Infallibly Accessible and Involuntary

My concern with belief is then a concern with narrow content belief, understood in the way made precise in the last section. Beliefs are mental states (and so, in a wide sense, events) in the sense that the believer has privileged access to them. In this sense sensations, occurent thoughts, desires, and purposes are also mental states. Whatever means others have or can acquire for learning about my sensations, and so on, I can also acquire. They can learn about whether I am in pain by studying my behaviour and my brain states. But I can also study my behaviour (on a film) and my brain states (through a complicated system of mirrors and microscopes). Yet I have an additional means of learning whether I am in pain—by actually experiencing the pain. Some mental states are conscious states—such that, if we are in those states, necessarily to some extent we are occurently aware of being in those states. Pain is plausibly such a state. But some mental states are continuing states—that is, ones that we can have without currently being in any way aware of them; but they are mental in that we can, if we choose, become aware of them by a means not open to others.

Beliefs are, I suggest, continuing mental states. Clearly they continue while the believer is unaware of them. I have at the present instant many beliefs, for example, about ancient history, which do not impinge on my consciousness while I am thinking about other things. But they are mental states because I can become aware of them if I so choose, by asking myself what I think about the issue in question; I can, as it were, 'look in' on them. And, by what I acknowledge to myself in sincere internal admission to myself when I ask myself what I think, I have a means of access to my beliefs not available to others. It might be useful in explaining someone's behaviour to postulate an internal state with propositional content that is part of its cause, but, unless that state is one to which the subject has privileged access, it would seem to me that it does not count as a 'belief' in the ordinary sense of the word. Much of my hostile behaviour towards some person might be usefully explained by the 'belief' that he killed my mother. But, unless that belief is one that I will acknowledge to myself if I force myself to be as honest as I can be, there seems every reason not to call it a belief. And it certainly does not play the normal role that belief plays in my life—I do not alter it in the light of new evidence, I do not ask myself whether I have grounds for it, I do not take it into account when working out what to do. My concern in this book with belief is a concern with 'belief' in the ordinary sense, and that is a state to which its possessor has privileged access.

And not merely privileged but infallible access. Since someone's belief about something just is the way that a certain aspect of the world looks to him at a particular time, he cannot at that time be in error about it—that is, about the content of his belief. True, a person may refuse to admit to herself, let alone to others, that she has a certain belief—beliefs may be repressed. But to repress a belief is to hide from oneself, not merely that one has that belief, but that one believes that one does have that belief. (Repression of belief notoriously involves concealing itself.) Yet to hide a state of oneself from oneself still involves being in that state. So, if I have a belief *B*, and I have a belief *C* about whether or not I have a belief *B*, *C* will be infallible—whether or not I repress *B* and *C*.

I may not be able to put my beliefs into words of a public language, even if I try to do so. For first I may have mistaken beliefs about the meaning of public words. I may think that a table is called 'a chair' in English, and so, trying to put into words my belief that I have a brown table, I may say 'I have a brown chair'. Or, secondly, I may have beliefs for which I do not have any public words. Animals and very young children clearly have beliefs before they have a language in which to express them. And even when we do have quite a full language we may come across new kinds of objects and properties such that we can recognize new instances of them, but have no word for them. And if I cannot always put my own beliefs into words, there is no reason to suppose that others can always do so.

Belief is a passive state; believing is a state in which you are, it is not a matter of you doing something. And it is an involuntary state, a state in which you find yourself and which you cannot change at will at an instant. I believe that today is Tuesday, that I am now in Oxford, that Aquinas died in AD 1274, and so on and so on. I cannot suddenly decide to believe that today is Monday, that I am now in Italy, or that Aquinas lived in the eighteenth century. That belief is involuntary was a claim of Locke, Leibniz, and Hume. 'Belief consists', wrote Hume, 'merely in a certain feeling or sentiment; in something that depends not on the will, but must arise from certain determinate causes and principles of which we are not masters.'[9] But

[9] D. Hume, *Treatise Concerning Human Nature*, Appendix. See also J. Locke: 'Assent is no more in our power than knowledge . . . what upon full examination I find the most probable I cannot deny my assent to' (*Essay Concerning Human Understanding*, 4. 20. 16). And

what these writers do not bring out is that this is a logical matter, not a contingent feature of our psychology. For suppose that I could choose my beliefs—that is, bring them about intentionally. To do something intentionally involves knowing that you are doing it. Yet, if I knew that what I called 'my beliefs' were the result of my choice, I would know that they were not forced upon me by outside forces, that what I 'believed' was in no way influenced by what was the case in the outside world; what I 'believed' was simply what I chose to believe. But then I would know that I had no reason or grounds for believing 'my beliefs' either to be true or to be false; (on any understanding of 'likely' or 'probable') they would be just as likely to be false as to be true. But, if I thought that of my beliefs, I would not really believe them. We believe our beliefs because we know that we do not choose them but because (if we think about it) we believe that they are forced upon us by the outside world. But, although we cannot alter our beliefs just like that, what we can do is to take steps to alter them over a period of time; and I shall consider when (if we are concerned to have true beliefs) this is a good thing to do in Chapter 7.

The Logical Relations of Beliefs to other Mental States

Although we have infallible access, I have claimed, to the content of our beliefs, we cannot have single beliefs in isolation from other beliefs and other mental states; and, for each belief with a certain content, in order to be that belief it must sustain certain logical relations to the subject's other mental states. Our infallible access is to the web of such states.

First, if a believer has a belief that some proposition p is true, he will need to have other beliefs that certain propositions that are entailed by p are true, or to acquire these other beliefs if the possibility of their truth is put to him. I could not believe that (p&q), unless I would also (if it was put to me) believe that p and believe that q. Nor could I believe that the figure on the board has ten sides, unless I would also believe (if it was put to me) that the number of its sides was greater than seven. Note that I do not claim that having one belief entails having another; only that it entails having it when the possibility is put to the subject. For, whatever might be the case with the former example, clearly I might have the belief that the figure has ten sides, without it ever having crossed my mind that the number of its sides is

G. W. Leibniz puts into the mouth of his spokesman Theophilus the claim that beliefs are 'inherently involuntary' (*New Essays on Human Understanding*, trans. and ed. P. Remnant and J. Bennett (Cambridge University Press, 1981), 520).

greater than seven. If that is thought irrelevant and no distinction is made between the beliefs one has, and the propositions that one would believe if they were put to one, it would follow immediately that all subjects have an infinite number of beliefs. In the last example, we would have to ascribe to the subject beliefs that the number of sides of his figure is less than eleven, less than twelve, less than thirteen, and so on ad infinitum. And any attempt to identify beliefs with current states of the subject, let alone hold that beliefs are correlated one–one with brain states, immediately becomes implausible. Of course, it is not always very obvious exactly where the line is to be drawn between what one does believe and what one would believe it were put to one. But exact lines of application of concepts are never easy to draw, and that fact casts no doubt on the existence of clear cases where a concept applies and clear cases where it does not. (By some proposition being 'put' to the subject, I mean it being, he believes, immediately and obviously relevant to which actions he believes that he should perform. Whether I believe p is put to me when I am asked whether I believe p, for (I believe that) whether I believe p or not makes a difference to how I should answer the question. But a proposition is also put to me if (I believe that) it makes any other immediate and obvious difference to what I should do.)

It is equally, if not more difficult, to say *which* logical relations to other possible beliefs a belief needs to have in order to have a given belief. For clearly none of us is consistent enough to believe each of the consequences of our beliefs that are put to us. And it may well be that there are beliefs, such that any two subjects differ in respect of which of the consequences of that belief they are prepared to acknowledge. So, if we want to say that sometimes two subjects have the same belief (and surely we do), we need to say that in order to have a given belief, there are only certain very immediate and obvious consequences that subjects need to believe (if they are, they believe, put to them) if they are to have that belief. Immediacy and obviousness again make it difficult to draw lines, but again that need not worry us.

Secondly, there are many beliefs that involve concepts that are introduced to us in part by our having apparent perceptual experiences of their instantiation. We acquire colour concepts by being told that perceptual experiences on certain occasions are perceptions of something that looks yellow, red, or whatever, and many other concepts are introduced to us in this way, and it becomes part of our understanding of the concept that it applies to objects that look, sound, feel, or whatever, a certain way, a way that we are shown by example. A house is not just a building for living in, but something that looks like this and that and the other. Something is square, not merely if it has four equal sides and four equal angles, but if it is something that looks like such-and-such. (This way of connecting the concept to experience helps us to understand which concepts 'side' and 'angle' and 'equal' designate.) So we connect a belief that such concepts are instantiated with the kind of perceptual experiences that would lead us to believe that we are perceiving their instantiation. The belief that this house is square is in part the belief it is because of the perceptual experiences that we believe would be experiences of seeing that this house is square, even if we are not currently having these experiences. (Because the experiences that help to make the belief the belief it is need not be the actual past experiences that caused us to have the relevant concepts, but the possible experiences with which we now associate the concepts, our access to them can be infallible.) My belief that *p* is the belief it is because I believe that such-and-such experiences would be experiences of seeing it to be the case that *p*.

Thirdly, for a kind of belief that I shall call a means–end belief, the belief entails by which short-term purposes the subject will seek to achieve his longer-term purposes. By a believer's purposes I mean the purposes that he is currently attempting to achieve by his intentional actions. Intentional actions include more basic or short-term actions—moving arms or legs in various ways, saying this word or writing this sentence; and less basic or longer-term actions—walking to the railway station, delivering a certain lecture, writing a chapter of a book. We do the less basic actions by doing the more basic actions. By the agent intentionally attempting to do an action, I designate that mental state that would be called 'trying' in the case of difficulty or failure, but that must be the same state whether or not external factors prevent the agent from performing the action. When I try to move my arm but find that I cannot because my efferent nerves have been cut, my mental contribution is the same as when my nerves are operating normally. Our means–ends beliefs are beliefs about which short-term actions are steps towards which long-term actions; which of the former are such that their achievement will make it more probable that we shall perform which long-term actions. Since most actions, and especially the longer-term ones, consist in bringing about some state of affairs that we may call their goal or end, means–end beliefs are beliefs about which short-term actions will make more probable the attainment of certain goals. Examples are my belief that, to walk to the railway station most directly, I need to walk along this street and then that street; and my belief that to write a good chapter on belief I need to write sections on this aspect and then on that aspect of the topic.

For purposes, as for beliefs, subjects have privileged access to what their purposes (described in terms of narrow content) are. This is because whatever the ways that others use to learn about my purposes (by studying my behaviour and brain states) I can also use, but I have an additional way of learning about my purposes—by introspection. And my introspection will be infallible. I cannot really be intentionally attempting to walk to the station, unless I believe that that is my goal. If I did not believe that, it would be an unintended result of my walking that I arrived at the station. As with other beliefs, I may be unwilling to admit to myself what I am intentionally attempting; but this very description of the situation involves my having a true belief about what I am attempting. Long-term purposes plus means–end beliefs explain short-term purposes. Because I am intentionally attempting to walk to the station by the most direct route and have the means–end belief that, by walking along this street and then that street, I shall get to the station most directly, I begin my walk by intentionally attempting to walk along this street. A purpose that is not explained by any longer-term purpose I will call an ultimate purpose. The agent does not seek to fulfil an ultimate purpose as a step towards any further goal. Most of us have at any one time more than one ultimate purpose, and some of them may not be very long term. I may have an ultimate purpose of writing a book (and so the shorter-term purpose of writing this paragraph) at the same time as an ultimate purpose of drinking a cup of coffee (ultimate, because I do not form it in order to forward some greater scheme). Or I may have an ultimate purpose of eating lunch at the same time as a purpose of talking agreeably to my companion.

The relation between purposes and means–ends beliefs becomes a bit more complicated when we take into account the strengths of different beliefs and purposes. I may have a number of beliefs about which means will attain which ends of different strengths—that is, put in probability terms, I ascribe different probabilities to different means attaining different ends. And, as first noted, I may be attempting to fulfil more than one ultimate purpose at the same time, but give greater priority to one over another.

If my one and only ultimate purpose in life is to get to London in my car, and I believe the left-hand road leads to London and the right-hand road does not, then I shall form the more basic purpose of taking the left-hand road. But this is a highly simplified situation, and the way in which belief affects more basic purposes usually depends on the relative strengths of the different beliefs and on the relative strengths of the different ultimate purposes that we have simultaneously. I may believe that the right-hand road also leads to London, but, so long as my belief that the left-hand road leads to London is stronger, I shall still purpose to take the left-hand road. Or rather I shall—so long as getting to London by car is my only ultimate purpose in life. But normally I shall have also other ultimate purposes—not to drive for too many hours, to drive via interesting scenery; and so on. Then other beliefs will enter in to determine what are the consequences of my ultimate purposes for my more basic purposes.

The relative strengths of various beliefs—which, I have argued, can usefully be explicated in terms of beliefs about relative probability—have the following consequences for more basic purposes, even when we cannot compare strengths of ultimate purposes:

> If *S* has ultimate purposes to achieve goals X_1, X_2, X_3, etc., which she believes incompatible (that is, attaining one entails not attaining the others), she will form the more basic purpose to do an action A_1 (rather than actions believed incompatible with A_1—A_2, A_3, etc.) in so far as she believes that the probability that:
>
> (1) A_1 will lead to the attainment of X_1
> is greater than the probability of any other statement of the form
> (1*a*) A_n $(n \neq 1)$ will lead to the attainment of X_1;
> and that:
> (2) A_1 will lead to the attainment of X_2
> is greater than the probability of any other statement of the form
> (2*a*) A_n $(n \neq 1)$ will lead to the attainment of X_2;
> and that
> (3) A_1 will lead to the attainment of X_3
> is greater than the probability of any other statement of the form
> (3a) A_n $(n \neq 1)$ will lead to the attainment of X_3.
> and so on.

If *S* believes that some of these conditions are satisfied, and that in no case the converse is satisfied (for example, that the probability a statement of the form of (2*a*) is greater than that of (2)), *S* will form the purpose to do A_1. In other cases, if *S*'s purposes to attain her different goals are of equal strength, she will form the purpose to do A_1 if she believes that it is more probable that A_1 will attain one of the goals than that any alternative action will attain one of the goals. But, if the purposes are not of equal strength, whether S will purpose to do A_1 will depend on whether her strongest purposes (the goals she seeks most to attain) are ones that, she believes, will more probably be attained by doing A_1 than by doing any incompatible action.[10]

Although beliefs about comparative probability (that *p* is more probable than *q*) are ones that subjects often have and ones about which they can have infallible awareness, most people do not have many beliefs about probabilities of propositions that have precise numerical values. Sometimes we may believe that the proposition that some future event will occur has a precise numerical probability (other than 1, 0, or $\frac{1}{2}$)—say that there is a 0.32 probability of the coin landing heads (because we have noted that 32 of the past 100 tosses were heads)—but this is unusual. The only beliefs that have immediate consequences for which combinations of ultimate and more basic purposes we can have are means–ends beliefs. But we normally hold means–end beliefs because they follow from other beliefs, including theoretical beliefs in the sense of beliefs about how the world is categorically (in contrast to hypothetical beliefs about what would happen if such-and-such). Yet any given means–end belief will follow from innumerable different conjunctions of other beliefs. My example of the previous page was oversimplified in not bringing out this point. 'The . . . road leads to London' in that example should be read more precisely as 'If I drive down the . . . road, I will get to London'. But I may hold that belief because I hold any one of very different conjunctions involving theoretical beliefs. I may hold it because I believe that the road goes to London and my car works well and has enough petrol to get to London (and a few other beliefs as well). Or I may hold it because I believe that there is a lorry at the end of the road that will pick up any car that comes down it and take it to London. Or I may hold it because I believe that the road goes to the house of a witch, who will wave a wand that will instantaneously take any car that passes to London. And so on. More generally, for any given ultimate purpose, any more basic purpose is compatible with the subject having any of many different sets of theoretical beliefs from which the relevant means–end belief follows.

All beliefs, however recondite in combination with some other belief, will have consequences for how someone should seek to execute some ultimate purpose. My belief that the Pharaoh referred to in the concluding chapters of the Book of Genesis was Ramses II may seem to have little by

[10] It is one of the roles of decision theory, which I discuss in Additional Note B, to draw out the consequences of our beliefs and ultimate purposes for our more basic purposes—that is, which actions we would attempt, if we were logically omniscient.

way of consequences for action. But all beliefs whatsoever, when combined with beliefs about the meanings of sentences, have consequences for what someone should purpose to say if they have the purpose of telling the truth. If I believe that you are asking me which in my view was the Pharaoh referred to in the Book of Genesis, then if I have the purpose of telling you the truth about my beliefs, and if also I have such beliefs as that 'Ramses II' denotes Ramses II (that is, the person whom everyone else called 'Ramses II'), I will purpose to say 'Ramses II'.

I noted, however, a few pages back that, while having a belief entailed believing some of its consequences (if they are put to one), it certainly could not entail believing all of its consequences, or indeed any particular one of them unless the issue of whether there was this entailment was put to one. In consequence, one may well have theoretical beliefs, of whose consequences for action one is unaware—especially if the consequences are somewhat remote consequences that follow from a combination of beliefs that one has. Hence some people may have beliefs that do not, together with their ultimate purposes, lead to the more basic purposes to which they would lead in other people who are better aware of the logical consequences of their beliefs.

So—in summary—a subject can have only a given belief (that is, one with a certain content) if it has certain relations to other beliefs of his, (in the case of perceptual beliefs) to the experiences that the subject regards as experiences of it, and (in the case of means–ends beliefs) to the ways in which he seeks to fulfil his ultimate purposes. His infallible access to the content of his beliefs is an infallible access to the web of mental states to which it belongs.[11]

[11] The account that I have given of how beliefs are the beliefs they are in virtue of their relations to other beliefs, to perceptual experiences, and to attempted actions, is similar in principle to the account given in outline by Christopher Peacocke in *A Study of Concepts* (MIT Press, 1992), esp. ch. 4. Thus for Peacocke (p. 107): 'the relations required of a state if it is to be a belief with a given content are fixed by the possession conditions of the constituent concepts of that concept . . . The possession condition will mention the role of the concept in certain transitions that the thinker is willing to make.' These transitions include both 'inferential transitions'—relations to other beliefs, and 'transitions from initial states involving perceptual experience'. He then goes on to suggest, more tentatively (p. 114), that we might 'write into the relational property required for a state of belief with a given content the requirement that there be desire-like states with which it is capable of interacting to produce intentions and actions'. His 'intentions' are my purposes, attempts to perform actions. For Peacocke, however, 'perceptual experience' is tied far more tightly to its public causes, and 'intentions' are tied far more tightly to their public effects than for me.

The Public Manifestation of Belief

But how are other people to have access to this web, to learn what a given person believes? The obvious answer is by means of the public input to and output from a person's belief-system. Thus, it may seem, we can have access to someone else's perceptual beliefs by their public cause. Your experience is an experience of a square object if it is one normally caused by a square object, if it is an experience you normally get when you look at a square object. Your experience is an experience of your house if it is an experience you normally get when you look at your house. Hence the belief you have caused by an experience normally caused by looking at your square house is the belief that your house is square; and a belief on any other occasion is that belief if it is the belief that could have been caused in that way.

One trouble with this answer is that some people do not notice what stares them in the face, or—if they do—do not have the same sensory apparatus or the same concepts as others for what they perceive to give rise in them to the same beliefs as it does in others. I may look at a magenta cummerbund, and that may cause a visual experience that gives rise to a belief. But, since I am partially colour-blind and unobservant, the experience represents itself to me as one of a brown tie, and so I acquire the belief that I am seeing a brown tie. Or even if I am not colour-blind or unobservant, if I do not have the concepts of 'magenta' or 'cummerbund', looking at the magenta cummerbund will still not give rise to the belief that I am seeing a magenta cummerbund. Among the public input to someone's belief-system is what they are told orally or in writing. But again they may not pay attention to what they are told, they may not be able to discriminate the words accurately, or they may not know what the words mean.

And why not suppose that some people are subject to much more massive malfunctioning? Maybe the colour experiences caused by blue objects in you are the same as the colour experiences caused by red objects in me, and vice versa. Or, worse still, maybe round objects look to you the way square objects look to the rest of us, and conversely. And so on. Why should not others acquire massively erroneous beliefs from their observation of the world?

An obvious answer is that such erroneous beliefs would show up in the subject's public behaviour. And it is its connections with public output that are often thought to provide the best public criteria for what a subject believes. Means–end beliefs plus ultimate purposes lead to basic purposes, that is attempted bodily actions—how I try to move my hands or legs or lips. And means–end beliefs plus ultimate purposes plus basic powers (which bodily movements I can make if I try) determine which bodily movements I do make and which (in virtue of being intentionally produced) are bodily actions—my moving this arm or that leg in such and such a way, or uttering this or that word. If we assume that all humans have roughly the same powers of direct control over their bodies (for example, that we can all move our legs at will but not make our hair stand on end at will) and that we do move parts of our bodies in the ways typical of voluntary motion only when we purpose to do so (for example, that never, when we try to move an arm, does the leg move instead), then means–end beliefs plus ultimate purposes will lead to certain bodily movements as opposed to others.

But even given the assumption about his basic powers, we can only infer from his actions to an agent's means–end beliefs, on some assumption about his purposes. If we suppose that my one and only purpose is to get to London in my car, and if I take the left-hand road, then I must believe that it is at least as probable that the left-hand road will get me to London as that the right-hand one will. But any stretch of public behaviour is compatible with the subject having any of innumerable alternative sets of means–end beliefs plus purposes. If I take some pills, that may be because I believe they will cure my headache and I have the purpose of curing it; or because I believe they will kill me and I have the purpose of committing suicide; or because I believe that they will give me a beautiful vision and I have the purpose of having a beautiful vision. Public behaviour will, however, rule out many combinations of purposes plus means–end beliefs. My taking the pills would rule out my having the belief that they will kill me together with the ultimate purpose of staying alive (and no other ultimate purposes). And so on.

The only beliefs that make a difference to which actions I perform in order to execute my purposes are means–end beliefs; and these, we saw earlier, may result from innumerable different combinations of more theoretical beliefs. If I believe that my house (which is in fact square) is round and also believe that material objects (including humans) are subject to certain sorts of expansions and contractions near the walls of the house, I will have the same means–end beliefs about which item of furniture I can fit into a room as I would if I believed that the house was square and there were no such disturbing forces. And any inference from people's means–end beliefs to the more theoretical beliefs lying behind them will have to take account of the possibility that those people may not draw out the means–end beliefs that follow from their more theoretical beliefs. All depends on how far they are aware of the consequences of their more theoretical beliefs; that can be guaranteed only where the consequences by way of means–end beliefs relevant to which action should be performed are immediate and obvious.

Among the behaviour by which we rightly seek to discover what someone believes are his utterances (in speech or writing). My answer to the question 'which Pharaoh do you believe was the one referred to in the Book of Genesis?'—'Ramses II'—will show you what I believe only if you assume that I have the purpose of telling the truth and a belief that 'Ramses II' refers to 'Ramses II' and a true belief about the meaning of the question. And, as mentioned earlier, even the very limited inferences we can make from their behaviour to people's beliefs assumes that they have similar basic powers. Maybe when I was trying to say 'Merneptah', believing that Merneptah was the Pharaoh referred to, the words 'Ramses II' came out of my mouth.

So is it not possible that we may be massively in error about other people's beliefs (and their purposes and the extent of their bodily powers)? My answer to this question is that this is indeed logically possible, but it is massively improbable. This is because (our inductive criteria are such that) the theory that leads us to expect the data that we observe, which is simplest, is the one most probably true; and the simplest theory about the public behaviour of others in response to input to their sense organs has the consequence that normally they have the same very general beliefs about the world as ourselves. Fuller argument in favour of these being the criteria we use (and are right to use) to reach probable conclusions about the causes of phenomena will be given in Chapter 4.

More specifically—we use the principle of simplicity in attributing to people relatively stable purposes, beliefs, and bodily capacities. We assume, other things being equal, that the beliefs and purposes manifested in a person's actions today and yesterday are similar; that different people including ourselves have similar purposes in similar situations and that people acquire similar beliefs when presented with similar stimuli in accord with some relatively simple belief-producing process whereby similar kinds of input produce similar kinds of belief (and that people have similar abilities to each other to control their bodily movements).[12] These assumptions are

[12] The fact that it is as such simpler to suppose that other people are much like ourselves in their purposes and ways of belief acquisition, and so—when they are on the whole in circumstances not too dissimilar from ours—that they have on the whole similar beliefs to ours, suggests Davidson's Principle of Charity: always assume that other people's general beliefs are much like ours, and so (since we must believe our own beliefs to be true), also true. Generally, the simplest theory of our own and other people's beliefs and purposes will attribute much the same general beliefs and purposes to all of us. But not necessarily or

then qualified in so far as is necessary to construct a theory of purpose and belief compatible with observed public behaviour, but qualified so as to complicate them as little as possible. Application of these principles allows us to reach conclusions very, very probably true, about what a person believes. If we show to a person *S* other people being killed by being shot in the heart, we reasonably suppose that *S* will come to believe that shooting kills (since we ourselves would come to hold that belief when shown what *S* was shown), and so, if we then see *S* shooting someone else *T*, we infer that he believes that he will kill *T*, and so (since shooting involves a bodily movement that we can control) that he has the purpose of killing *T*. We assume that purposes do not come and go completely randomly, and so, if failing to hit *T* with his shot, *S* then tries to strangle him, we infer that *S* believes that strangling kills (because *S*'s purpose of killing *T* has remained). And so on. Further, we attribute to believers the simplest set of more theoretical beliefs that will entail the means–end beliefs we attribute to them; or, more precisely, the simplest set that includes a hypothesis about the extent to which normally they are aware of the consequences of their more theoretical beliefs. What people say about their more theoretical beliefs is often the best guide to what these are, because the simplest theory of their verbal behaviour in most circumstances is normally one that attributes to them the purpose of telling the truth, and having the linguistic competence to do so. But, if the simplest overall theory of their beliefs and purposes has the consequence that certain people tell lies on certain matters, we should hold that.

Assumptions about bodily powers can also be qualified if making the qualification allows us to adopt a simpler theory of an agent's purposes and beliefs than we would otherwise be able to have. If most of the things you say are what you would not say if you have the purposes that other people have (for example, to talk in some way relevantly) and the beliefs they have (for example, about what things are relevant), we may reasonably suppose that you do not know what you are saying—the words simply come out of your mouth unintended by you—as in Wernicke's aphasia.

always. The simplest theory might lead us to radically different theories of the purposes and beliefs of another community from our own (if that community is situated in very different circumstances from ours, or if its members behave in very different ways). And, in so far as, consistently with their behaviour, we could attribute the same purposes and beliefs to both groups, this might involve postulating that the others acquired their beliefs in a very complicated way. So Davidson exaggerates in claiming that 'charity is forced on us; whether we like it or not, if we want to understand others, we must count them right in most matters' ('On the Very Idea of a Conceptual Scheme', in Donald Davidson, *Inquiries into Truth and Interpretation* (Clarendon Press, 1984), 197).

The public evidence that we should take into account in reaching a view about someone's beliefs should include (if and when we discover that) evidence about their brain states. For, since beliefs cause behaviour by causing brain states, which in turn cause behaviour, and are caused by observable phenomena by the latter causing brain states that in turn cause beliefs, any evidence of different brain states underlying their beliefs in different people when their behaviour or the public observable phenomena are the same will be evidence (via the principle of simplicity) of difference of belief. We seek the overall simplest theory that leads us to expect the data—of brain states as well as of public behaviour, and that is the one most probably true.

In practice, when we are interpreting the behaviour (and, in so far as we know them, the brain states) of other human beings, we surely often reach a theory of them that is very probably true indeed (because massively simpler than any other theory that will lead us to expect that behaviour and those brain states). Yet I suggest that it is logically possible that we may be mistaken in undiscoverable ways. Someone tells *S* that a certain pill will kill people. *S* has not been getting on well recently with his wife, and is short of money. If *S*'s wife dies, *S* will inherit her money. His wife reports having a headache; he gives her the pill, she takes it and dies. The simplest explanation of *S*'s behaviour is that he believes that the pill will kill and he sought to kill his wife by giving her the pill. But maybe he misheard what he was told about the pill—maybe he thought that his informant said that it would cure headaches. That is, maybe what *S* was told caused in *S* the belief that the pill cures, not that it kills. In that case, *S*'s action is to be explained by a purpose of helping. The simplest explanation of the public phenomena may not be the true one; and that remains the case, however much further public evidence we get about brain states and subsequent behaviour. Yet the subject who has infallible access to his beliefs and purposes may know more than the public evidence shows.[13]

[13] Many philosophers hold that, to have a 'factual meaning'—i.e. to state a possibly true contingent fact—in a public language, a proposition must be in some degree verifiable or falsifiable; or at least that the concepts involved in it must on other occasions occur in propositions which are in some degree verifiable or falsifiable. My view that it is logically possible that we may be incorrigibly mistaken about the purposes and beliefs of others does not fall foul of either of these public requirements, so long as 'in some degree verifiable' is understood as 'rendered probable by the publicly observable evidence' and 'in some degree falsifiable' as 'rendered improbable by the publicly observable evidence'. For all of the claims I discuss are rendered probable by one sort of public evidence and improbable by another (given that—as I shall be arguing at length in Chapter 4—simplicity is evidence of truth). And so we can identify which proposition about someone's mental life we are discussing, by which public evidence would make it probable and which public evidence would make it improbable. It can still happen that our public evidence is such that a proposition about

It follows that what makes a (narrow content) belief the belief it is is internal to it and is logically independent of its physical causes and effects. For, with respect to each of two different beliefs, it is logically possible that that belief be correlated with a brain state with a certain physical nature and certain causal links to other brain states and to the world outside the body. Nevertheless, I have been arguing, the brain states and behaviour causally connected with a subject's beliefs constitute very strong evidence of what those beliefs are.[14] So beliefs (and, by a similar argument, purposes) are not physical events, these being events individuated solely by public criteria.

There are Beliefs

So far I have been assuming that there are such states of affairs as beliefs and I have been examining what makes it the case that a belief has this content rather than that one. But a number of modern philosophers known as 'eliminativists' hold that there are no such states as beliefs—or purposes or desires or thoughts or any other mental states[15] (although they acknowledge that it is more convenient in ordinary conversation to talk as if there were such states). The view that there are such states and that they explain our behaviour is regarded by these philosophers as an out-of-date psychological theory that they call 'folk psychology'. For, the argument goes, the vast success of physical science makes it immensely probable that all physical events (including bodily movements) are caused solely by other physical events; and so beliefs can explain any events only if they are the same as physical events. I have argued above that beliefs, and likewise purposes,

someone's mental life improbable on that evidence is nevertheless true; and the subject having privileged access to his mental life can know that. To demand that the principle of meaning be understood in less liberal terms—to demand that to have factual meaning a proposition must be conclusively verifiable or falsifiable—leads to well-known implausibilites. For example, no proposition of the form '(x) $(\exists y)$ $(x\ Ry)$' (e.g. 'everyone has someone who loves them') when x and y range over possibly infinite sets would have any meaning. For such propositions are neither conclusively verifiable nor conclusively falsifiable.

[14] This is a very brief argument for a view that is the subject of an enormous amount of philosophical controversy. My excuse for its brevity is that my view of the nature of belief is not of enormous importance for most of the argument of this book about the justification of belief. For much fuller argument that beliefs, purposes, etc., are not the same events as any brain events, see my *The Evolution of the Soul* (rev. edn., Clarendon Press, 1997), pt. I.

[15] See e.g. P. M. Churchland, 'Eliminative Materialism and Propositional Attitudes', *Journal of Philosophy*, 78 (1981), 67–90.

are mental events, distinct from physical events (although, of course, in causal interaction with them). But, suppose (as eliminativists as well as others would claim) that my argument is mistaken. It would then follow that, if there are beliefs and purposes, each token belief (that is, each belief on a particular occasion when someone has it) would be the same event as some brain event, and each token purpose would be the same as some other brain event. But there is no reason to suppose, the argument goes, that for each public action we can conveniently divide up its causes in the brain into two separate components, a belief and a purpose, such that all brain events that are beliefs have something in common with other brain events that are beliefs but differ from them in a way correlated with the way in which the content of one belief differs from the content of another belief (and similarly for brain events that are purposes). The brain is not like that; it does not have states that can be put into one-one correlation with our beliefs and purposes. Really, says the eliminativist, there are just brain events. Beliefs, like phlogiston and witches, do not really exist.

This argument seems to me to have some plausibility once its assumption is granted that beliefs and purposes (if they exist) just are physical events. But, given my arguments against that, there is no reason for going along with the eliminativist. And indeed the (to my mind) obvious falsity of his conclusion seems to me to be very strong further evidence against his initial assumption. For it is more obvious than is almost anything else that we have purposes to achieve goals by our actions. We could do that only if we have beliefs about which actions will (probably) achieve which goals. Eliminativism is at most a bold guess about the result of future science. That we seek to attain goals by contrast stares us in the face as an evident fact. So I stick with the common-sense view that there are beliefs. But I emphasize that they are not the same as brain events, although causally sustained by brain events and (together with purposes) causing other brain events.

The Value of True Belief

True belief is undoubtedly a good thing to have. Only with true beliefs can we achieve our purposes. Only if I have a true belief about where Latimer Road is can I achieve my purpose of getting there. And true beliefs about people and things close to you or central to human history are intrinsically valuable. It matters that I shall have true beliefs about whether my wife is faithful, who my parents are, whether the Earth is the centre of the

Universe, or whether it is sometimes right to torture people—whether or not such beliefs make any difference to my conduct. (It makes a difference to my character what are my beliefs about the morality of torture, whether or not I ever torture anyone or encourage anyone else to do so or discourage them from doing so.) And strong true belief is better than weak true belief. For weak true belief will be weaker and so less influential in conduct than any somewhat stronger false belief. If I have the weak true belief that this road leads to Latimer Road, and a stronger false belief that that road also leads to Latimer Road, I shall take the latter road—and so not achieve my purpose. And, if true belief has intrinsic value, it seems intrinsically good that it be strong; for that amounts to seeing clearly rather than cloudily how things are.

Stephen Stich[16] has argued that true belief has no value. His argument, however, depends crucially on the view that the only events are physical events; there are no events other than brain events that influence our conduct. He allows that maybe (contrary to eliminativism) we can map beliefs (and purposes) onto brain events by some function that picks out some token brain event as a particular belief (or purpose), in virtue of its place in a network of causal relations to other brain events and to the world outside the body being parallel to the logical relations of that belief (or purpose) to other beliefs and purposes of the subject and to their extra-bodily causes and effects. More precisely, the function just maps brain states onto sentences of some natural language that express the propositions that form the content of the supposed beliefs and purposes. On this model it is not that brain states provide evidence of which beliefs we have (as I have claimed), but that which beliefs we have just is a matter of the function that correlates them with brain states (chosen perhaps on grounds of simplicity, but only so by convention; not because simplicity is evidence of something beyond the brain state). Stich then reasonably claims that philosophers could easily invent many different functions that would correlate brain states with sentences in very different ways, which would explain (with varying degrees of simplicity perhaps, we should add) the same behaviour. How we map brain states onto sentences will, however, make no difference to our behaviour, which will be caused by brain states alone; and so will make no difference to our prospects for survival and happiness—and so why should it matter how we do the mapping and so what beliefs we have?

Stich's conclusion, like that of the eliminativist, certainly follows from his premisses. But the conclusion is so implausible that it casts further

[16] See his *The Fragmentation of Reason* (MIT Press, 1990), ch. 5.

doubt on his premisses, including the crucial premiss that the only events that influence our conduct are brain events, individuated by public criteria—a view that I have already given reason to reject. It seems overwhelmingly evident that it is because of the content of our beliefs and purposes that we act as we do. It is because I believe that Headington Road leads to Latimer Road that I drive along Headington Road, when I have the purpose of getting to Latimer Road. With a belief (or purpose) with different content I would not be driving along Headington Road. Since it would follow from Stich's view that beliefs individuated in part by their content, something to which we have privileged access, do not affect behaviour, it follows from the falsity of the latter that Stich's argument fails.

So much for the nature of beliefs. I pass now to the central issue of this book—when is a belief a justified belief.

3

Probability

The adequacy of grounds is often expressed in terms of probability—both by the externalist and by the internalist. The grounds for a belief are adequate to the extent to which they render the belief probable. (And if the grounds for one belief *B* consist of another belief *C*, then, for *B* to have adequate grounds, *C*'s grounds must make *B* probable. I assume this qualification throughout, without mentioning it on each relevant occasion.) Adequacy is thus a matter of degree, and one needs some level of adequacy for the belief to become justified. For the normal case where belief that *p* is belief that *p* as opposed to not-*p*, the natural level to suggest for the adequacy of its grounds to make the belief justified is that the grounds give it probability of greater than $\frac{1}{2}$. As we saw in the last chapter, where people are sufficiently sophisticated to have beliefs about the probabilities of other beliefs, belief that *p* is best explicated as belief that *p* is more probable than not-*p*. Probabilities of alternatives (which are exclusive and exhaustive) sum to 1 (see later) and so, if the probability of *p* is greater than that of not-*p*, it is greater than $\frac{1}{2}$. So a belief that *p* (as opposed to not-*p*) is justified if it really does have a probability greater than $\frac{1}{2}$ (which is what the believer will believe about it if he is sophisticated enough to have a belief about its probability). The belief is better justified (the grounds are more adequate), the more that probability exceeds $\frac{1}{2}$ and the closer it is to 1. However, internalists and externalists have very different understandings of the kind of probability involved, and so we need to spell out what are the different kinds of probability. (I shall sometimes use 'likely' as a synonym for 'probable'.)

Physical Probability

First there is physical (or natural) probability, sometimes called by contemporary philosophers of science 'chance'.[1] This is a measure of the extent

[1] Although I think that 'physical probability' is the least unsatisfactory name for this kind of probability, I draw attention to the awkwardness that there may be a 'physical

to which some particular outcome is predetermined by its causes at some earlier time. An event having a probability of 1 is it being predetermined to happen; an event having a probability of 0 is it being predetermined not to happen. Intermediate values measure the extent of the bias in nature towards the event happening or not happening. To say that the probability now of this atom of C_{14} decaying within 5,600 years is $\frac{1}{2}$ is to say that, given the whole state of the world now, it is not predetermined whether the atom will decay within 5,600 years, but that nature has an equal propensity to produce decay and to produce no decay within that time. A physical probability of 1 we may call physical necessity, and a physical probability of 0 physical impossibility. Physical probability is relative to time—as the time at which the event is predicted to happen or not to happen draws near, so (if that probability is not 1 or 0) the probability of its occurrence may change.

The operation of determinism within a period of time *T* is then best represented as the claim that for every event *E* (within *T*) there is at each prior time *t* within *T* an event *C* (which may be a state of the whole universe), such that *C* has a physical probability of 1 of causing *E*; indeterminism is the claim that for some *E* (within *T*) and some *t* (within *T*), there is an event *C* for which that does not hold.[2]

Statistical Probability—Actual and Hypothetical

Then there is statistical probability. A statistical probability is simply a proportion of events, either in an actual class or in a hypothetical class, that is a class generatable by a repeatable process. Ordinary language expressions in which the probability is said to concern 'a' member—that is, any member—of some class are naturally interpreted in one of these two ways. 'The probability of a registered voter in New Hampshire in the year 2000 voting for the Republican presidential candidate is 0.56′ is naturally interpreted as a claim that 56 per cent registered voters in New Hampshire in 2000 voted for the Republican presidential candidate. This is a claim about an actual proportion in a finite class. There can also be claims about actual proportions in an

probability' for the occurrence of mental states. In saying this, I am using this expression solely in the sense defined above, and am not implying any physicalist account of the mental.

[2] Events include both changes of states, and unchanging states. The localization of determinism to a period of time allows for such possibilities as that the universe may be deterministic now, even if it began with an uncaused 'Big Bang'.

infinite class—for example, about the proportion of stars more than 5 billion years old, where—let us suppose—there are an infinite number of stars. I shall, however, assume (unless stated otherwise) that an actual statistical probability is a proportion in a finite class. By contrast, 'the probability of *a* toss of this (newly minted) coin being heads is $\frac{1}{2}$' is naturally interpreted as an assertion about a proportion in a class generatable by a repeatable process—namely, tossing the coin. It is not a claim that at some time the physical probability of any toss is $\frac{1}{2}$—for that is obviously most unlikely. The world is at any rate nearly deterministic and physical probabilities of such outcomes are likely to be close to 1 or 0, according to the initial conditions (angle of toss, momentum imparted to coin, and so on). Rather, it is a claim about a proportion of outcomes of a procedure, but not an actual proportion—for the coin may not have been tossed and may never be going to be tossed. It is a claim about a proportion that would result if it were tossed. It is vague how many times a process would need to be repeated in order to yield the proportion with which such hypothetical statistical probabilities are concerned. But it is convenient to make the notion more precise in the way that mathematicians often do, to suppose that it concerns the proportion in an infinite class; and I shall assume (unless stated otherwise) that a hypothetical statistical probability is a proportion in an infinite class. In that case there must normally (if the assertion is to have clear content) be an understanding of the order in which members of the class are taken; and the assertion is then to be read as claiming that, when more and more members of the class are taken in that order, (eventually) the proportion diverges less and less from the stated value.[3] Consider the infinite class of natural numbers (1, 2, 3 . . .). What is the probability of a member of that class being an even number? If the numbers are arranged in their normal order (of increasing magnitude), the probability is $\frac{1}{2}$, because as you take more and more numbers (eventually) the proportion gets and stays closer and closer to half ($\frac{1}{2}, \frac{1}{3}, \frac{2}{4}, \frac{2}{5}, \frac{3}{6}$ . . .). But they can be arranged differently. Suppose that you arrange them in the order of even numbers (of increasing magnitude), inserting two odd numbers (in order of increasing magnitude) after each even number. Then your series begins 2, 1, 3, 4, 5, 7, 6, 9, 11, 8, 13, 15 . . . The probability of a number being an even number is then $\frac{1}{3}$. The order in which members are taken does not matter when we are dealing only with a finite class. Here the probability of an *A* being *B* is given by the proportion of *A*s in

[3] More precisely: to say that the proportion of *A*s that are *B* in an infinite class of *A*s (taken in a certain order) is p is to say that, for every finite number $d>0$, there is some number of *A*s n_d such that, for any $n>n_d$, where there are n *A*s (that is, the first n *A*s in the order), r of which are *B*, $p+d>\frac{r}{n}>p-d$.

the whole class of *B*s. But 'proportion in the whole class' is an expression that will not have a meaning when we are talking about an infinite class unless the order of selection is specified[4] (except in some cases, where the order of selection makes no difference to the proportion).

There must also, if an assertion of hypothetical statistical probability is to have clear meaning, normally be an understanding of what must remain constant and what is allowed to vary (and how) when new members of the class are generated. As we have noted, the world is deterministic (or very nearly so)—that is, which event occurs at a given time is fully determined by each previous state of the universe (within some interval of time). Then if we specify fully enough the conditions in which each toss of a certain coin is to be made—which face is upward when the toss is made, the exact angle of toss, distance above the table of the toss, momentum imparted to the coin, distribution of air molecules in the room, and so on, and that any wear and tear to coin or room is repaired, the probability of it landing heads will be 1 for many sets of conditions, and 0 for many other sets of conditions (or values very close to these values). When we claim that the probability of a toss of the coin landing heads is $\frac{1}{2}$, which sets of conditions are we assuming to hold? Clearly neither. We suppose that these conditions may vary. But how? In the proportions in which, when people normally toss coins, they do actually vary in such a way as to make a difference to the result. That is, since most coin-tossers do not choose at which angle to toss their coin, it will lie equally often within areas of equal angular width within a range from say 90° to the floor to 30°. And so on for all the other conditions that affect the result. (Since the proportions of relevant conditions in which people normally toss coins surely do not vary significantly according to the spatio-temporal region in which we measure them, we can speak without ambiguity of 'the proportions'.) Given this ordinary context, then the probability of heads may indeed be $\frac{1}{2}$. But it may not be beyond the skill of a practised tosser who wants the coin to land heads to toss a coin in a very calm room at a chosen angle with a chosen momentum at a chosen height above the ground in such a way as to ensure that the proportion of heads is quite different—for example, $\frac{3}{4}$ or $\frac{1}{4}$. (It is to guard against practised tossers that, when issues in a game depend on the toss of a coin, one person tosses and his opponent 'calls' which toss is to constitute a win for him while the coin is in the air.)

[4] Some writers insist that one can talk about statistical probability only in a class selected by a 'random' process. For this requirement, and reasons for rejecting it, see Additional Note C on Randomness.

What are the logical relations between physical and statistical probability? Statistical probability is concerned with what actually happens, or would happen under certain circumstances. Physical probability is concerned with what is inclined to happen, and so—in extreme cases—with what has to happen. The one entails deductively very little about the other. Only physical probabilities (at some time) of 1 or 0 are guaranteed to make a difference to what happens. If each *A* has a physical probability (at some time) of 1 of being *B* (at a later time), then the statistical probability (actual or hypothetical) of an *A* being *B* (at the later time) is 1. If each *A* has a physical probability of 0 of being *B*, then the statistical probability of an *A* being *B* is 0. In an infinite class, if each *A* apart from a finite number of *A*s has a physical probability (at some time) of being *B* (at a later time) of 1, then the statistical probability of an *A* being *B* (at the later time) will be 1 also (and, if the physical probability is 0, the statistical probability will be 0 also). One may rightly think that in some sense it is immensely probable that various other relations hold—for example, that, that if each *A* in an infinite class has a physical probability of *p* of being *B*, then the statistical probability of an *A* being *B* (whatever the order of selection of *A*s) will be *p*. But it is logically possible that this will not hold—what is physically improbable may go on happening for ever. The sense in which it is nevertheless immensely 'probable' that relations such as that mentioned will hold will be analysed in due course as 'logically probable'.

Conversely, statements of statistical probability entail virtually nothing about physical probability. There can be a hypothetical statistical probability of $\frac{1}{2}$ of tosses of this coin (taken in their temporal order) being heads, even if alternate tosses of coins have physical probabilities (at some earlier time) of heads of 1 and 0 respectively. However, in ways that I will analyse in due course, statements of statistical probability give varying degrees of logical probability to claims about physical probability, and statements about actual statistical probability give varying degrees of logical probability to claims about hypothetical statistical probability, and conversely.

'Laws of nature' are concerned with what has to happen, or has a physical propensity to happen, to all things of certain kinds. They are, therefore, naturally construed as generalizations about physical probabilities. Let us call a statement lawlike if it claims that for certain *A*, *B*, *p*, and *n*, at all times *t*, every actual and in some sense physically possible,[5] A has a physical prob-

[5] I suggest, as a natural construal of 'a physically possible *A*', an *A* that, there is a physical probability other than 0, could result from a rearrangement of the existing matter or other constituents of the universe. For David Lewis (see Additional Note D), unlike most writers, the statistical probability involved needs to hold only for the class consisting of each actual *A*.

ability p of being B at time $(t+n)$. A lawlike statement that is true will state a law of nature. In universal laws, p is 1 or 0. Thus the claim that it is a universal law that all photons travel in straight lines in empty space is the claim that every photon, actual or physically possible, has at every time t a physical probability of 1 of travelling in a straight line at that time (that is, $n=0$). In probabilistic laws p has a value other than 1 or 0. It is a probabilistic law that 50 per cent atoms of C_{14} decay within 5,600 years; which means that every atom of C_{14} has a physical probability of ½ at every time t of decaying within 5,600 years (of being decayed after 5,600 years).[6]

Statistical probability is often called 'objective probability', but this is a misleading name that I shall avoid. It is misleading, because the value of the probability of some other kinds is just as objective a matter. The value of a physical probability is objective; and so, as I shall argue shortly, is the value of one kind of inductive probability. When from the seventeenth century onwards people began to talk about things being 'probable' in something like modern senses and reflected on what they meant, they (and especially mathematicians) sometimes supposed that there was only one kind of probability, and sometimes they supposed that there were two kinds—one a feature of the physical world, and the other the probability on evidence that something was the case in the physical world.[7] Among modern philosophers, the distinction was made most forcefully and influentially by Rudolf Carnap,[8] who called the former 'probability$_2$' and the latter 'probability$_1$'. For Carnap, 'probability$_2$' was what I have called 'statistical probability'. Other writers have spelled out the former kind of probability as what I have called 'physical probability'. Yet other writers have thought of these latter two kinds of probability as conceptually distinct, even if some of them have held (see Additional Note D) that one kind could be reduced (in some sense) to the other.[9] Likewise, as we come to probability on evidence, we shall need—unlike most writers—to distinguish several concepts under this general heading.

[6] For further analysis of the relation between laws of nature and physical probabilities of individual events, see Additional Note D on laws of nature.

[7] See Ian Hacking, *The Emergence of Probability* (Cambridge University Press, 1975), ch. 2, for some of the thinkers of the seventeenth century and thereafter aware of this distinction.

[8] Rudolf Carnap, *Logical Foundations of Probability* (University of Chicago Press, 1950).

[9] Detailed modern explications of statistical probability begin with John Venn's *Logic of Chance* (1886) and continue through the writings of Richard von Mises (*Probability, Statistics and Truth* (German edn., 1928)) and Hans Reichenbach (*The Theory of Probability* (University of California Press, 1949)). What I have called physical or natural probability seems to be the kind of probability that the Propensity Theory of Probability sought to explicate. See e.g. Karl Popper, 'The Propensity Interpretation of Probability', *British Journal for the Philosophy of Science*, 10 (1960), 25–42.

Inductive Probability

Inductive probability is a measure of the extent to which one proposition *r* makes another one *q* likely to be true (*r* and *q* may be complicated conjunctions or disjunctions of other propositions). Typically, *r* will report some observable datum, our evidence; and *q* will be some hypothesis about the cause of *r* or some prediction for the future. But scientific or other hypotheses may make it probable that we will observe some datum in future, in the same sense of probability. And, if we understand by our 'evidence', as is most natural (as I shall develop in Chapter 5), what we already believe or could discover, then inductive probability must not be described as concerned only with the probability of hypotheses on evidence. It is concerned with the probability of one proposition or another, where the second, if true, would give reason for believing the former. We assume the second proposition to be true, and measure how much reason it provides for believing the first proposition to be.

The inductive probability of *q* given *r*, or of *q* on *r* (measuring how probable *r* makes *q*), has the value 1 when *r* makes *q* certain (that is, when given *r*, *q* is certainly true) and the value 0 when *r* makes not-*q* (the negation of *q*) certain, and intermediate values as *r* gives intermediate degrees of support to *q*. Inductive probability (unlike statistical or physical probability) does not normally have an exact numerical value—it is just high or low, or more than half, or less than the probability of some different proposition *s* on a certain other proposition *t*. Where one proposition *r* makes another proposition *q* no more likely to be true than it would be anyway (that is, *r* is irrelevant to *q*), we can still talk of the probability of *q* on *r*, but it will be the same as the probability of *q* 'anyway'. By the latter we may mean either the probability of *q* on a certain other proposition that we have not bothered to mention, or its intrinsic probability (which I shall express as its probability on a mere tautology—that is, if the only thing we assume to be true is a mere tautology). The importance of this notion of intrinsic probability will be developed later. So every proposition will have some probability on every other proposition. These propositions that give or receive probability may include propositions reporting statistical or physical probabilities.

Let me illustrate these points by examples of cases where we have evidence that we may plausibly think renders probable to some degree some hypothesis, such as a scientific theory or a prediction—for example, that the next toss of this coin will land heads, or that a certain photon sent from a source through a screen with two slits towards a photographic plate passes through the left slit. For the latter we may have evidence that the photon at emission had a physical probability of $\frac{2}{3}$ of passing through the left slit; we may also have evidence as to where it impacted afterwards on the plate. Each of these pieces of evidence, if they were the only pieces of evidence, would give a particular (and normally different) inductive probability to the hypothesis that it passed through the left slit. Together they might give a different probability, from either probability separately, to that hypothesis. When we are considering the hypothesis that this coin will land heads next time, we may have various pieces of evidence in the form of statistical probabilities about proportions of heads in finite classes of observed tosses of various kinds, the proportions of tosses of all coins that land heads, of tosses of all coins by me that land heads, and so on and so forth. The probability that this coin will land heads when tossed next time may not be the same as any of these, but in some complicated way a function of all of them. Thus, suppose our evidence is that this coin is one of two biased coins, one with a statistical probability (in a large finite observed class) of $\frac{2}{3}$ of landing heads and the other with a statistical probability (in a large finite observed class) of $\frac{2}{3}$ of landing tails. On that evidence, (plausibly) the probability of the next toss of this coin being heads is $\frac{1}{2}$. Also, of course, hypotheses about physical probability and about hypothetical statistical probability are themselves hypotheses about which we may have evidence in the form of actual statistical probabilities. That 562 tosses out of 1,000 tosses of this coin (in such-and-such a set-up) have been heads makes it (plausibly) inductively more probable that the hypothetical statistical probability of heads in an infinite series of tosses (with such-and-such a set-up, given that any wear on the coin is replaced etc.) is 0.562 than that it has any other value. But that evidence makes it not much less probable that the value is 0.561 or 0.563 than that it is 0.562. However, it (plausibly) gives a value of 0.562 to the inductive probability of the hypothesis that the next toss will be heads.

Now there is a sense in which it is often contingent that one proposition gives such-and-such a value to the probability of another proposition. That a particular fingerprint on a surface makes it probable that someone with a corresponding pattern on their fingers touched the surface is contingent on the uniqueness of finger patterns and the durability of patterns and prints. But what this contingency amounts to is that the probability has one value if a proposition reporting the uniqueness and durability of prints is added to the original second proposition (the particular print being on the surface), and a different value if it is not. For the purpose of assessing the inductive probability of q or r, the (simple or complex) second proposition must be delineated clearly. Then it is probability relative to that proposition alone that is being assessed. The value of that is a function of what the first and second propositions are (and in some cases—see below—of the beliefs and capacities of a subject), but quite independent of other facts about the objects referred to in those propositions.

We do think that there are (very roughly—a qualification that I shall assume throughout subsequent discussion but not normally bother to repeat) right and wrong ways to assess how probable one proposition *r* makes another one *q*, and the philosopher of induction tries to codify the right ways. Reflecting, for example, on what kinds of evidence make what kinds of hypothesis probable and make one kind of hypothesis more probable than another, and (in so far as we have clear views about this) how much probability some evidence gives to some hypothesis, he codifies the criteria that we almost all (including scientists) use and believe to be correct. If we do not think that there are such criteria, then we must hold that no one makes any error if he regards any scientific theory compatible with observations and any prediction or retrodiction whatsoever from those observations as as probable on the evidence as any other. On the basis of our evidence of what has happened so far, it would be as sensible to believe that cyanide will nourish and bread poison tomorrow, or that if we stand on concrete we shall sink into the ground, as to believe the opposite of these things. Given the evident implausibility of thinking thus of scientific theories and their predictions and retrodictions, I conclude that there are correct inductive criteria that often give clear results, at any rate for claims of comparative probability (that is, claims to the effect that proposition *q* given *r* is more probable than proposition *s* given *t*).

Of course, even when we have a correct understanding of what kinds of thing make other kinds of thing probable, we may misapply our criteria through a failure to realize what are the relevant logical possibilities and necessities—what, for example, are the possible scientific theories in some area; or, through a failure to realize what are the deductive or correct inductive consequences of our evidence. But that measure of inductive support that would be reached by a logically omniscient being (that is, one who knows what are all the relevant logical possibilities and knows what they entail, and has correct inductive criteria) is what I shall call *logical probability*. It has a value determined by the content of *q* and *r*, which measures the total force of *r* with respect to *q*; to which we try to conform our judgements of inductive probability on evidence but about the value of which we may make mistakes. That this measure has a value that is determined a priori is brought out by the possibility of counter-inductive worlds in which the probable never happens. It may well happen that whatever horse is judged by the experts in this sense most likely to win never does. And that may remain the case, even when, at each stage, the experts add to their evidence, evidence about the failure of the most recent prediction. Yet, what the experts predicted may nevertheless have been probable on the evidence available to them, at each stage. Or, similarly, consider the man determined to break the bank at Monte Carlo by studying the frequencies with which a certain roulette wheel lands in the red or black sections. At the end of each day, he places a bet on the section on which the wheel has landed most frequently so far (on that day and previous days). It is surely more probable that the section on which the wheel has stopped most frequently in the past will be the one on which it stops again. But, alas, the gambler could lose every bet. If he does, the evidence of this happening over such a long period may give a certain probability to the hypothesis that the wheel is rigged so that at the end of the day it lands on the section on which it has landed least frequently in the past. If the gambler adjusts his betting to take account of this, he may still lose every bet. The logically probable may never happen, but of course it is always logically probable that the logically probable will happen.

I shall be examining in the next chapter in detail what are the correct inductive criteria. In order to spell out a sharp concept of logical probability, we need to understand the vague definitions of 'the probability of q on r is 1' as 'r makes q certain', and 'the probability of q on r is 0' as 'r makes not-q certain' more precisely. I shall understand 'r makes q certain' as 'r entails q';[10] and 'r makes not-q certain' as 'r entails not-q'. (I point out in Additional Note G that one slightly looser understanding of these phrases would be very difficult to use in a coherent way.) Given these definitions, there are certain principles that are forced upon us by what has already been said. Representing propositions by lower-case letters, by $P(x|y)$ the probability of x on y, by N the modal operator 'necessarily' (that is, of logical necessity), by '$\rightarrow$' 'implies' and by '$\leftrightarrow$' 'mutually implies', these principles can then be stated as follows (where p, q, and r are any propositions at all).

1. $P(q|r) \geq 0$

1*a*. $P(q|r) \leq 1$

2. If $N(p \leftrightarrow q)$, $P(r|p) = P(r|q)$

[10] 'Entails' is being used in the sense of 'strictly implies'. p strictly implies q, if it is not logically possible that (p and not-q). Where q is itself logically necessary, it will never be logically possible that (p and not-q).

2*a*. If $N(p \leftrightarrow q)$, $P(p|r) = P(q|r)$
3. If $N(r \rightarrow q)$, $P(q|r) = 1$

(I have labelled some of the principles with a simple numeral—e.g. '2'. These ones I shall need as axioms of the probability calculus when I set it out more fully in the next chapter. Those of the principles labelled with an '*a*'—for example, '2*a*', I shall not need as axioms. They will follow as theorems from the complete axiom set that I shall propose in the next chapter).

Principles 1 and 1*a* simply state that logical probability has a maximum value of 1 and a minimum value of 0. To ascribe a probability of 1 to some proposition on some other proposition is to say that on that proposition it is certainly true (in the sense now made precise); no proposition can be more certainly true than that. To ascribe a probability of 0 to some proposition on some other proposition is to say that on that proposition it is certainly false (in the sense now made precise); no proposition can be more certainly false than that. Principles 2 and 2*a* say that logically equivalent propositions always have the same probability on any proposition, and always give the same probability to any proposition. Our principles concern the measure of support that would be reached by a logically omniscient being. Such a being will know of any logically equivalent p and q that they are logically equivalent—that, of logical necessity, whenever one is true, the other is true. So he will know that to the extent to which some proposition r supports p and so supports the claim that the world is a world in which p holds, it supports the world being (since it is the same world) a world in which q holds, and thus supports q. By a similar argument logically equivalent propositions give the same support to any given proposition. Principle 3 follows directly from the definition of a probability of 1.

Since all logical truths are entailed by any other proposition, the logical probability of every logical truth on any proposition will (by Principle 3) be 1. Also, since every proposition e is logically equivalent to its conjunction with any logical truth q, by Principle 2 $P(h|e) = P(h|e\&q)$, and so in the calculation of logical probability every logical truth will in effect function as evidence and the value of the probability of h will have been calculated in a way that takes account of every logical truth. So no discovery of any deductive consequence of e (including logical truths), can affect the value of $P(h|e)$, construed as a logical probability. Yet it does often seem that the probability of a scientific hypothesis is affected, not merely by the discovery of new observational evidence, but by the discovery of a new hypothesis that leads us to expect the old evidence. Ptolemy's theory of astronomy (h_1) had a certain degree of probability on the evidence (k) available before the sixteenth century. Then Copernicus propounded his theory (h_2) and (to oversimplify things a bit) showed that h_2 entailed k; that made h_1 less likely to be true, because it suggested a better explanation than h_1 for the occurrence of k. But what Copernicus discovered (e) was a new logical truth—that h_2 entailed k. Yet, if we think of probability being thus affected by logical discoveries, we are dealing with a kind of probability on evidence that is not logical probability.

Likewise, because any logical truth is entailed by any other proposition, any true mathematical conjecture will have a logical probability of 1 on any evidence; and any false conjecture a probability of 0. A logically omniscient investigator could work out, for every mathematical conjecture (that is, every suggested mathematical theorem), whether its probability is 1 or 0. But there is also a sense in which one can have logical and contingent evidence for or against mathematical conjectures, which can increase or decrease their probability. Goldbach's conjecture (that every even number is the sum of two prime numbers)—put forward in the eighteenth century but so far neither proven true nor proven false—would seem to have its probability increased by the logical evidence that it holds for the first trillion numbers; and by the contingent evidence (if there was such) that some otherwise truthful great mathematician claimed to have proved it.

So we have reached a kind of inductive probability in which the addition of logical truths to contingent evidence makes a difference to its value; and in which the value is dependent on the extent of human deductive capacities to deduce more and more remote consequences of the evidence.[11] It is a measure of the support by some proposition (a conjunction of a contingent proposition and a logical truth) to some other proposition that a certain human (or group of humans) would ascribe—given that they have the

[11] As, interestingly, Keynes, the founder of the 'logical theory of probability', suggested that it should be: 'Probability is . . . relative in a sense to the principles of *human* reason. The degree of probability, which it is rational for *us* to entertain, does not presume perfect logical insight, and is relative in part to the secondary propositions which we in fact know; and it is not dependent upon whether more perfect logical insight is or is not conceivable. It is the degree of probability to which those logical processes lead, of which our minds are capable; or . . . which those secondary propositions justify, which we in fact know. If we do not take this view of probability, if we do not limit it in this way and make it, to this extent, relative to human powers, we are altogether adrift in the unknown; for we cannot ever know what degree of probability would be justified by the perception of logical relations which we are, and must always be, incapable of comprehending' (J. M. Keynes, *A Treatise of Probability* (MacMillan and Co., 1921), 32). The trouble with this passage, however, is that different humans have different 'powers' of 'logical insight'. So we get as many species of this kind of probability as there are groups of humans with the same powers. See Alvin Plantinga, *Warrant and Proper Function* (Oxford University Press, 1993), 150–1 for the difference between logical and epistemic probability.

right criteria for what is evidence for what but only limited ability to work out the consequences thereof. I shall call this notion epistemic probability. The epistemic probability of a hypothesis is relative not merely to evidence but to the logical competence of the investigator. But the notion is extraordinarily vague—there seems only the very vaguest of understandings of what can reasonably be expected of a particular investigator by way of having worked out the consequence of applying agreed criteria to certain evidence. It might indeed be possible to index the different kinds of epistemic probability. We might begin with the correct criteria of logical probability, axiomized in some simple way. For some particular set of such axioms and some unique way of measuring the number of deductive steps from premiss to conclusion, we can then generate an infinite spectrum of kinds of epistemic probability as follows. A proposition *q* has on a proposition *r* (which may include both contingent evidence and known logical truths including the logical truths of which theories there are that entail certain data) as its epistemic probability of kind *s*, whatever logical probability can be deduced by *s* steps from *e* and the axioms; otherwise its probability is indeterminate between whatever values can be calculated by *s* steps as its maximum and by *s* steps as its minimum.[12]

Once we allow the probability of a mathematical conjecture to be affected by considerations other than whether the axioms of mathematics entail it or its negation, as well as logical evidence, contingent evidence will also make a difference. The contingent evidence might include evidence of a statistical kind about logical relations—for example, that certain kinds of mathematical conjecture usually turn out to be true. Or it might include evidence that certain techniques for guessing logical entailments usually work (for example, that the first guess a trained mathematician makes after a good holiday usually turns out to be correct).[13]

[12] For discussion of systems of probability that are in effect systems of epistemic probability in the writings of Daniel Garber and Richard Jeffrey, see Additional Note E.

[13] A number of recent writers have drawn our attention to the fact that for even a large computer to prove deductively some theorem from a small axiom set might often take an enormous amount of computer time, whereas to make a calculation whether the theorem is valid by some fallible probabilistic strategy might take a very small amount of computer time. Analogously, if humans are to work things out using a relatively small number of neurones within a short time, they often need 'quick and dirty' strategies rather than totally reliable ones. See e.g., Christopher Cherniak, 'Computational Complexity and the Universal Acceptance of Logic', *Journal of Philosophy*. 81 (1984), 739–58. Studies by various psychologists, beginning from the work of A. Tversky and D. Kahneman, have shown that humans do frequently use such strategies even when they could use deductively valid procedures. See e.g. R. Nisbett and L. Ross, 'Judgmental Heuristics and Knowledge Structures', repr. (as is Cherniak's paper) in H. Kornblith (ed.), *Naturalizing Epistemology* (2nd edn., MIT Press,

The trouble is that, even given an index such as I have proposed, there seems so little reason to use epistemic probability of kind 22 to assess the probability for subject *A* and probability of kind 46 to assess the probability for subject *B* of a given hypothesis on given evidence. Maybe subjects can be expected to have taken as many steps as they have in fact taken. But how are we to assess how many further steps they ought to have taken? And similar difficulties will arise with any other systems that make the probability of a hypothesis to depend on the logical capacities and knowledge of an investigator. Nevertheless, we do seem to have a very vague notion of epistemic probability—the inductive probability of one proposition on another as assessed by correct criteria of logical probability with a certain limited logical competence to see alternative theories and their consequences, which a subject with certain knowledge and abilities can be expected to have.

The probability on evidence both logical and epistemic, of which I have been writing so far is, I repeat, the probability, given correct inductive criteria, whatever they are (even if not all investigators have the logical competence to apply these criteria fully). Those who hold that there are no such objectively correct criteria will have no use for the concepts of logical and epistemic probability in the senses in which I have defined them. I do, however, as stated earlier, find it difficult to take such thinkers seriously. Surely no one really believes that any way of extrapolating data and reaching predictions about the future is as likely to give true results as any other. But, of course, people have somewhat different views about what the objectively correct criteria are. So we can go on to talk of an inductive probability relative to different inductive critreria (that is, criteria for what are the correct logical probabilities) and so one can generate a whole further range of inductive probabilities. If probability is relative to evidence, one's evidence may surely be reasonably construed as including evidence (that is, what seems to one to be the case) about what is evidence for what. But, if we are going to allow a probability relative to various inductive criteria, we ought also to allow a probability relative to various deductive criteria. Our characterization of epistemic probability assumed that, although subjects might be limited in their ability to draw deductive inferences (and so in their knowledge of logical truths), at any rate they did not have any invalid

1997). The initial use of such a strategy would not as such yield a belief rendered epistemically probable by its evidence; the resulting belief would be a mere guess—unless, for other reasons, other of the subject's evidence rendered the belief probable. But, once the subject's evidence includes evidence that the strategy usually works, then the use of it will lead to a belief rendered epistemically probable by its evidence.

rules of inference or false logical beliefs. A more liberal concept of probability will drop these requirements also. And so we come to a concept of probability in which probability is relative, not merely to logical knowledge and capacity, but also to a set of inductive and deductive criteria. I will call this kind of inductive probability, subjective probability. It is only if, given his logical capacities, he makes an error in reasoning by his own deductive and inductive criteria that a subject could be mistaken about what is the subjective probability (on his criteria) of some proposition on given evidence. For the subjective probability of a hypothesis on evidence is just the force that the evidence has for someone with a certain way of assessing that evidence, and a certain ability to do so. But now we have the problem, not merely of assessing for a given subject what his logical capacities are, but of assessing what are his criteria. If he makes what we consider to be a mistake in (deductive or inductive) inference, we need to be able to distinguish between his misapplying his own criteria, which are the same as ours, and his applying correctly his own criteria, which are different from ours. By cross-questioning the subject we may be able to see which is happening, but drawing the line is not easy.

Many writers who write today about inductive probability call it 'subjective probability', and think of it as subject-relative. They understand it as probability by a subject's own inductive criteria, tailored in the minimum respect that they conform to the axioms of the probability calculus—which I lay out in the next chapter—and use correct deductive criteria. (There can be more than one way of knocking a person's criteria of what is evidence for what into this minimum logical shape.) This is a kind of inductive probability, midway in certain respects between the various kinds I have distinguished; but not one with which I shall find it useful to operate. For, given that (as I have argued that we all believe) there are correct criteria of what is evidence for what, it seems arbitrary to have a kind of probability defined partly by correct criteria (the criteria captured in the axioms of the probability calculus) and partly by a subject's own criteria. Misassessments of the correct inductive probability resulting from failure to conform to the axioms of the calculus may cause subjects to fail to realize some of their purposes, but so may misassessments of any other kind. So I distinguish from the primary kind of inductive probability[14]—logical probability, the

[14] The classical account of inductive probability is that given by J. M. Keynes in *A Treatise on Probability*. Keynes seems in general to be talking about 'logical probability' in my sense, and he is thought of as the founder of the 'logical theory of probability'; but the quotation in my n. 11 shows that there is a 'relative to human capacities' element in his account of what makes what probable. Carnap's classical *Logical Foundations* was

two kinds—epistemic and subjective. The latter are the assessment of logical probability by subjects of varying lack of capacity to apply correct criteria of logical probability, and varying degrees of false belief about what these are.[15] I shall come in the next chapter to consider what are the correct criteria of logical probability. Meanwhile, we can see how different theories of justification use different kinds of probability in assessing the adequacy of grounds for belief.

Adequacy and Probability

I noted at the beginning of this chapter that writers often express their account of the adequacy of grounds for belief in terms of probability. A belief has adequate grounds if those grounds make the proposition believed probable. Now that we have distinguished various kinds of probability, we can see that an externalist account of adequacy will need to be spelled out in terms of an externalist kind of probability—physical or statistical—and an internalist account of adequacy will need to be spelled out in terms of an internalist kind of probability—inductive probability of some kind.

Physical probability is an intrinsic propensity in a particular event to produce another. To use it to express the adequacy of grounds would involve saying that grounds are adequate in so far as they make it physically probable that a true belief results. But, given that, in fact, in our world, physical probabilities of events (on the large or medium scale) are almost always 1 or 0 or extremely close thereto, for almost any actual belief, it

concerned almost entirely with inductive probability, his 'probability$_1$'. He wrote of this there as a 'logical' relation ('a partial logical implication'). But his later short work *The Continuum of Inductive Methods* (Chicago University Press, 1952) explored the consequences for the probability of hypotheses on evidence of various different criteria of inductive probability. In my terminology, it was a study of different kinds of subjective probability for hypotheses on evidence, expressible in a very limited language.

[15] A subject's beliefs about what is made logically probable by correct criteria will also be his beliefs about what is made logically probable given his capacity to work this out, and also his beliefs about what is made logically probable given his beliefs about what the criteria are. Hence he will believe the same propositions to be logically probable, epistemically probable (relative to his capacities), and subjectively probable (given his criteria)—that is, to have values of these probabilities greater than $\frac{1}{2}$. But it will not always be the case that he believes the exact value of the logical probability of some proposition to be the same as its epistemic or subjective proabability. For, as noted in the text, while we may believe every mathematical conjecture to have a probability on any evidence of either 1 or 0, we may ascribe to such conjectures intermediate values measuring the epistemic or subjective probability that it will have the former value.

would be very probable that it would have been produced. So virtually all actual true beliefs would be very highly justified; and virtually all actual false beliefs would be almost totally unjustified. And that seems so far away from our normal understanding of justification that talk of probability in all externalist theories is best regarded instead as talk of statistical probability of some of the many possible kinds.[16] A belief has adequate grounds if it is statistically probable that a process of belief-production from grounds of that kind will yield a true belief. Then we have different externalist theories, according to the kinds we take. We can construe the classes very generally (a belief resulting from perception) or very precisely (a belief of this kind resulting from perception by me in a dark room); and construe the beliefs and grounds as beliefs and grounds of the actual world, or of possible worlds of different kinds (for example, ones with the same laws of nature as our world, but circumstances varying in the kinds of way they do in the actual world). The different kinds of theory entertained by an externalist such as Goldman considered in Chapter 1 in effect all understand adequacy in terms of different kinds of statistical probability.

For an internalist, however, the adequacy of grounds is a matter of inductive probability. A belief is justified in so far as its grounds render it inductively probable that the proposition believed is true (that is, give it a probability greater than ½). What makes it the case that a sensation or belief makes another belief (that is, the proposition believed) probable depends on the logical relations between the content of the sensation *s*, or the premiss belief, *e*, and the conclusion belief, *h*. But the issue is: are these the relations knowable by a logically omniscient individual; or the relations knowable by an individual of limited logical competence who operates with correct inductive principles; or the relations that an individual reaches by utilizing with his limited competence his own understanding of inductive probability? That is, is the inductive probability logical, epistemic, or subjective probability? (In the latter two cases it is the competence or

[16] (Pre-1993) Alston is explicitly externalist about what constitutes grounds being adequate. Although he does not give any explicit account of the kind of probability required for grounds to be adequate, the use of the words 'kinds' and 'tendency' in the passage below, clearly adumbrates a statistical account: 'The ground must be such that the *probability* of the belief's being true, given that ground, is very high. It is an objective probability that is in question here. The world is such that, at least in the kinds of situations in which we typically find ourselves, the ground is a reliable indication of the fact believed. In this paper I will not attempt to spell out the kind of objective probability being appealed to. Suffice it to say that I am thinking in terms of some kind of "tendency" conception of probability, where the lawful structure of the world is such that one state of affairs renders another more or less probable' (*Epistemic Justification* (Cornell University Press, 1989), 232. See similar remarks in his *Perceiving God* (Cornell University Press, 1991), 75).

standards of the subject in question that determine the kind of epistemic or subjective probability.) Very different results follow according to the kind of inductive probability involved. Were the Greeks justified in believing Ptolemy's theory of astronomy that sun, moon, and planets revolved around the earth? For the internalist that is a matter of whether their evidence make Ptolemy's theory probable. The very fact that there is a rival theory that does (we now all see) provide a simpler explanation of the observed data available to the Greeks—a logical fact—entails that their evidence did not make Ptolemy's theory logically probable. However, they were unable to work out that there was a rival theory with this property. As far as they could see, Ptolemy's theory provided the simplest explanation of the evidence—on the correct criteria of what makes what probable. Their understanding of the simplicity of a theory was not, I suggest, significantly different from ours. Hence (relative to their logical capacities) Ptolemy's theory was epistemically probable on their evidence. But, suppose that they had had a very different understanding from ours of what makes for the simplicity of a theory, and believed that any theory that attributed great influence and importance to the sun was very simple and so had high prior probability, even if the laws that determined just how it exercised that influence were very complicated. Suppose, too, that they had had available to them such a theory, which led them to expect the observed evidence, then by their criteria Ptolemy's theory would not have been rendered subjectively probable on their evidence (because it did not place the sun in the centre of the universe). So, whether an internalist is to say that the Greeks were justified in believing Ptolemy's theory depends on the kind of inductive probability that he uses.

4

The Criteria of Logical Probability

So what are the correct criteria for what makes what probable? I suggest that we reach (and are right to reach) our beliefs about what will happen in the future, did happen in the past, or is happening somewhere else or is too small to be observed, by means of some explanatory hypothesis—some hypothesis that purports to give a causal explanation of what we observe or have observed (or, in a wide sense, experienced). The explanatory hypothesis will tell us the past or underlying causes of what we have observed, and allow us to infer its future and distant consequences. It is via an explanatory hypothesis that we reach beliefs about the unobserved, even though the hypothesis may be of such a primitive, low-level, and obvious kind that we hardly notice its role. For example, we and our ancestors have observed the sun to rise (relative to the earth) at approximately twenty-four-hour intervals for very many years without exception. We therefore judge that the sun always rises at approximately twenty-four hour-intervals; and we go on to judge that there is some law at work making the sun rise. That allows us to predict that it will rise again tomorrow. If we did not believe that there was some law (albeit one operative only under certain conditions and not a fundamental law) that the sun rises always at twenty-four-hour intervals, we would judge our past observations of this having happened to be merely observations of some large-scale coincidence and so not to license any prediction to the future.

So we must look first at the criteria for what kind of evidence supports what kind of explanatory hypothesis. These should be revealed by reflection on the procedures of scientists, historians, detectives, and so on, procedures that in general the rest of us think to be correct.

The Nature of Explanation

I suggest that there are two basic patterns of explanation: inanimate explanation, characteristic of the physical sciences and of much ordinary-life explanation; and personal explanation, characteristic of history and psychology and also of much other ordinary-life explanation. In purported explanations of both kinds, a phenomenon—that is, the occurrence of an event—is explained by a cause (or causes) and some principle (or principles) in virtue of which the cause (in the conditions then operative) brought about the event as effect. The explanation is true if the cause and principles did operate to produce the effect. The components of inanimate explanation are normally analysed as initial conditions, one of which we may designate in a somewhat arbitrary way as the cause, while calling the other initial conditions the conditions under which the cause operated; and laws of nature making it physically necessary or probable to some particular degree that events of the former kind are followed by events similar to the effect. The explanation is a full one if the laws make it physically necessary that effect would occur; a partial one if the laws make it probable to a degree less than 1 that the effect would occur.[1] Thus the explanation of why a certain barrel of gunpowder exploded on a certain occasion is that it was caused by the gunpowder being ignited at a temperature and pressure within certain ranges in the presence of oxygen, and the law that all gunpowder ignited in such circumstances explodes. Philosophers differ about whether laws of nature and initial conditions are ultimate constituents of the universe that causally affect what happens, or whether talk about laws of nature (as well as talk about initial conditions) is analysable into talk about the powers, liabilities (and other properties) of substances, which are the only ultimate constituents of the universe.[2] But, as little for present purposes turns on whether such an analysis is correct, I will ignore this issue and operate simply with the account of the constituents of inanimate causal explanation as laws and initial conditions.

In a personal explanation of some phenomenon, it is persons (or other animate beings) who are the causes, and the principles in virtue of which they cause include their powers (to act intentionally), beliefs, and purposes. As we saw in Chapter 2, whether they exercise some power will depend on their beliefs about the effects of doing so, and their purposes to bring about or not bring about this or that effect. The explanation of why

[1] This classic account of inanimate explanation is due to C. G. Hempel. Explanation in terms of universal laws (ones that in my terminology make the effect physically necessary) was called by Hempel deductive–nomological (D–N) explanation. Explanation in terms of probabilistic laws was called by Hempel inductive–statistical explanation. (See 'Aspects of Scientific Explanation' in C. G. Hempel, *Aspects of Scientific Explanation and Other Essays in the Philosophy of Science* (Free Press, 1965).)

[2] See Additional Note D for fuller discussion of what is involved in laws of nature being ultimate constituents of the universe.

my hand moved on some occasion is that I (the cause) intentionally made it move; and that I did so because I have the power to make it move intentionally (that is, I will make it move, if I purpose to), and because I believed that thereby I could catch someone's attention and that I had the purpose of catching their attention.

The purposes of people follow from their desires and beliefs. I understand by a person having at some time a desire to do action *A* (at that time or at some appropriate time) or have happen to him state *Z*, his having an inclination to form a purpose to do action *A* either at that time or when he believes it appropriate, or to have the purpose of allowing *Z* to happen to him when he believes it begins to do so. To have a desire to cross one's legs now is to have an inclination to form a purpose to cross one's legs now; to have a desire now to get rich is to have an inclination now to form purposes to acquire money when—the person believes—the opportunities arise to acquire money. To desire to sleep is to have an inclination to let falling asleep happen to you when it begins to do so. An inclination to form a purpose will lead to the formation of the purpose at that time or when believed appropriate, either with physical necessity or with some lesser degree of physical probability. One desire is stronger than another in so far as it is physically more probable that it will lead to the formation of a stronger purpose. The main criterion for one purpose being stronger than another is the person's public behaviour given his purposes and beliefs (see Chapter 2). If, for example, a person believes that he cannot fulfil both of his only two purposes but has the power to fulfil either of them, the purpose that he fulfils is the strongest. Desires are inclinations to act with which one finds oneself. Most humans have relatively constant long-term desires (for example, for a stable home and family), and desires that occur regularly under standard circumstances (for example, to sleep every twenty-four hours). They may, however, change in strength gradually or suddenly over time, and one cause of their changing influence is the subject's own choice to make some effort to diminish the influence of one desire and to increase the influence of another.[3]

[3] This simplified model of human psychology is all that is needed for present purposes. A more accurate model will, I believe, contrast desires to act and beliefs about the moral worth of actions, and see the human agent as acting on his strongest desire in the absence of moral beliefs (that is his beliefs about what is most worth doing), and on his moral beliefs in the absence of desires, and choosing between the purpose promoted by desire and that promoted by moral belief where there is conflict. See my *The Evolution of the Soul* (2nd edn., Clarendon Press, 1997), esp. ch. 6. I have simplified this picture here by treating moral beliefs as desires.

Explanation may be deep or superficial. It is superficial in so far as the principles invoked are limited ones operative only in a narrow range of circumstances, their operation under those circumstances being explicable by a deeper principle. Lower-level laws (such as Kepler's laws) are (approximately) derivable (for relevant circumstances—that is, for massive bodies with the kinds of masses, distances apart, and initial velocities of the sun and planets) from higher-level laws (such as Newton's laws); and the derivation may be deductive or (see below) inductive. Higher-level laws have more content (that is, carry consequences for far more kinds of phenomena than do lower-level laws), and often fit together into an overall theory. Higher-level laws provide deeper, more fundamental explanations of events, and the highest-level laws of all provide the most fundamental inanimate explanation. Likewise, some piece of human behaviour may be explained by the agent's purpose, brought about by his most immediate desire—my going to the door is explained by my purpose to go to the kitchen, together with my belief that the kitchen lies through the door and my power to walk, and my purpose is brought about by my desire to go to the kitchen; but this desire is in turn explained by my desire for food together with my belief that there is food in the kitchen. Ultimate desires (desires derived from no higher desire) explain the ultimate purposes in an agent's current actions (what he is trying in the end to achieve by his current actions), and also the purposes that he would seek to execute when circumstances are, he believes, appropriate (for example, the desire to get rich explaining actions of seeking to make money when occasions arise).

The Criteria of Downward Inference

Before we come to consider the criteria for the degree to which some phenomenon renders probable some explanatory hypothesis (the criteria of 'upward inference'), we need to consider briefly the criteria for the degree to which an explanatory hypothesis renders (logically) probable the occurrence of some phenomenon (the criteria of 'downward inference'). A hypothesis of inanimate explanation consists, we have seen, of certain suggested laws of nature (a scientific theory), and certain suggested initial conditions. The basic rule of 'downward inference', for the logical probability that such a hypothesis gives to a phenomenon, is captured by a simple version of what David Lewis called 'the Principal Principle'.[4] This simple

[4] See David Lewis, 'A Subjectivist's Guide to Objective Chance' (in his *Philosophical Papers*, ii (Oxford University Press, 1986)) and the later 'Humean Supervenience

version, put in my terminology, says that (for any t and any n) the logical probability of this being B (at $t+n$), on the hypothesis (taken by itself) that the physical probability (at t) of an A being B (at $t+n$) is p and this is an A (at t), is p. (I omit the temporal qualifications from subsequent examples, for the sake of simplicity of exposition. It will be evident how they can be reinserted.) 'There is a physical probability of 0.9 that a photon emitted under conditions *C* will pass through slit *S*', and 'this is a photon that has been emitted under conditions *C*' gives a logical probability of 0.9 to 'this will pass through slit *S*'. Given the account of laws of nature in Chapter 3, it then follows that 'it is a law of nature that all *A*s have a physical probability p of being *B*'; and 'this is an *A*' gives a logical probability of p to 'this is a *B*'. More detailed consequences follow about statistical probabilities, about the proportion of *A*s that will be *B* in a finite (or infinite) class. 'It is a law of nature that all *A*s have a physical probability of 0.9 of being *B*, and there are 100 *A*s here' (taken by itself) gives a high logical probability to 'approximately 90 of the *A*s here are *B*'. (Just how 'high' will depend on how precisely we read 'approximately'. More detailed rules for calculating this will follow from the axioms of logical probability, to be presented later in the chapter.) And, I suggested in the previous chapter, 'in some sense it is immensely probable . . . that if each *A* in an infinite class has a physical probability of p of being *B*, then the statistical probability of an *A* being *B* (whatever the order of selection of *A*s) will be p'. We can now specify what that sense is—it is logical probability. This kind of downward inference is involved also in inference from high-level laws to their certain or probable consequences by way of low-level laws for particular kinds of situations (for example, from the laws of Quantum Theory to their consequences for the behaviour of atoms of particular kinds—for example, hydrogen atoms).

This rule of inference can be extended more generally. Any statistical probability (even if it forms no part of an explanatory hypothesis), taken

Debugged' (*Mind*, 103 (1994), 473–90). Lewis's 'credence' is my 'logical probability', and his 'chance' is the nearest thing in his system to my 'physical probability'. The principle then states—to put it loosely—that the credence of an event *A*, given its 'chance' and any other knowledge of the history of the world up to the time in question, has the same value as its chance. Lewis's actual versions (in the earlier and later work) are then complicated by various factors. One is that (as I comment in my Additional Note D), the chance of a particular event just is the statistical probability of an event of that kind over all time (the kind being picked out in terms of the categories used in the best scientific theory). So—loosely—the chance of a particular event occurring in certain circumstances just is the proportion of similar events that have occurred or will occur in similar cirucmstances. And that, to my mind, obliterates the destinction between what does happen and what has to happen or is inclined to happen.

by itself, gives a corresponding logical probability to any instance. 'The statistical probability of an *A* being *B* is *p*', and 'this is an *A*' makes it logically probable to degree *p* that 'this is *B*'. In this case, as in all cases, and as we noted in Chapter 3, the words 'taken by itself' are crucial. The addition of further evidence may always affect the value of a logical probability, except when that value is 1 or 0. If we add to 'the statistical probability of an *A* being *B* is $\frac{2}{3}$' and 'this is an *A*' that 'a totally reliable observer observed that this was not *B*', the probability of 'this is *B*' changes from being $\frac{2}{3}$ to being 0. But, when one proposition gives a logical probability of 1 to another proposition (as does, for example, 'The statistical probability of an *A* (the class of *A*'s being finite) being *B* is 1, and this is an *A*' to 'this is a *B*'), this probability remains 1, whatever further information we add to the first proposition.

Returning to personal explanation—if we know some person's desires and their strengths, and know in what circumstances they believe they are situated—we can infer their purposes, often with logical probability 1. And, if we know their means-end beliefs, and their basic powers, we can then infer their actions. If we know of Jones that he desires to eat lunch at 1 p.m. each day, has no other desire that leads to a different purpose at 1 p.m. today, and believes that it is 1 p.m. now, we can infer that he will form the purpose of going to lunch. From that, his belief that lunch is obtainable most readily in the lunch room and his having the power to move thither, we can infer (with probability 1) that he will go to the lunch room. When (as is more normal) people have beliefs and purposes of different strengths, the inference to what (given their basic powers) they will do in various circumstances becomes more complicated. And, if it is not physically necessary, but merely a matter of physical probabilities less than 1 whether desires will lead to purposes of certain strengths, then the downward inference will give logical probabilities of less than 1 to conclusions about people's actions.

So much for the (fairly obvious) criteria of 'downward inference', for the logical probabilities that different explanatory hypotheses give to various (possible and actual) phenomena. But, of course, we can rely on hypotheses to predict phenomena only to the extent to which we have evidence for those hypotheses, and so I turn to the (less obvious) criteria of 'upward inference' for when and how much phenomena render probable different explanatory hypotheses.

The Criteria of Upward Inference

There are, I suggest, two a priori and two a posteriori criteria that determine the extent to which phenomena render some explanatory hypothesis probable. That three of these operate is not subject to much philosophical dispute, and so I shall not devote a great deal of space to defending their status; but the operation of the fourth—the criterion of simplicity—is the subject of considerable dispute, and so I shall need to defend my claim about its status at greater length. My claim is that, among incompatible purported explanations, one that satisfies the criteria better on the whole is more probably true, and so the one that satisfies the criteria best on the whole is the one that is most probably true. It provides, in the weak sense of explanation as 'purported explanation', the best explanation of the data. In this chapter, I shall use 'data', 'phenomena', and 'evidence' interchangeably, names for whatever particular pieces of information we think we have discerned, immediately relevant to some hypothesis that we are considering. 'Background evidence' means everything else that we believe we know about the world. These are very loose holding-accounts. In the next chapter I shall be examining the different ways in which 'evidence', and so 'background evidence', may be understood. The results of this chapter will hold whichever of these ways are adopted.

On the a posteriori side, there is, first, the criterion of yielding the data—that is, leading us to expect for certain initial conditions (the conjunction of) many observed data with high logical probability (ideally with probability 1—that is, certainty). If a hypothesis predicts that in certain circumstances certain observations will be made, and they are made, that is evidence that the theory is true. The higher the probability with which the hypothesis predicts the data, and the more data it predicts with high probability, the more probable it is that the hypothesis is true. A hypothesis incompatible with the data is certainly false. Suppose that we know that some coin has either two heads, two tails, or a head and a tail. We toss it five times, and it lands heads each time. The second theory is incompatible with the data and so is eliminated. The data are far more probable on the first theory (where they have a probability of 1) than on the third theory (where, in the absence of any other evidence, the probability of five heads in five tosses is $(\frac{2}{3})^5 = \frac{1}{32}$). The more times we toss the coin and obtain only heads, the greater the probability of the first hypothesis (even though, given the hypothesis, the probability of the data remains the same: 1). Or—to take a more real-life scientific theory—Newton's theory of gravity is more probably true in so far as, for given initial conditions, it makes highly probable not merely the observed data of periods taken by planets to revolve around the sun, but data about the periods of moons of Jupiter and Saturn, of eclipses of the sun and moon, of the intervals between high and low tides on earth, and so on. And, in so far as Newton's theory makes the occurrence of the data more probable than does any rival theory, then—other things being equal—Newton's theory is more probable than any rival theory. When a prediction concerns the value of a continuous variable, there are limits to the accuracy of prediction that we can measure, even of a true deterministic theory, owing to our ignorance of many very small unconnected interfering factors (atmospheric disturbance, imperfection of measuring apparatus, and so on) that constitute part of the initial conditions. But, given our limited knowledge of the initial conditions, the narrower the range of values of a variable that the theory predicts successfully with a given high probability, in effect the more data it yields. (It seems to me irrelevant to whether some evidence *e* makes some hypothesis *h* probable whether *e* is discovered first and then *h* is put forward as a hypothesis to explain it, or whether *h* is first proposed as a hypothesis and *e* (which *h* predicts) is observed subsequently. But, as many writers have thought that *h* is much better 'supported' in the latter case, I discuss this issue in the Appendix on Predictivism. My use before then of such expressions as '*h* predicts *e*' is not meant to carry the implication that *e* was discovered subsequently to the formulation of *h*; only the timeless implication that *h* renders *e* probable. Nor, unless '*e*' is described as 'evidence' or 'observed', do I imply that the prediction is successful).

The second criterion on the a posteriori side is that a hypothesis is more probably true in so far as it fits with our 'background evidence', that is—loosely—with everything else we believe about the world. If a theory about the behaviour of some newly discovered planet of our solar system claims that it moves in a circle centred on a point 10m miles from the sun, then the fact that it fits badly with the evidence that all other planets of our system move in ellipses with the sun at one focus makes it much less probable. Or—to take an example from personal explanation—a hypothesis that Jones had a desire to steal stronger than any other desire, a belief that there was money in the safe (which did not belong to him), the power to break open the safe, leading to his stealing money from the safe, is much more probable in so far as it fits with our other evidence (obtained on other occasions) of his character at other times (for example, that he stole from safes frequently) and much less probable in so far as it fits badly with that evidence (for example, that he had never stolen anything before).

On the a priori side, there is, first, scope. The greater the scope of a hypothesis, the less it is likely to be true. The scope of a hypothesis is a matter of how much it tells us (whether correctly or not) about the world—whether it tells us just about our planet, or about all the planets of the solar system, or about all the planets in the universe; or whether it purports to predict exact values of many variables or only approximate values of few variables. The more claims you make and the more detailed your claims, the greater the probability that your claims will contain some falsity and that so the conjunction of these claims will be false. There is no precise way of measuring scope, but we can compare scope. If one hypothesis entails another but is not entailed by it, the former has greater scope than the latter. And rough comparisons at any rate, and sometimes precise comparisons, are possible between theories not thus logically related. A hypothesis that predicted all the positions of Mars for the next century within some given limit of accuracy would have the same scope as one that predicted all the positions of Venus for the next century within the same limit. Conversely, a hypothesis that predicted all the positions of Mars for the next year would have smaller scope than one that predicted all the positions of Venus for the next century; and so clearly (as such—that is, barring better satisfaction of the other criteria) be more likely to be true. However, the influence of this criterion is not very great when we are dealing with hypotheses that satisfy the other criteria very well. A theory of very great scope—such as General Relativity, concerned with the behaviour of matter–energy at all points of space and time—may still be judged very probable, despite that great scope, if it satisfies the other criteria very well.

And then, finally, there is the a priori criterion of simplicity, which I believe to be of immense importance—other things being equal, a simpler hypothesis is more probably true and so the simplest hypothesis is the one most probably true. Since the role of this criterion, unlike that of the others, has been the subject of much dispute, I shall shortly say quite a lot about its nature and role in order to make my claims about it plausible.

If one hypothesis is superior to another in yielding the data to a higher degree of logical probability, or in yielding more data to the same degree of probability, then as such it is more likely to be true, but any greater simplicity of a rival hypothesis is a compensating factor that could lead to equal probability overall or even to the greater probability of the rival. Again, a hypothesis with smaller scope is as such more likely to be true. But greater ability to yield the data or greater simplicity may come in as compensating factors to make a difference to which is the more probable—except in a case where the hypothesis with greater scope entails the theory with lesser. (In this latter case, the probability of the latter cannot be less than the former, since any evidence that a whole hypothesis is true is evidence that any part of it is true.)

And, again, if one hypothesis fits better with background evidence than does another—for another example, if one theory about the behaviour of argon at low temperatures fits better with our evidence about what other inert gases do at low temperatures than does another—that is reason for supposing it true; but the other factors may come in as compensating factors with the consequence that the theory that fits less well with background evidence is the one more probably true.

The Criterion of Simplicity

Let me begin my discussion of the role of this criterion by showing it at work in choosing among scientific theories of equal scope fitting equally well with background evidence and yielding the same data with the same degree of logical probability. Let us suppose that we are investigating a new area and there is no background evidence to guide us as to the form of theory to be expected to hold in this area. We study the relation of two variables—x and y. We collect a finite number of observations of values of y for integral values of x. We find the following results:

x	0	1	2	3	4	5	6
y	0	2	4	6	8	10	12

A formula suggests itself as to how x and y are connected that will allow us to extrapolate to the future: $y=2x$. The formula yields the data in the respect that from it and from any observed value of x we can deduce the observed value of y. Consequently it satisfies the criterion of yielding these data maximally well. But $y=2x$ is not the only formula that does so. For example, all formulae of the form

$$y=2x+x(x-1)(x-2)(x-3)(x-4)(x-5)(x-6)z$$

yield those data equally well, and there are an infinite number of formulae of that form, according to the filling you give to z, which may be a constant or some function of x or any other variable. All these different formulae, although agreeing in yielding the values of y (for given values of x) observed so far, make totally different predictions for the future. Why prefer one formula rather than another? The obvious answer is that we prefer the simplest ($y=2x$) (obtained by putting z equal to 0). We believe it to be more likely to be true than any other formula of the stated form—as can be seen by the fact that we believe its predictions to be as such more likely to be true than those of any other formula of that form. If our life depended on predicting the correct value of y for $x = 9$, we would think it utterly irrational to make any prediction other than $y = 18$.

The comment is often made in discussions of this sort of example that none of the 'wild' theories—for example, ones generated by giving non-zero values to z, would be seriously put forward by scientists. The comment is, of course, true. But my concern is with why the wild theories would not be seriously put forward, and my answer is that scientists implicitly use a principle of simplicity.

People used to say that the answer to this problem was that we should assume that the future will resemble the past. But the future always resembles the past—in some respect. Whatever the next value of y observed, for a given value of x, there will be some mathematical formula that yields that value as well as values of y observed so far. Suppose that when, given the initial data of our previous example, we go on to measure the value of y for $x = 7$ and find that $y = 5{,}054$. Then the future will have resembled the past in that the past and the future values of y all conform to the formula reached from the above formula by puting $z = 1$: the formula $y = 2x + x(x-1)(x-2)(x-3)(x-4)(x-5)(x-6)$. The criterion 'Choose the theory that postulates that the future resembles the past' is empty. To give it content we must amend it to 'Choose the theory that postulates that the future resembles the past in the simplest respect'.

Some people, faced initially with this issue, suggest that we might test between alternative theories by making a new observation—for example, find the value of y for $x = 7$. If it is 14, then the theory $y = 2x$ is confirmed. However, although, by making the new observation, an infinite number of theories will be shown false, an infinite number will remain, agreeing in yielding all observations so far (including the new one, $y = 14$), yet predicting differently for the new future. All theories of the form of the previous theory where z is such that $(x - 7)$ is a factor of it are like this. In claiming, however, that the simplest theory that yields the data is most probably true, I do not, as I have made clear, rule out that theory being shown false by subsequent observations. When we measure y, for $x = 7$, the value might turn out to be 5,054 or any other number at all. If that happens, we need to move to the simplest remaining theory that yields the new observations, as well as the old ones. This process can move science in the direction of a theory quite complicated relative to the theory with which we began. But the point remains that, however many theories you eliminate by finding falsifying observations, you will always be left with an infinite number of theories that yield the observations made up to that time, and of those, I claim, we prefer, and are right to prefer, the simplest as the most probable.

The criterion of simplicity is at work, not merely when we postulate a generalization correlating observations; it is also at work when we postulate the underlying causes of observable data, and, among the infinite number of theories that will do this (in such a way as to yield the data), it tells us (roughly) to postulate few entities and few kinds of entities behaving in mathematically simple kinds of way. If you have a theory that leads you to expect the existence of many thousands of chemical substances in terms of a hundred kinds of atom combining and recombining in various regular patterns, prefer that theory to a theory that also leads you to expect the data but that tells you that each substance is made of varying numbers of atoms of kinds never found in any other substances, which have annihilated each other in complicated ways to produce new atoms forming new substances so far, but are not guaranteed to do so in the future. And, of course, to make the point again, theories normally compete, not merely in respect of simplicity, but in respect of the three other criteria as well; and a theory may be more probable on its evidence than a simpler theory, because it satisfies the other criteria better.

So far I have merely illustrated by a couple of examples one theory being simpler than others. What, more precisely, is it for the one theory to be simpler than another? Before giving my positive account, I need to rule out a quite different understanding of simplicity, which often gets confused with simplicity in my sense, and which clouds the discussion and seems to make my claim about the role of the criterion of simplicity implausible. This is the understanding of a theory being simpler as it having greater scope. It was Popper, more than anyone, who championed an understanding of this kind. He began by equating simplicity with degree of falsifiability. He wrote: 'The epistemological questions which arise in connection with the concept of simplicity can all be answered if we equate this concept with degree of falsifiability.'[5] He claimed that the 'empirical content'—in my terminology, the scope of a theory—'increases with its degree of falsifiability'.[6] He compared[7] four theories of heavenly motion: 'all orbits of heavenly bodies are circles' (p), 'all orbits of planets are circles' (q), 'all orbits of heavenly bodies are ellipses' (r), and 'all orbits of planets are

[5] K. R. Popper, *The Logic of Scientific Discovery* (Hutchinson, 1959), 140.

[6] Ibid. 113.

[7] Ibid. 122.

ellipses' (s). He claimed that, since planets are only one kind of heavenly body, and circles are only one kind of ellipse, p ruled out more possible states of affairs than did the others, and q and r each ruled out more states of affairs than s. p was thus easier to falsify than, for example, q—because an observation of any heavenly body, not just a planet, not moving in a circle would suffice to falsify it; and, for that reason, p told you more, had greater scope, than q. For similar reasons, p had greater scope than r and s; q and r each had greater scope than s.

Now there may be a lot to be said for having theories simpler in this sense. Big claims are theoretically more important than small ones; and, if they can be falsified easily, at any rate some progress can often be made. Theories with great scope are, however, as such, as I have already noted and as Popper boldly proclaimed, more likely to be false than theories with small scope. And there is no point in taking the trouble to falsify theories that are almost certainly false anyway.[8] It is at this point that simplicity in a different sense comes in, as a criterion of probable truth. In my terminology a theory that a planet moves in a circle, for example, does not as such have greater simplicity than the theory that it moves in an ellipse; it just has less free parameters (a circle being an ellipse with a particular eccentricity, zero), and thus has greater scope. The theory that it moves in a circle, however, may well be simpler in my sense than the theory that it moves in an ellipse of a particular non-circular shape (where both have the same number of free parameters).

What is it then for a hypothesis to be simpler in my preferred sense? I shall describe what this criterion amounts to more fully and discuss its jus-

[8] Elliott Sober's understanding (in *Simplicity* (Clarendon Press, 1975)) selects much the same theories as simpler than other theories, as does Popper's understanding. For Sober, the simplest theory is the most informative theory in the sense of the one with respect to which you need to obtain less additional information in order to be able to answer your questions. He claims that his account of simplicity allows us to discriminate between equally precise equations, such as $y=3x+6$, and $y=5x^4+4x^3+75x+168$. While both theories need to have added to them merely the value of x in order to answer the question 'What is the value of y?', they do not require the same amount of extra information in order to answer the question 'What is the value of dy/dx?'. The first theory needs no extra information to tell you this, whereas the second theory needs to have added to it the value of y (or x). Now, of course we want theories that answer the questions in which we are interested. But the crucial point is that we want those answers only if the theories are probably true, and it is to the determination of that, that simplicity in my sense is crucially relevant (and simplicity in Sober's sense is irrelevant). (Note incidentally that Sober's account makes simplicity question-relative; what is simple in a community depends on what their scientific interests are. The second equation enables us to answer, without requiring extra information, 'What is the value of $y-(5x^4+4x^3+75x)$?' The answer is 168. But the first equation requires us to have the value of y (or x) before we can answer that question.)

tification by limiting myself mainly to cases where the hypothesis at stake is a scientific theory consisting of one or more purported laws of nature; and then go on to the point that my account of simplicity and its role applies to hypotheses of all kinds. The same hypothesis, in the sense of one postulating the same entities, properties, and relations between them, may be expressed in different logically equivalent formulations—a formulation of a hypothesis being any collection of sentences that claim that things are (in contingent respects) as the theory claims. One hypothesis is simpler than another if (and only if) the simplest formulation of the former is simpler than the simplest formulation of the latter. There are various facets of simplicity. They are, to speak strictly, facets of formulations of hypotheses. But, in the case of a facet where any formulation of a hypothesis will have the same degree of that facet as any other formulation of the same hypothesis, I shall speak straightforwardly of the simplicity of hypotheses. (The first two facets will be seen to have this property—for example, any formulation of a hypothesis will postulate the same number of entities as any other.)

The first facet of simplicity is just a matter of number of things postulated. A hypothesis that postulates one entity (or property of an entity) rather than two, two rather than three, is (other things being equal) simpler. When there is damage to livestock in some vicinity, it is simpler to postulate that it is caused by one puma escaped from captivity than by two. The principle of simplicity says that, if the former hypothesis yields the data just as well as the latter does, it is more probably true. (The application of this facet in choosing theories is simply the use of Occam's razor. Note that the two suppositions have equal scope—they are both claims about exactly how many pumas there are. The difference between them making for the greater probability of the former is a matter of relative simplicity.)

Secondly, number of kinds of thing. A hypothesis that postulates three kinds of entities (or properties of entities) is (other things being equal) simpler than one that postulates six, and so on. A scientific theory that postulates three kinds of quark is simpler than one that postulates six kinds of quark; and one that postulates that quarks have just certain properties such as spin is simpler than one that postulates that they have these properties and also colour-charge as well.[9]

[9] A 'theory' with few variables might seem often to have an additional advantage over a theory with many variables of a kind to which Glymour drew our attention. This is that the value of a variable of the former can be calculated from different parts of the data by different routes. Plausibly, if the two ways of calculating it yield the same value, that confirms the

Thirdly, a formulation of a hypothesis that contains a predicate (descriptive of a property) whose sense can be grasped only by someone who understands some other term (when the latter can be understood without understanding the former) will be less simple than an otherwise equally simple formulation of a hypothesis that contains the latter term instead. Thus, if 'grue' can be understood only by someone who understands 'green' but not conversely, then 'all emeralds are green' is simpler than 'all emeralds are grue'.[10] The general force of this requirement is, of course, other things being equal, to lead us to prefer predicates designating the more readily observable properties rather than ones a long way distant from observation. We cannot grasp the sense of the physicist's terms 'enthalpy' or 'isospin' or 'hypercharge' unless we understand some of the consequences of a system having a certain amount of enthalpy, or a quark

theory. (See Clark Glymour, *Theory and Evidence* (Princeton University Press, 1980), *passim.*) But this is in fact an advantage possessed by families of theories (i.e. 'theories' in which values of variables are yet to be determined) over other families. It is not, for example, an advantage possessed by one fully determinate theory postulating many properties with precise values over one postulating few properties with precise values, which is what the first and second facets of simplicity described in the text are concerned with. To the extent to which a theory (i.e. a family of theories) T_1 possesses Glymour's advantage over another theory T_2, then T_1 rules out more combinations of observations than does T_2. For if there are two kinds of observation each of which allows us to calculate the value of a certain variable of T_1, then, for each value of one kind of observation, all values except one of the other kind of observation are ruled out. If this does not hold for T_2, T_2 rules out less than does T_1. So T_1 predicts more precisely than does T_2. Glymour's advantage thus comes under the heading of my third criterion of greater scope rather than under the heading of simplicity in my sense. Glymour himself acknowledges that his 'bootstrap procedures . . . do not seem to help the [curve fitting] problem much more than a whit' (p. 340).

[10] See the famous example introduced into philosophical discussion by Nelson Goodman (in his *Fact, Fiction, and Forecast* (2nd edn., Bobbs-Merrill, 1965)). The original example has usually been altered slightly in subsequent discussion, so that an object is defined as 'grue' at a time *t* if (and only if) it is green and *t* is before some named date, let us say AD 2050 or it is blue and *t* is after 2050. Hence all emeralds observed so far (i.e. before 2050) are green, and also now grue. But the extrapolation from those data to 'all emeralds are (always) green' seems better justified than an extrapolation to 'all emeralds are (always) grue'. The former hypothesis would have the consequence that emeralds after AD 2050 would be green; the latter hypothesis would have the consequence that emeralds after AD 2050 would be blue. If the term 'grue' is introduced into our language by this definition, our conception of grue is a more complicated conception than that of green since in order to grasp what it is to be grue, we have first to grasp what it is to be green, but not vice versa. Hence our preference for the former hypothesis can be explained in terms of our preference for the simpler hypothesis. If, however, 'grue' is introduced not by definition but by examples of objects that are grue, then the problem of conflict between the two hypotheses will not arise. For the examples by which (before AD 2050) 'grue' is introduced will be the same as those by which 'green' is introduced, and no one will have any reason (before AD 2050) for supposing that it has a different meaning from 'green'.

having isospin or hypercharge, in terms closer to observation or unless there are analogies to these properties among more observable properties.

Of course, which properties are observable depends on who is doing the observing and what apparatus they have to help them; but there remains a logical dependence of the observability of some properties on the observability of others. For any given language-using community in which words are given a sense, that sense may be tied to one means of observing or to a process that involves all of a number of means of observing, including the former means. Whether or not a track crosses a photographic plate depends on the way it looks to most observers, but whether or not a fundamental particle has a negative charge or not depends (in part) on the results of very many diverse kinds of observation including whether it leaves a track on a photographic plate in certain circumstances. In that sense, tracks on photographic plates are more readily observable than the charges of fundamental particles. The less readily observable is as such more theoretical—the attribution of greenness to an object carries less consequences by way of big theory than does the attribution of charm. This facet of simplicity says: do not postulate underlying theoretical properties, unless you cannot get a hypothesis that yields the data equally well without them.[11]

Fourthly, a formulation of a hypothesis in the form of a theory consisting of a few separate laws is (other things being equal) simpler than one consisting of many laws. Kepler's three laws of planetary motion (plus a proposition for each planet, stating its mean distance from the sun) enabling

[11] David Lewis ('New Work for a Theory of Universals', *Australasian Journal of Philosophy*, 61 (1983), 343–77) has claimed that simple theories should have predicates that designate 'natural' properties: 'We should ask how candidate systems compare in simplicity when each is formulated in the simplest eligible way; or, if we count different formulations as different systems, we should dismiss the ineligible ones from candidacy. An appropriate standard of eligibility is not far to seek: let the primitive vocabulary that appears in the axioms refer to perfectly natural properties' (p. 367). And, of course, the problem then arises as to how we are to recognize these 'perfectly natural properties'. My answer is that only comparative talk is in place—one can recognize properties postulated by one theory as more natural than those postulated by another. They are either the more readily observable properties (ones that are designated by predicates that an investigator can grasp, while needing to grasp the sense of fewer other predicates); or properties that have worked better in other theories. The former are natural because they contain intrinsically simpler properties; the latter derive their naturalness from theories that incorporate them fitting well with successful background theories—it is background evidence that determines their naturalness. So far I have been concerned to hold background evidence constant (e.g. because there is no background evidence relevant to the field of enquiry; or because theories up for consideration fit it equally well). If we ignore background evidence, naturalness is a matter of ready observability.

deduction of the paths and periods of all the planets relative to earth was (in this respect) simpler than Copernicus' or Ptolemy's forty or so laws, which also enabled these to be deduced. Fifthly, a formulation of a theory in which individual laws relate few variables rather than many is simpler. Consider a formulation of a theory T_1, which has three laws, one relating two variables (x and y), one relating two other variables (w and z), and one relating two further variables (r and v). Compare it with a formulation T_2, which also has three laws, each of which relates all six variables. T_1 is, in respect of this facet, the simpler formulation.

And finally (other things being equal) a mathematically simpler formulation is simpler. This facet is illustrated by my earlier example of $y = 2x$ being simpler than any formula of the form $y = 2x + x(x-1)(x-2)(x-3)(x-4)(x-5)(x-6)z$, for all fillings of z other than 0.

Two sub-facets are involved in this facet of mathematical simplicity. One is that fewer terms make an equation or description of some state of affairs simpler: $y = z + x$ is simpler than $y = z + x + x^2$. Secondly, other things being equal, an equation or description of some state of affairs is mathematically simpler than another in so far as it uses simpler mathematical entities or relations than that other. A mathematical entity or relation Q is simpler than another one Y if Q can be understood by someone who does not understand Y, but Y cannot be understood by anyone who does not understand Q. Thus 0 and 1 are simpler entities than 2, 2 than 3, and so on. For you cannot grasp the notion of 2 *A*s unless you can grasp the notion of 0 *A*s. (You would not know what it is for something to be an *A* in the room unless you knew what it was for there to be 0 *A*s in the room). Conversely, 0 must be understood together with 1, but 1 can be understood without 2 being understood. For this reason $y = z + x$ is a simpler equation than $y = z + 2x$. (But, while small numbers are thus simpler than large numbers and non-integral numbers, this aspect of simplicity seems to make a very small difference to relative overall simplicity compared to that made by the numbers 1 and 0 or by different kinds of mathematical function. It does, however, operate, as can be seen by our preference for a theory stating that a force was proportional to $\frac{ee'}{r^2}$ over a theory postulating that the force was proportional to $\frac{ee'}{r^{1.997}}$ if both were equally good at yielding the data.) My definition has the consequence that multiplication is a less simple relation than addition, power than multiplication, vector product than scalar product; rational numbers are less simple entities than integers, real numbers than rational numbers, tensors than vectors, and so on. Hence $y = x$ is a simpler equation than $y=\sqrt{5}x$. (Note that this criterion of mathematical simplicity concerns the preferable form of a description of quantitative values of certain given non-mathematical entities and properties or an equation relating them, and is different from the earlier criterion that concerned the preferability of a hypothesis postulating fewer non-mathematical entities and properties.)

In order to compare hypotheses, we need to compare their simplest formulations. But it is not always clear which is the simplest formulation of a hypothesis. For it is always possible to give a formulation of a hypothesis that makes it simpler in one respect at the cost of loss of simplicity in another respect. We can, for example, reduce many laws to few by introducing variables with more components (scalars such as mass having only one component, vectors such as velocity in three-dimensional space having three components, tensors having many more), and so compressing the information into a shorter form. Maxwell is known for having propounded *four* laws of electromagnetism, but Maxwell used only vectors and scalars. Put his theory in tensor form, and you can express it with only two laws. But the gain in simplicity in fewness of laws is balanced by the loss involved in introducing variables—that is, values of properties, more remote from observation (you cannot grasp the concept of an electromagnetic field tensor without grasping the concepts of electric field and magnetic field, but not vice versa); and more complex mathematical entities. Formulations of hypotheses may or may not become simpler when there is a loss in respect of one facet but a gain in respect of another.

Just as it is the simplest formulation of a hypothesis that we should use when comparing hypotheses in respect of their simplicity, so it is their simplest formulation that we should use in comparing hypotheses in respect of their scope. A theory 'all ravens are black', in making a precise claim about the colour of each bird of some species, certainly seems to have more scope than a theory 'all swans are either white or green or blue', which makes a much less precise claim about the colour of each bird of some species. But, if we invent a word 'whue' defined as 'either white or green or blue' and reformulate the second theory as 'all swans are whue', it might seem to have just as much scope as the first theory. But intuitively it does not. We can explain that intuition in terms of the later formulation of the second theory being less simple than the earlier one by satisfying the third facet of simplicity less well; and the simplest formulation of the theory revealing its nature more clearly.

To revert to our main present topic of the comparison of hypotheses in respect of simplicity—even if it is clear that you have hypotheses in their simplest formulations, all too often a new hypothesis whose simplest formulation is simpler than the simplest formulation of its predecessor in respect of one facet will be more complex in respect of another. Take again that well-worn example of Copernicus' theory of planetary motion (with its many epicycles, deferents, and moving eccentrics, carrying the planets round the sun) versus Kepler's theory of non-circular elliptical motion of planets around the sun. In (what are fairly evidently) their simplest formulations, Copernicus' theory has laws covering some forty separate circular motions, whereas Kepler's theory has far fewer laws. But non-circular elliptical motion is more complex than circular motion—there are more terms in an equation of non-circular elliptical motion. How can we weigh the facets against each other? With the benefit of hindsight, I am inclined to say that Kepler's theory is simpler than Copernicus'; the gain in having so few separate motions is not outweighed by the small addition to the complexity of individual motions. But that was not obvious in the seventeenth century.

It is, I suggest, normally objectively clear which is the simplest formulation of a hypothesis and which hypothesis is the simplest, when simplest formulations differ only in respect of one facet of simplicity. And, while the criteria for comparing facets of simplicity are in no way clear, there is, I suggest, plenty of consensus over a range of cases about how to weigh greater simplicity in one respect against less in another; although I do not think that any general formula can be produced for calculating this that would command any widespread agreement.[12] My ground for supposing that there is this general consensus is this. Take some standard scientific theory T_1, produce another theory T_2 that yields the data equally well and has equal scope, and has some marginal advantage over T_1 in respect of one facet of simplicity at the expense of disadvantage in respect of another. It will normally be evident to any scientist (even if he knows nothing about the particular field in question) which is the simpler theory and the one to be adopted if they fit equally well with background evidence. But there certainly remains a borderland of pairs of formulations of theories about the relative overall simplicity of which scientists will differ.[13] Yet, if we have only a few theories about whose relative probability on the data (because of

[12] One formula in circulation for measuring simplicity is the computation formula, that the simplest hypothesis is the one that can be expressed in fewest symbols. This formula gives an account of simplicity that largely but not entirely coincides with mine. I compare and contrast the two accounts in Additional Note F, and defend there my account as capturing our intuitions better in those cases where the two accounts conflict.

[13] T. S. Kuhn, often considered (on the basis of his classic work, *The Structure of Scientific Revolutions* (University of Chicago Press, 1962)) as holding that there are no common criteria among scientists of different cultures for judging the worth of theories, in his later

disagreement about which is the simpler) there is dispute, such disagreement can be resolved by finding more data, probable on one theory but improbable on the others. What holds for scientific theories can, I suggest, be generalized to hypotheses of other kinds.

The account that I have given of simplicity was reached by reflecting on the a priori considerations (additional to scope) that lead us to recognize one hypothesis as more probable than another. Nothing turns for the purposes of the main argument of this book on whether I have captured them with perfect accuracy. But it should be evident that considerations of the kind that I have described are operative, and that the word 'simplicity' is a natural one for describing the overall criterion that you get when you put all these considerations together.

Simplicity is the only criterion of choice among hypotheses of equal scope with equal ability to yield the data, when there is no background evidence—that is, evidence of how things behave in neighbouring fields of enquiry. When we are considering very large-scale theories, there will be no such background evidence. A general theory of the mechanical behaviour of matter, such as was Newton's, attempted to explain so much that there were no theories of neighbouring areas with which it could dovetail. And the same point applies, even more strongly, to the even more all-embracing theories developed since Newton that seek to explain all things known to science. The only criterion for choice among such theories that yield the data equally well is that of simplicity.

Consider Newton formulating his theory of gravitation to account for the data of terrestrial gravitation (incorporated in Galileo's law of fall), of collision (formulated by Huyghens), of planetary motion (captured by Kepler's laws), of the motions of the moons of Jupiter and Saturn, of tides and comets. His three laws of motion and his law of gravitational attraction—that all bodies attract each other with forces proportional to the product of their masses (m and m') and inversely proportional to the square of their distance apart

$$(r) - F = \frac{mm'}{r^2},$$

were such as to allow people to deduce for innumerable observed values of variables other values, which they could observe to hold (to the limit of accuracy that could be measured); his theory yielded a vast number of data very

collection of essays *The Essential Tension* (University of Chicago Press, 1977, 322) listed simplicity among five 'standard criteria for assessing the adequacy of a scientific theory', along with accuracy, consistency, scope, and fruitfulness. He commented that individually the criteria are imprecise and they often conflict with each other.

well. But equally successful and of equal scope would have been any theory that replaced the law of gravitational attraction with a law of the form

$$F = \frac{mm'}{r^2} + \frac{Kmm'}{r^4},$$

where K is a very small constant, such that the data available to Newton would not have been sufficiently accurate to allow discrimination between the predictions of the two theories. Indeed, sixty years later, when data had been obtained that did seem sufficiently accurate to discriminate between Newton's theory and a certain theory of the latter form, they seemed to Clairaut to be such as to favour the latter, and he tentatively proposed such a theory—but only because of the (as it seemed to him) inability of Newton's theory to yield the data then available;[14] otherwise his preference for Newton's theory was clear. Among other theories that yield the data available in the eighteenth century (to as great a degree of accuracy as could then or can now be measured) are all theories obtained from Newton's theory by replacing the law of gravitation by a law of the form

$$F = \frac{mm'}{r^{2.000...(100\ \text{zeros})\ ...1}}.$$

So too do many theories in which

$$F = \frac{mm'}{r^2} + Km,$$

where K is a variable whose value depends on the average distance apart of the galaxies. As, in consequence of their mutual recession arising from the 'Big Bang', the galaxies get further apart, they will, such a theory may suggest, eventually reach some critical level (for example, in AD 2050). K, we may suppose, has the value zero until then, in AD 2050 it has value 1, and thereafter it has a value that measures the proportional increase since AD 2050 of the average distance apart of the galaxies. Such theories will be just as good at yielding the data obtained then or now as is Newton's theory. Of course, none of these theories is rendered at all probable by the data, but why they are not rendered probable is not because they do not yield the data (in the sense that I defined), for they do; but because they are obviously less simple than another theory that does yield the data.

However, it may reasonably be urged, this is not the normal situation. Most hypotheses between which we have to choose are less all-embracing, and then it will often be the case that one fits better with our background

[14] See e.g. A. Pannekoek, *A History of Astronomy* (George Allen & Unwin, 1961), 303.

evidence then do many others. The all-important point to be made at this stage is, however, that it is the criterion of simplicity that determines which proposed theory 'fits best' with those neighbouring hypotheses. 'Fitting better' is 'fitting more simply', and thus making for a simpler overall view of the world. The requirement of simplicity thus involves the requirement of coherence in our belief system, on which coherence theories of justification (and knowledge) rightly insist.[15] (But, as we noted in Chapter 1, coherence theories neglect the point that some beliefs are rightly basic, and thus have a privileged (though not incorrigible) status that must be respected in securing the coherence of our system.)

Suppose you are studying the structure of some chemical substance *x*. Chemical theory already tells you the element atoms of which all other chemical substances are built, their valency, and the kinds of bond that can exist between them. Experimental evidence may be provided of some of the substances out of which *x* was formed and into which it decomposes. Does not this evidence already fix the parameters in terms of which the chemical formula of *x* is to be stated? Perhaps a finite number of experiments will eliminate all possibilities except one. Not so. Maybe *x* has a component atom never found elsewhere in the universe, formed out of its special kind of quark, which comes into being when *x* is formed and disappears when it decomposes. Maybe there are kinds of bond that bind together the atoms of *x* and no other substance. And so on. But this sort of supposition is absurd. Of course it is. But why is it absurd? Because the supposition that in one substance there exist kinds of atoms formed in kinds of ways and forming kinds of bonds unknown in the rest of the universe amounts to a supposition that our general chemical and physical laws are vastly less simple than we had otherwise supposed them to be. They would have the form not '*L*1 . . . *L*20' (where these are relatively simple laws applying to all chemical substances) but the form of '*L*1 . . . *L*20, except in x where *L*21 . . . *L*24', where *L*21 . . . *L*24 are laws of a totally different form from *L*1 . . . *L*20. It is the criterion of simplicity that tells us to have theories that 'mesh' with theories of neighbouring and wider fields; and it does so by insisting that overall theories be as simple as possible. The criterion of background evidence—that that theory of some field T_1, which fits better with theories

[15] Laurence Bonjour, developing a coherence theory of justification, expounds the notion of coherence as follows: 'Intuitively, coherence is a matter of how well a body of beliefs "hangs together": how well its component beliefs fit together, agree or dovetail with each other, so as to produce an organized, tightly structured system of beliefs, rather than either a helter-skelter collection or a set of conflicting subsystems' (*The Structure of Empirical Knowledge* (Harvard University Press, 1985), 93).

established for neighbouring fields T', T'' ... etc., than do other theories of the former field T_2, T_3, T_4 ... etc., is (other things being equal) more likely to be true than the latter theories, boils down to the criteria of yielding the data and of simplicity. For the claim is that that conjunction of theories (T_1 with T', T'' ... etc.; rather than T_2 with T', T'' ... etc.), which is the simplest theory to yield the data in all fields (with a given degree of probability), is (among theories of equal scope) that most likely to be true.[16]

In holding simpler theories to be more probable than complex theories, the enquirer is holding it to be more probable that the world as a whole is simple than that it is complex. Hence, we should postulate, on grounds of simplicity, as most likely to be true, that theory of a narrow region that makes our overall world theory the simplest for the total data. That theory may not be the simplest theory of the narrow aspect of the world, considered on its own. When it is urged that there are grounds for postulating many entities rather than few, or a complex equation rather than a simple one, even when a simpler theory yields the data equally well, those grounds will, I suggest, be found to consist in the fact that theories of neighbouring fields postulate many entities in similar circumstances, or equations of similar form to the complex equation; and so the overall picture is simpler if we postulate in a new region the same kind of complexity as in the others.[17]

[16] Boyd has claimed that judgements of projectability, i.e. in effect simplicity in my sense, are judgements of 'theoretical plausibility' (i.e. of fit with other existing theories), 'where the determination of the relevant respects of resemblance is itself a theoretical issue', i.e. that what constitutes 'fit' is in some way itself determined by the background. (See Richard Boyd, 'Realism, Approximate Truth and Philosophical Method', repr. in D. Papineau (ed.), *The Philosophy of Science* (Oxford University Press, 1996), 223–4.) His view seems to arise from regarding background as consisting not merely of scientific theories in the ordinary sense but also of principles of inference; and this conglomeration of two very distinct things seems to arise from a claim that empirical data can provide evidence not merely for theories but for principles of inference. But these principles of inference so established cannot be all the ones that there are—for then there would be no principles left in virtue of which the empirical data could provide evidence for them. Science must have some a priori contribution. If it is suggested that the procedure of establishing principles of inference is entirely circular, then a scientific theory well supported on its own principles of inference by its data and any crazy theory well supported on its crazy principles of inference by the same data would be just as likely to be true—which is manifestly false.

[17] This is the answer to the objection of Colin Howson that use of the simplicity postulate is 'at odds with reasonable procedures. In the case of hypotheses generated in economic forecasting, to take an extreme example, simple hypotheses would normally be regarded as very unlikely' ('On the Consistency of Jeffreys's Simplicity Postulate and its Role in Bayesian Inference', *Philosophical Quarterly*, 38 (1988), 68–83; see p. 78). But the reason why such hypotheses are very unlikely is that very simple hypotheses have worked poorly in the past in social and economic theory, while the simplest among hypotheses of a certain kind and degree of complexity have done better; and so a new hypothesis, to fit well with

Note, of course, that an investigator can make a choice only between the hypotheses that have occurred to him or to his colleagues (if only to be dismissed as absurd). There may be simple theories of which some scientist has not thought, and his judgement that a certain theory is the one most probably true on the evidence may arise through a failure to realize that there is a much simpler theory that yields the data. In that case, the scientist's theory will be only epistemically probable (for a certain kind of epistemic probability) but not logically probable. For the same reason, a scientist may misjudge which theory fits best with background evidence, through a failure to realize the simplicity of some overall connections. In this case, his error will affect his judgement of the comparative worth of theories, not merely his judgement of the absolute worth of the theories available to him. For it may be that a theory T_1 of a narrow area fits better with background evidence B than does a theory T_2 of that area—although the scientist has made the opposite judgement, through a failure to see that there is a very simple overall theory Θ of which (B and T_1) is a consequence.

My claim—that, for given fit with background evidence among hypotheses of the same scope that yield the data equally well, the simplest is that most probably true—has been argued so far mainly for inanimate explanation and, holding initial conditions constant, mainly for scientific theories. But the same considerations apply when we hold scientific theories constant, and compare hypotheses about initial conditions; or when both theories and initial conditions are allowed to vary, and we seek the most probable account overall of what are the initial conditions and what is the true theory. Assuming Newton's theory to be true, Leverrier wondered why Uranus moved along a path that was irregular in comparison with the path that Newtonian theory seemed to predict for it. On the supposition that the only other planets were the five known to the ancients together with Uranus, the irregularities were not to be expected. So Leverier postulated a seventh planet, which pulled Uranus out of its regular orbit when close to it.[18] He could have postulated 726 tiny planets with a common centre of gravity at the position at which he postulated Neptune, but the former supposition (while having equal scope—telling us how many planets there were and of what mass) was simpler (in virtue of the first facet that I described). Or he could have put forward a yet more complicated proposal, amending Newton's theory and postulating two

the latter hypotheses, will have to postulate the same kinds of complex interactions—in other words, a new relatively complex hypothesis will make for a simpler overall theory than does a new very simple hypothesis.

[18] See e.g. Pannekoek, *History of Astronomy*, 359–62.

further heavenly bodies at the same time. But, of course, he would not have supposed that the evidence supported that complicated hypothesis. The simplest overall hypothesis (of theory and initial conditions) was that most probably true. When we are assessing the relative simplicity of initial conditions, the crucial facets that determine this are the first, second, third, and the mathematical facets. A hypothesis that postulates more entities and properties, or kinds of entities and properties, described in ways more remote from observation or mathematically more complicated is, as such, less likely to be true.

The same considerations apply to personal explanation; I have already illustrated this in Chapter 2, when considering the grounds for attributing beliefs to human persons. In considering hypotheses seeking to explain the occurrence of certain data through the intentional agency of a person, we prefer, among those that yield the data, other things being equal, the simplest. We find certain pieces of metal all having on them the same outline of a human head. A possible explanation is that each of them was caused intentionally by the same person, exercising (by holding a chisel) normal human bodily powers, having the purpose to make a coin and believing that a piece of metal with such marks would be a coin; this person had a continuing desire to make coins that gave rise over time to his different actions. There are many other possible explanations that would lead us to expect the phenomena—maybe each of the marks on the pieces of metal was made by a different person at a different period of history with a different belief to fulfil a different purpose, arising from a different desire, and that it was in consequence a coincidence that all the marks had the same shape. While detailed hypotheses of this kind can satisfy the criterion of leading us to expect the observed phenomena, as well as does the former hypothesis, clearly they satisfy the criterion of simplicity far less well—for they postulate many persons, desires, and beliefs, rather than one person, one desire, and one belief. Of course, in these and all other examples that we consider, 'other things' may not be 'equal'. The criterion of fit with background evidence may effect crucially the assessment of such hypotheses; evidence, for example, about how and when and where people make coins. (After all, they normally make coins by melting metal and pouring it into a mould. But maybe that hypothesis would not make the data as probable as does the chiselling hypothesis. Maybe the marks on the coin are typical chisel marks.) So too may the criterion of scope. The former hypothesis attributing the marks to the agency of one person with certain desires and beliefs is more probable than a hypothesis that purports to tell us a lot more about who that person was and what were his other desires and beliefs.

In assessing a much wider range of phenomena in terms of their intentional causation by human persons we build up a picture of the phenomena as caused by few persons with powers and desires and beliefs that are constant or change in regular ways (that is, vary in a mathematically simple way with variations in the values of few kinds of variable—for example, sensory stimuli)—as few persons and as simple ways of change as we can. If we can explain two events as brought about by a human in order to fulfil the same desire, we do not invoke a quite new desire to explain the second event. If we can explain an event as brought about by a person in virtue of bodily powers of the same kind as other humans have, we do not postulate some novel power—we do not postulate that some person has a basic power of bending spoons at some distance away if we can explain the phenomenon of the spoons being bent by someone else bending them with his hands. And so on.

And, if the issue is whether certain phenomena are brought about intentionally by a person at all, rather than being caused by some inanimate process, the issue turns on whether there is a simple personal explanation that leads us to expect these phenomena. If we go to a distant planet and find some object with appendages moving around and causing effects, the question arises whether we have here a person (or animal), or just an inanimate object. The issue then turns on whether we can attribute to this object a small set of constant desires, and beliefs about how to fulfil them sensitive to sensory stimuli, with a set of powers to act intentionally guided by beliefs and desires, in such a way as to lead us to expect the phenomena that we observe, and whether such an explanation is simpler than any inanimate explanation. If so it is probably (but not certainly) correct.

Attempts to Deny the Fundamental Role of Simplicity

Among philosophers who allow this—hard to resist—claim that simplicity plays the crucial role that I have described in choosing between hypotheses, there are three kinds of unsatisfactory reaction. I illustrate and respond to these reactions by considering the context in which they are most discussed—where the hypotheses are scientific theories. The arguments can be generalized to cover other kinds of hypothesis.

The first is to claim that our preference for simpler theories is for reasons other than their greater probable truth. The obvious version of this is that we prefer simpler theories because it is more convenient to operate with them.[19] It may be more convenient, but it is not always that much more convenient. It would not be too difficult in these days of computer-aided calculations to work out the predictions of some theories more complicated than the simplest theory (of given scope that yield the data to a given degree of probability) if it were important to do so. Yet, even given the predictions of quite a large number of different theories worked out in advance for us, we would still think it right to rely on the predictions of the simplest theory. Our main interest in predictions is an interest in probable truth. We need to know whether the bridge will break if we drive a lorry over it, whether the drug will kill or cure, whether the nuclear explosion will set up a chain reaction that will destroy all humanity, and so on. If there are two theories that yield the observations made so far, one predicting that all life in the northern (but not the southern) hemisphere will be destroyed tomorrow and the other predicting that all life in the southern (but not the northern) hemisphere will be destroyed tomorrow, and there is no time to test further between them but the latter is complicated and the former is simple, any northerner would be on the aeroplane to the south tonight and think that he was highly rational to do so. He would be on the aeroplane because he believes that the predictions of the former theory are as such probably true, and that is because he believes the former theory itself is probably true and is more probably true than the latter theory.

But, given that there is no escaping the fact that scientists use simplicity as a criterion of probable truth, the second unsatisfactory philosophical reaction is to claim that there are empirical grounds for their doing so. It is, the argument goes, the fact that in general simpler theories have worked well in the past that justifies us in assuming that they will work well in the future. To put the claim formally—consider any set of data available at some moment of past history *t*, and any pair of theories that yield those data equally well, T_A and T_B (either actual theories that were constructed, or theories that could have been constructed at *t*), such that T_A is the simplest theory that yields the data and T_B a more complex theory; then normally T_A has or would have subsequently proved the better predictor. We can generalize from these past results to: usually, simplest theories predict better than more complex theories, which in turn makes it probable that on some new occasion the simplest theory will predict better, and so makes it more probable that a simplest theory is true than that a more complicated

[19] Thus Newton-Smith: 'The case for simplicity is pragmatic. It simply is easier to calculate with simpler theories. But there is no reason to see greater relative simplicity of this sort as an indicator of greater verisimilitude' (W. H. Newton-Smith, *The Rationality of Science* (Routledge & Kegan Paul, 1981), 231).

theory is true. True, sometimes the simplest theory has not proved the better predictor. Equally able to yield the rough data known to Boyle about how the temperature (T) of a gas varied with its pressure (p) and volume (v) of gases were no doubt both Boyle's law, $pv = RT$ (R being a constant that varies with the gas) and (if it had been formulated then) Van der Waal's law $\left(p+\frac{a}{v^2}\right)(v-b)=RT$ (a and b being constants that vary with the kind of gas). Yet Van der Waal's law proved the better subsequent predictor. But the claim was only that usually the simplest theory has proved the better predictor, and that would justify the assertion that probably a given simplest theory will prove the better predictor on some future occasion than some given less simple theory, and so is more probably true.

However, even this modest claim about the history of science—that usually the simplest theory has proved the better predictor—seems very doubtful. In many areas of enquiry the simpler 'laws' that served well in the past have been replaced by more complicated laws—the story of Boyle to Van der Waals is hardly unique. But, even if simplest theories have usually proved better predictors, this would not provide a justification for subsequent use of the criterion of simplicity, for the reason that such a justification would already rely on the criterion of simplicity. There are different ways of extrapolating from the corpus of past data about the relative success that was had by actual theories and that would have been had by possible theories of different kinds, if they had been formulated. 'Usually simplest theories predict better than more complex theories' is one way. Another way is an extrapolation of the form 'Usually theories formulated by Greeks in the bath, by Englishmen who watch apples drop, or Germans who work in patent offices . . . etc., which initially appeal to the scientific community, predict better than other theories'.[20] An extrapolation of this kind, spelled out at great length, would yield the data of the past history of science just as well as the extrapolation that connects predictive success with simplicity. It would provide a rival explanation of the past data that we could use to determine which future theories that yielded the data were more probably true. But, of course, this kind of extrapolation is an absurd way of extrapolating from the past data concerning the relative success of theories. And why is it absurd? Because it is far less simple than the obvious way of extrapolating. We have assumed the principle (that the simplest way of extrapolating from data yields a more probably true law) in

[20] Supposedly Archimedes formulated his law in his bath, Newton formulated his theory after watching an apple drop, and Einstein once worked in a patent office.

providing its justification! Any other purported empirical justification of use of the criterion of simplicity will prove equally circular.

Finally, there is the reaction of claiming that it follows from some theorem of the traditional probability calculus or even more obvious logical truth that the simplest theory will probably predict best, and so is more likely to be true than other theories. This is a more sophisticated way of putting the old claim that a deductive justification can be provided for supposing that induction will probably work. But the past evidence is just a finite collection of data. How could it be a logical consequence of that, either what will happen, or what will probably happen? As Hume, of course, affirmed: 'there can be no demonstrative arguments to prove, that those instances of which we have had no experience, resemble those, of which we have had experience',[21] and I add, to tighten the argument, 'in any given respect'.[22]

Quite obviously, so many of our judgements about which scientific theory is more probably true than which other scientific theory are correct. That can only be if the criteria that I have analysed in this chapter are (at any rate approximately) the correct ones; and that means that, among theories of equal scope (fitting equally well with background evidence) that yield the data observed so far with equal probability, a simpler one is more probably true. That cannot be established empirically, and hence it must be an a priori principle. We do not use it because it follows from some more obvious a priori principle. Hence it must be a fundamental a priori principle.

Bayes's Theorem

I have been arguing in this chapter that we have a pattern of inference from particular data to their causal explanation—either in terms of initial conditions and laws of nature, or in terms of other persons, their desires, beliefs, and basic powers; a set of criteria that we employ and think it right to employ for which phenomena make which explanations logically probable. I do not imply that this is the only way in which we can learn about any of the explanatory factors. It may be a basic datum that certain initial

[21] David Hume, *Treatise of Human Nature*, 1. 3. 6.

[22] Philosophers do still go on trying to produce proofs that the criterion of simplicity follows from the traditional axioms of the calculus. For a recent attempt, see Malcolm Forster and Elliott Sober, 'How to Tell when Simpler, More Unified, and Less *ad hoc* Theories will Provide More Accurate Predictions', *British Journal for Philosophy of Science*, 45 (1994), 1–35; and the crucial response to it by A. Kukla, 'Forster and Sober on the Curve-Fitting Problem', *British Journal for the Philosophy of Science*, 46 (1995), 248–52.

conditions held (we may have observed them), or that another person had some purpose (that too might be so obvious as a result of observation as not to need more obvious evidence). I will come in Chapter 5 to the issue of whether there is a privileged set of starting points by which our beliefs should be made logically probable. But the particular starting points (our 'evidence' or 'data') with which I have illustrated my account of the criteria of 'upward inference' are typical public phenomena that we would naturally describe as 'observable' on particular occasions by particular humans with our sort of capacities.

The workings of the criteria that I have set out are captured very well in the formulae of the traditional calculus of probability, used as a calculus of inductive probability[23]—that is, for measuring the probability of one proposition on another. I set out in the previous chapter three axioms to which any calculus of logical probability must correspond: for any propositions p, q, and r

1. $P(q|r) \geq 0$
2. If $N(p \leftrightarrow q)$, $P(r|p) = P(r|q)$
3. If $N(r \rightarrow q)$, $P(q|r) = 1$

We get a full set of axioms for the traditional calculus by adding to them (representing 'and' by '&', and 'not' by '~'):

4. If $N \sim(p\&q\&r)$ (viz. not all three can be true together), and $\sim N \sim r$ (viz. r is logically possible), then $P(p \vee q|r) = P(p|r) + P(q|r)$
5. $P(p\&q|r) = P(p|q\&r) \times P(q|r)$

From the axioms[24] themselves, sometimes called the 'Bayesian' axioms, there follow various theorems. These include the principles called, in Chapter 3, '1*a*' and '2*a*'. There also follows Bayes's theorem, which I will state in terms of the probability of a hypothesis h on evidence e and background evidence k.

$$P(h|e\&k) = \frac{P(e|h\&k)P(h|k)}{P(e|k)}$$

This theorem holds, whatever h, e, and k are. But, for present purposes, h will be taken to be an explanatory hypothesis: e usually represents new

[23] Most textbooks of statistics use it as a calculus of statistical probability.

[24] Axiom 4 is called the Axiom of Finite Additivity. It is often suggested that we should add to the axiom set a stronger version of this axiom, called the Axiom of Countable Additivity. I endorse the case for this in Additional Note G, but, for the sake of simplicity of exposition and because nothing further in this book turns on it, I do not put this axiom in the text here.

more direct or observational data: k usually represents our background evidence in the sense of our very general evidence about the world, taken for granted when investigating e. Evidence may, however, be divided as we choose between e and k; we may put all our relevant logically contingent evidence into e, and k then becomes mere tautological knowledge—namely, irrelevant. $P(h|e\&k)$ is the 'posterior probability of h', $P(h|k)$ the 'prior probability of h', $P(e|k)$ the 'prior probability of e'. If $P(h|e\&k) > P(h|k)$—that is, if e raises the probability of h—I shall follow an established usage in saying that e 'confirms' h. To accept that Bayes's theorem governs all claims about the support given by evidence to hypotheses does not involve holding that the various probabilities can be given exact numerical values (and, as I noted earlier, inductive probabilities do not normally have exact numerical values.). One can think of them as having rough values, values within certain limits; and the theorem, as putting limits on the values of some probabilities, given the limits on others. Or, more usefully, one can think of it as a matrix for generating theorems of comparative probability—for example, that, for two hypotheses h_1 and h_2 and $P(e|k) > 0$, if $P(e|h_1\&k) = P(e|h_2\&k)$, then $P(h_1|e\&k) > P(h_2|e\&k)$ if and only if $P(h_1|k) > P(h_2|k)$.

One important such theorem (which holds given that neither $P(h|k)$ nor $P(e|k) = 0$), known as the relevance criterion, is that $P(h|e\&k) > P(h|k)$ if and only if $P(e|h\&k) > P(e|k)$. (And similarily that $P(h|e\&k) = P(h|k)$ if and only if $P(e|h\&k) = P(e|k)$; and $P(h|e\&k) < P(h|k)$ if and only if $P(e|h\&k) < P(e|k)$.) What this says is that evidence raises the probability of a hypothesis only if it is more probable that that will occur if the hypothesis is true than if we do not make that assumption. Understanding by 'confirms' 'increases the probability of', and by 'disconfirms' 'decreases the probability of', this says that e confirms (disconfirms) h if and only if e is more probable given h than if we do not assume h—from which it follows that e confirms h if and only if e is more probable given h than given not-h. And the confirmation is greater the more $P(e|h\&k)$ exceeds $P(e|k)$ or $P(e|{\sim}h\&k)$.

If e represents our data of observation, and h our hypothesis, $P(e|h\&k)$ is, then, a measure of how probable the hypothesis renders the data, given our background evidence. Bayes's theorem thus captures one aspect of our first criterion that a hypothesis is more probable (its posterior probability is higher) in so far as (given background evidence k) it renders the observed data probable. $P(h|k)$ is a measure of how probable is h, given background evidence alone. If k contains contingent background evidence, then $P(h|k)$ will depend in part on how well h fits with k, which—as we have seen—is a matter of how simple is the conjunction $(h\&k)$. But if we put all the contingent evidence into e, then k becomes some bare tautology. In that case $P(h|k)$ is what we may call the intrinsic probability of h; it will depend solely on factors intrinsic to h. If we give to the intrinisic probability of h a value that is greater the simpler is h, and smaller the greater the scope of h, $P(h|k)$ thus allows us to capture the extent to which the other three criteria set out in this chapter for when a hypothesis is rendered probable by its evidence are satisfied.

$P(e|k)$ measures how probable it is that the data will be found on background evidence alone—that is, if we do not assume that our theory h is true. It follows from the axioms of the calculus that this is equal to the sum of the probability of e on h (and k) and the probability of e on $\sim h$ (and k):

$$P(e|k) = P(e|h\&k)\ P(h|k) + P(e|{\sim}h\&k)\ P({\sim}h|k)$$

This in turn equals the sum of the probabilities of e on h and on each of the hypotheses rival to h (which together exhaust the possible alternatives—that is, at most and at least one of them must be true), each multiplied by the prior probability of that hypothesis. More formally:

$$P(e|k) = P(e|h\&k)\ P(h|k) + P(e|h_1\&k)\ P(h_1|k) + P(e|h_2\&k)\ P(h_2|k) + \ldots$$

There will, of course, be an infinite number of possible hypotheses alternative to h, but, the lower the values for some h_n of $P(e|h_n\&k)\ P(h_n|k)$, the more we can ignore them. The first term of the right-hand side of the above formula repeats the top line of Bayes's theorem. The other terms state the probability of e coming about by some other route than via h. The smaller the value of these terms—either because the rival hypotheses do not make e in the least probable, or because their prior probability is very low—the lower the value of the bottom line of Bayes's theorem, and so the more probable is our hypothesis h. So a hypothesis h is more probable on evidence e, the less probable it is that e would occur if h were false and so some hypothesis rival to h were true.

It is by $P(e|k)$ that Bayes's theorem takes account of the other aspect of my first criterion stated earlier in the chapter that, the more data there are to which a hypothesis h gives a given positive amount of probability, the more probable is h. Bayes's theorem yields this result because, the more such data there are, the less probable it is that they come about by some route other than h. Suppose that you have data e_1, to which both h and h_1 give a degree of probability p ($P(e_1 h\&k) = p$, and $P(e_1 h_1\&k) = p$). Then you acquire further data e_2. Now, in neither case can that increase the probability of the total data on the hypothesis. It cannot be more probable on any hypothesis that you would observe both e_2 and e_1 than you would observe

e_1 (though, of course, it might be more probable that you would observe (e_1 and e_2) than that you would observe (e_1 and not-e_2)—but that is not relevant.) This follows from the calculus, but should in any case be obvious.

So the addition of new data can only either leave the probability of the data on the hypothesis unchanged or decrease it. $P(e_1\&e_2|h\&k) \leq P(e_1|h\&k)$. Now, for each new piece of evidence e_2, there will be some rival to h that entails not-e_2 (that is, that predicts that with a probability of 1). For example, suppose h is 'all ravens are black', and e_1 is 'a, b, c, and d are ravens, and a is black, and b is black and c is black', e_2 is 'd is black'. $P(e_1\&e_2|h\&k) = P(e_1|h\&k)$ and has some value between 0 and 1. But there are many hypotheses inconsistent with h that entail that d is not black. For these hypotheses h_n $P(e_1\&e_2|h_n\&k) = 0$. More generally, the more data there are entailed by h, the more data there will be ruled out (or rendered improbable) by rival hypotheses, and so the smaller will be $P(e|k)$ and so the larger will be $P(h|e\&k)$. Of course, many such rivals may be very 'implausible' and what that amounts to is that their prior probability is low ($P(h_n|k)$ is low). In that case, the additional evidence will not make much difference.

The more plausible alternatives to h will be ones that are not too much less simple than h or fit in fairly well with contingent background evidence. There may be areas for which almost all these rival theories claim that objects will show rather different patterns of behaviour from those that they show in the common area where they make the same predictions as h. In such a case, the ability of h to make true predictions for different areas adds even more to its probability than its ability to make more true predictions for the same area (in which the more plausible rivals to h do not almost all diverge from h in their predictions). Theories rival to Newton's in the seventeenth century that made accurate predictions claimed that the motions of objects in the region beyond the moon were due to different forces from the ones that determined motion on earth—celestial spheres or vortices carried the planets round the earth while (in some form) gravity led to objects on earth falling to the ground. Such theories were by their very nature (postulating two kinds of force) less simple than Newton's (postulating only one force—gravity) and so had less prior probability. Theories postulating the same kind of force for both regions would have been (in this respect) equally simple with Newton's theory. But they would not have been able to make predictions nearly as accurate as Newton's theory. Hence the ability of Newton's theory to make more accurate predictions both about the heavens and the earth added much to the probability of that theory. For the total predictions e to which Newton's theory (h)

gave significant probability, $P(e|k)$ was not too much higher than $P(e|h\&k)$ $P(h|k)$.

So, if we allocate values to the intrinsic probabilities of hypotheses h (and to conjunctions $h\&k$) in the ways stated, Bayes's theorem captures the criteria for when evidence supports hypotheses set out in this chapter.[25]

Probability of Predictions

So far, in seeking to set out the criteria of logical probability, I have sought the criteria for how data or evidence give different degrees of logical probability to different theories purporting to explain the occurrence of that evidence. The theories will include prior observable causes and underlying unobservable causes; and my account shows how we can reach beliefs about these. But (as we shall see) not all retrodiction need be a matter of explaining some present evidence in terms of its past cause; and no prediction involves citing some future event as part of the explanation of a present event. So what are the criteria of logical probability that give probability to this or that prediction about the future or to this or that retrodiction that is not part of an explanation? I claimed at the beginning of this chapter that all prediction goes via an explanatory hypothesis. I can predict where the moon will be tomorrow night, because I have observed where it is tonight, and I have a theory (rendered probable by past observations) of its path and velocity that enables me to calculate from its position and the positions of sun, earth, and other planets tonight where they will cause the moon to be tomorrow. Or I can retrodict to some past event as a cause of some present event, and then—using the physical probabilities embodied in some theory—infer what other events (past, present, or future relative to us, but future relative to it) it will cause.

Although all prediction goes via explanation, it often goes via what I may call a 'dummy hypothesis'. That is, we infer by the criteria of upward inference that the explanation of certain data is of a certain kind (though we cannot infer exactly what the explanation is in detail), and this is sufficient for prediction. Suppose we have tossed a coin 1,000 times and 700 heads

[25] There are many statisticians who do not think that we can measure the support given to hypotheses, because we cannot allocate to them prior probabilities, let alone intrinsic probabilities. These 'non-Bayesian' statisticians normally hold that nevertheless satisfactory rules can be given for when we should 'accept' or 'reject' hypotheses, and they normally develop some variant of Neyman–Pearson theory for this purpose. For discussion of the deficiencies of such theories, see Additional Note H.

have resulted. We conclude that the logical probability of heads next time is $\frac{7}{10}$. But clearly we reach this conclusion because we suppose that the evidence of its past performance shows that—to speak very loosely—the coin has a measurable tendency of $\frac{7}{10}$ of landing heads. To speak less loosely, that evidence gives a very high logical probability to the statistical probability of a toss of this coin in a hypothetical infinite class of tosses (under normally varying tossing conditions—see p. 59) being heads of approximately $\frac{7}{10}$. But this tendency may arise through various alternative causes. Our background evidence from all we know about mechanics is that which face lands upwards is a function of the momentum imparted to the coin, angle of toss, distance above ground, and so on. So to account for the observed data we require a hypothesis of how such initial conditions combine with physical probability to yield the outcome; any such hypothesis must have the stated consequence about the statistical probability of tosses in a hypothetical infinite class. There are many different such hypotheses. The coin may have physical probability of landing heads of $\frac{7}{10}$ under all conditions; or—more likely—it may have a physical probability of 1 of landing heads under 70 per cent of conditions, and a physical probability of 1 of landing tails under 30 per cent of conditions; or there may be some more complicated mixture of physical probabilities and initial conditions. The background evidence and evidence of the coin's past performance merely give very high logical probability to the 'dummy hypothesis' that some hypothesis of the above kind (that is, one that has the stated consequence for the statistical probability of the coin) is true. The statistical probability then (taken by itself) gives a logical probability of $\frac{7}{10}$ to the next toss being heads. This may seem an extremely complicated account of a simple inference, but we can see that that is what is involved in predictions of this kind when we reflect that it is only because we think the evidence of past tosses shows something about the constitution of the coin and the circumstances of its tossing that we can make this judgement about what it shows about what is in some sense likely to happen next time. My account reveals, I hope, in detail, how it does this.

The double step of inference (to explanatory hypothesis and then to a consequence thereof) brings a complexity into the probability of predictions (and to retrodictions obtained by the double step. For simplicity of exposition I will avoid mentioning the latter each time; the same points apply to them.) Different explanatory hypotheses have different degrees of probability on the evidence; they give different degrees of probability to their predictions. Sometimes these hypotheses will be dummy hypotheses that give logical probability to a value of a statistical probability, which in turn gives a logical probability to a prediction; and so the step from evidence to prediction is a triple step. Having noted this role of dummy hypotheses, we can now ignore it and note that in effect often evidence in the form of an actual statistical probability (a proportion in a finite class) gives different degrees of probability to different theories about the statistical probability in a hypothetical infinite class, which in turn gives different degrees of logical probability to particular predictions. To get the probability of a certain prediction, we have to take the weighted sum of its probability on each possible hypothesis, the weighting being by the logical probability on its evidence of that hypothesis. Thus in a normal case, where there is no greatly relevant background evidence—to put the matter in rather loose non-mathematical terms—all hypotheses of the form 'the hypothetical statistical probability of an *A* being *B* (in an infinite class) is approximately *p*' will have roughly equal intrinsic probability, for all *p* between 0 and 1. The evidence that in a finite class $\frac{2}{3}$ of *A*s were *B* will be rendered quite probable by the hypothesis that in the infinite class $\frac{2}{3}$ of *A*s are *B*, and less probable by hypotheses in which *p* is further and further away from $\frac{2}{3}$. And so, in virtue of my first criterion of upward inference, the evidence renders hypotheses of the form 'the hypothetical statistical probability of an *A* being *B* is *p*' more probable, the closer is *p* to $\frac{2}{3}$. Each of these hypotheses 'the hypothetical statistical probability of an *A* being *B* is *p*' gives (by the Principal Principle) a logical probability of *p* to the next *A* being *B*. But, since hypotheses have greater probability on the evidence, the closer is the *p* in them to $\frac{2}{3}$, this weighting gives a total logical probability of about $\frac{2}{3}$ to the next *A* being *B*.

There is, however, no guarantee that (as in the example just discussed) the predictions of the most probable hypothesis will be the most probable predictions—though, normally, that will be so. Suppose we have background evidence (of a kind unavailable in my previous example) that our coin is (with equal prior logical probability) one of three kinds—it is either one with a hypothetical statistical probability (in an infinite class) of heads of 0.45, or one with such a probability of 0.49, or one with such a probability of 0.51. (I shall consider in the next section how we might be in a position to have such evidence.) We toss it a number of times and the evidence of the tosses (say 46 heads out of 100) is such as to make the first hypothesis more probable than the others, but such as to make the other two hypotheses not too much less probable. What is the probability of heads next time? It is plausibly, as before, the posterior probability of the first hypothesis being true multiplied by the probability of heads next time, given the first hypothesis; plus the posterior probability of the second hypothesis multiplied by the probability of heads next time on it; plus the prior probability of the third hypothesis multiplied by the probability of heads next time on it. That probability will be much closer to that yielded by the second hypothesis alone than to that yielded by the most probable hypothesis, the first hypothesis, alone—that is, closer to 0.49 than to 0.45.

These results about the probability of predictions are also captured by Bayes's theorem. They are summarized in the formula given on p. 105:

$$P(e|k) = P(e|h\&k)\ P(h|k) + P(e|h_1\&k)\ P(h_1|k) + P(e|h_2\&k)\ P(h_2|k) + \ldots$$

if we let k be the evidence that gives different degrees of posterior probability to the different hypotheses h, h_1, h_2, and so on; and let e be a prediction made by the different hypotheses with different degrees of probability. The formula allows us to calculate the probability of rival predictions e_1, e_2, e_3, and so on, if we substitute them for e throughout. It will be apparent that the prediction e_n, which is most probable on the most probable theory h_m (the one for which $P(h_m|k)$ is highest), is not necessarily the one whose probability on k is the highest.

All Propositions have Intrinsic Probabilities

As we have seen, simplicity and scope are a priori factors that give to different scientific theories different intrinsic probabilities, and without such we cannot assess the force of contingent evidence in support of the theories. Exactly the same applies when we consider the probabilities of different hypotheses about initial conditions and the elements involved in personal explanation. I seek now to illustrate this, for initial conditions, in order to bring out—since every contingent proposition including those involved in personal explanation (other than those that state the principles governing the behaviour of things, and are thus possible constituents of scientific theories) may form part of a set of initial conditions—that every contingent proposition has an intrinsic probability, a probability in advance of empirical discoveries that may increase or decrease that probability. As every necessarily true proposition has an intrinsic probability of 1 and every necessarily false proposition has an intrinsic probability of 0, it follows that all propositions whatsoever have intrinsic probabilities.

When we have not observed whether some state of affairs occurred, we may infer back to it from what we now observe and some established scientific theory. Then (see pp. 97–8) the simplest (theory + initial conditions) that leads us to expect what we observe is probably true. It could in principle happen that the simplest scientific theory of many data allows only one retrodiction from any given datum—that is, there is only one way allowed by the theory in which some given datum can have come into existence. Our universe might be two-way deterministic (that is, every total state of the universe at one time causes at each later time a unique determinate total state; and each total state at one time has at each earlier time a unique determinate total state as its cause). There is no good reason to suppose that the true global scientific theory will have the consequence that the universe is two-way deterministic, but let us suppose that it does, and let us also suppose that we have discovered this—such a theory being the simplest theory of all the data we have. However, it is evident that no human being can observe more than a few aspects of the state of the universe in his local region at a certain time; and so innumerable different total universe states at that time will be compatible with these aspects of the local region. Each of these possible present universe states would have been caused by a different earlier universe state. It remains logically possible that each of the states of the universe that contain at some time some local event *E* would have been caused (in accord with the global theory) by some state at some earlier time that contained an event *C*, and no state not containing *E* would have been so caused. Then we could identify *C* as the cause of *E*. However, it rather looks as if in our universe there are no events *E* observable by ordinary humans at some time that, even given a global two-way deterministic theory, would yield a unique retrodiction of this kind. The (contingent) reason for this is that causes have effects in distant places very rapidly, and which effect they have depends on which other events were happening at the time of the cause. So to retrodict *C* we would need detailed knowledge of a very wide state of the universe at the time of the occurrence of *E* in order to retrodict the other events (call them *D*) with which an event such as *C* might be interacting, which we would need to know in order to know what effects *C* would have. This latter retrodiction would pick out a unique set of events *D* with which *C* was interacting only if we knew enough about the surroundings of possible sets of events such as *D* in order to retrodict the true *D* from their present effects. A much wider set of observations at the present time would enable us to discover the true *D*—but only if we knew enough about their surrroundings *F*... And so ad infinitum.

In practice there will always be, even if we suppose that we know the true two-way deterministic global scientific theory, innumerable alternative possible causes of any present state of the universe that we can observe, and—I can add—even if we include in the present state our apparent memories of what we have observed in the past and the written records purporting to record the observations of others. And by 'causes' I mean causes that make physically necessary that present state. Fortunately, we can still make judgements about which alternative causes are more probable than others, and so gain probable knowledge of the past. We can do that only if such possible initial states have different prior probabilities—and these prior probabilities must be intrinsic probabilities, because they are all such as to lead us to expect the present data we find and there are no other data. A priori considerations can alone settle the issue. And the difficulties of retrodiction are multiplied, and so the need for a priori criteria greatly increased if we suppose—more realistically—that we have limited knowledge only of what are the true relevant scientific theories, and that suggests that they are not (even one-way) deterministic theories; and so initial states will bring about later states only with physical probabilities less than 1.

I take a very simple example to illustrate these abstract arguments, which involves (as retrodictions typically do) inference both to inanimate and to personal explanation. Suppose that we are looking for the cause of a rail crash. A train has passed a signal that should have been at red (stop) and ploughed into the back of another train. We have a limited amount of data—the crushed railway carriages, the twisted rail lines, the signalling system in its present state, and the reports of the living witnesses. The driver was killed in the crash, and the signalling system was slightly damaged. To make the example as simple as possible, let us suppose that there are only two possible causes—the signal was not working properly and showed green (instead of red), or the signal showed red but the driver did not notice the signal. No amount of evidence will enable us to eliminate either of these hypotheses if we are prepared to 'save' them by means of other hypotheses that will also be unfalsifiable by presently observable evidence.

The undamaged parts of the signal are working well, but maybe there was a loose electrical connection in the damaged part. We inspect the damaged part. If there is now a loose connection, maybe it was loosened in the crash. If there is no loose connection, maybe the crash had the unusual effect of tightening a previously loose nut—unusual because that effect would have been produced only given a certain exact position of the loose nut and the train having a momentum within a very narrow band. The driver would not have noticed the signal if he had been thinking about something else. Did he have domestic problems on his mind that might have distracted him? His family deny that he did, but maybe they are trying to save his reputation. If we add the right extra hypotheses[26] to each of

[26] These extra hypotheses are often called *ad hoc* hypotheses, hypotheses added to the original hypothesis *ad hoc*—that is, for the particular purpose of 'saving' the original

our original hypotheses about the cause, we can save both of the original hypotheses; and, if any evidence turns up that is improbable given the new hypotheses, we can add yet more extra hypotheses so as always to leave us with alternative sets of hypotheses that are such as, given our scientific theories, will lead us to expect all our evidence with the same very high logical probability. But it may be the case that one of the original hypotheses needs a lot of precising and complicating in order to save it, while the other does not. One may need to be made very precise—the train having a momentum within a very narrow band—and so it will have greater scope. One may need to be made more complicated—we may need to postulate lying by the driver's relatives quite out of line with their normal behaviour (as evidenced by a wider set of data). And, of course, accident investigation tribunals make their judgements on the basis of such considerations. They and we judge that scope decreases and simplicity increases the probabilities of hypotheses about states of affairs. These are intrinsic features of hypotheses, in no way dependent on their relation to empirical data, and so determine an intrinsic probability. Since, for any state of affairs C that could be postulated to explain some data *E* that we might discover, since *E* will always be such that many other possible states of affairs than *C* would with equally high probability lead us to expect *E*, it follows that *C* and every other state of affairs must have intrinsic probabilities (arising from scope and simplicity) if we are ever to make probably true retrodictions of phenomena.

This very same need for hypotheses to have intrinsic probabilities arises where those hypotheses concern statistical probabilities. Consider the example of the coins (on p. 109), where we began with an assumption that a coin had an equal prior probability of being one of three kinds—one with a hypothetical statistical probability of heads of 0.45, one with such a probability of 0.49, and one with such a probability of 0.51. Given that allocation of prior probabilities, evidence of tossing gives to each hypothesis that the coin has a particular statistical probability a different posterior probability (and so gives to a prediction of heads a certain posterior probability). How could we determine empirically what those prior probabilities were? We could have contingent background evidence about other coins found in the region—say that all the coins found in the region so far had statistical probabilities in large finite classes of heads of either 0.45 or 0.49 or 0.51, and that coins with the different statistical probabilities had been foundin equal quantities. This background evidence would give a high

hypothesis. But the purpose for which someone proposed a conjunction of hypotheses is irrelevant to whether evidence supports that conjunction. I argue this more fully in the Appendix on 'Predictivism'.

logical probability to a dummy hypothesis that the process of coin production in the region was such as to yield in equal numbers coins with one of the three stated statistical probabilities. This dummy hypothesis could be true either because almost all the coin-making devices (persons or factories) made equal numbers of all three kinds of coin, or because there were equal numbers of devices each making all of the three different kinds of coin in equal numbers, or because of some mixture of these factors. This dummy hypothesis in turn would give equal logical probability to a given coin having a particular such statistical probability.

However, the background evidence (of the coins found in the region) will have this effect only if the prior logical probabilities of finding any particular distribution of statistical probabilities among the coins were the same. For, if there was a high logical probability that most of the coins in the region would have a statistical probability of 0.99 of heads, then, although the contingent evidence from the coins discovered having no such statistical probability would make the former less probable, it could still be more probable than not that most of the coins in the region had a statistical probability of 0.99 of heads, and so make a crucial difference to the logical probability that a given coin would have a certain statistical probability. But we could have empirical evidence (pre-background evidence) that makes it equally probable that we will find any particular distribution of statistical probabilities among coins of the region. This could be, for example, that coin-producing devices have been found in other regions that produce coins with many different statistical probabilities in approximately equal numbers. But then this pre-background evidence will have the stated effect only if the prior probability of an even distribution of statistical probabilities among coin-producing devices (in all regions) was as probable as any other distribution. And so on!

In this kind of example, as in examples of all other kinds, it should now be clear that, if allocation of prior probabilities to initial conditions (and so generally to states of affairs) is to be done on the basis of contingent evidence, we would need to take in a wider and wider amount of evidence until we included everything in any way relevant. But then we would have to stop. At that final stage we would need to assess the logical probability that all this relevant contingent evidence gave to various hypotheses (for example, about the distribution of different kinds of coin-making devices, or whatever), and we can assess the effect of this evidence on these hypotheses only if we have a view about the prior probabilities of these hypotheses. If all members of some set of (exclusive and exhaustive) hypotheses have equal prior probability, then the one that renders the evidence most probable (that is, that makes the best predictions) will itself be the most probable. But, as we have seen, that will not necessarily be the case if some have greater prior probability than others. Yet at this stage there is no relevant contingent evidence left to help us to determine prior probabilities. They can be determined only on a priori grounds (by considerations of simplicity and scope). There must be intrinsic probabilities if there are to be any prior probabilities, and only if there are prior probabilities can there be posterior probabilities of initial conditions. In this example, we would expect to say at some stage that any distribution of some kind is equally probable—either of statistical probabilities among coins in the region or of statistical probabilities of coins produced by devices in other regions, or of some wider phenomenon; and we have to make that claim on a priori grounds. For, once we have assembled all the empirical evidence relevant to determining probabilities, only a priori criteria can tell us how to assess its effect.

Anyone who denies that there are correct ways of ascribing intrinsic probabilities to states of affairs will have to face the same kind of vastly implausible consequences as the person who denies that there are correct ways of ascribing intrinsic probabilities to scientific theories. For, just as one cannot justify one prediction rather than another on the grounds of what one presently observes without claiming that theories can be weighted by correct prior probabilities (ultimately dependent on intrinsic probabilities), so one cannot justify one retrodiction rather than another on the basis of what one presently observes without claiming that both theories and initial conditions (and the factors involved in personal explanation) can be weighted by correct prior probabilities (ultimately dependent on intrinsic probabilities).

The Principle of Indifference

The role of intrinsic probabilities of different states of affairs is most evident, not when it is involved as a hidden presupposition determining how contingent background evidence about initial conditions should be taken into account, but where there is no such background evidence making it more probable that there will be one initial state of affairs rather than another. In this situation a major tool for discovering the intrinsic probabilities of particular states of affairs is the Principle of Indifference. (This principle, though not its name, is due to Laplace.[27]) This states that two

[27] P. S. Laplace, *A Philosophical Essay on Probability* (first published 1814), trans. F. W. Truscott and F. L. Emory (Dover, 1951).

'events' (that is, states of affairs) are equally probable if we do not know any reason why one should occur rather then the other. Thus in the coin example (as originally formulated on p. 109), if there are only three kinds of coin, and we do not know of any reason why a coin would be of one kind rather than another, we should ascribe equal probabilities to each event. This principle would be empty if we had no conception of what constitutes such a reason, but, of course, we do have such a conception—which I have been spelling out for the last several pages. A reason may be provided by contingent background evidence (in the way illustrated earlier) or by the greater simplicity or smaller scope of the propositions reporting the events. So we should read the Principle as claiming that two events have equal intrinsic probability if background evidence does not give greater probability to any theory that favours one over the other, and they do not differ in scope or simplicity.

But, it is normally claimed, there are all too often equally rational ways of cutting up the cake of possibilities into events, such that we have no reason to suppose that the one would occur rather than the other, but where these different ways yield (by the Principle of Indifference) incompatible prior probabilities.[28] Examples designed to show this are known as variants of 'Bertrand's paradox'. I suggest that, when we look at these examples carefully, we will see that there are very often good reasons for cutting up the cake of possibilities in one way rather than another, so that no incompatibility arises. These are reasons of the kind I have been discussing—that many ways of cutting up the cake of possibilities yield sets of events, some of which are more probable than others by the criteria of simplicity and scope.

To take just one example, a variant produced by Howson and Urbach.[29] They ask us to consider 'a parameter *T* about which nothing is known'

[28] Keynes put a restriction on the Principle of Indifference that it 'is not applicable to a pair of alternatives, if we know that either of them is capable of being further split up into a pair of possible but incompatible alternatives of the same form as the original pair'. Thus you could not suppose to be equiprobable the alternatives that some swan is black or that it is 'whue' (as defined above, p. 91), because the latter alternative can be split into possible but incompatible alternatives of the same form as 'the swan is black'—namely, the alternatives 'the swan is white', 'the swan is green', and 'the swan is blue'. But the notion of 'of the same form' needs spelling out, e.g. as 'of the same form in the simplest respect'; and this restriction will not deal with some variants of Betrand's paradox such as the one discussed in the text. So we need an account of when the Principle applies, and this I have sought to provide. See J. M. Keynes *A Treatise on Probability* (first published 1921; Macmillan, 1963), 60–4.

[29] Colin Howson and Peter Urbach, *Scientific Reasoning: The Bayesian Approach* (2nd edn., Open Court, 1993), 60.

except that its value lies between some values a and b. Then it might seem reasonable to suppose that it is equally likely to lie within any interval of equal length—for example, that it is as likely to lie within the interval from a to $(a+1)$, as within the interval from $(a+1)$ to $(a+2)$. But then consider the parameter T^2, which, it follows, may have any value between a^2 and b^2. It seems just as reasonable to suppose that *it* is equally likely to lie within any interval of equal length—for example, that it is equally likely to lie within the interval from a^2 to (a^2+1), as within the interval from (a^2+1) to (a^2+2). The trouble is that the former way of cutting up the cake for T into equiprobable alternatives entails a different way of cutting up the cake for T^2 from that just described. Given that T is equally likely to lie within the interval a to $(a+1)$ as within the interval $(a+1)$ to $(a+2)$, then T^2 is equally likely to lie within the interval a^2 to (a^2+2a+1) as within the interval (a^2+2a+1) to (a^2+4a+4). But, if T^2 is equally likely to lie within any interval of equal length, it is equally likely to lie within the interval a^2 to $a^2+(2a+1)$ as within the interval $a^2+(2a+1)$ to $a^2+(4a+2)$. But this yields a different second interval equiprobable to the first interval, from that yielded by the previous formula. So, say Howson and Urbach, 'we now have a contradiction'.

However, only one of these ways of cutting up the cake of alternatives yields alternatives of equal scope. For, I urged earlier, in order to compare the scope of theories, we should use their simplest formulation. The formulation that T lies within a certain interval is simpler than the logically equivalent formulation that T^2 lies within a certain different interval. So we must say that it is any claim that T lies within any interval of the same length that is equiprobable, and not any claim that T^2 lies within any interval of the same length.

So, in this variant and—I believe—in most other variants of Bertrand's paradox, arguments will show that either contingent background evidence or considerations of simplicity and scope of the above type will show that only one way of distributing intrinsic probabilities among the ways suggested by the 'paradox' is the correct one. The Principle of Indifference should be applied in the simplest possible way. Occasionally contingent background evidence and considerations of simplicity and scope may give equal support to two or more incompatible ways of cutting up the cake of possibilities into alternatives. In such a case arguments of the above type show that we should allocate intrinsic probabilities by an average of the incompatible ways.

Among the implausible consequences of supposing there to be no correct way to allocate intrinsic probabilities would be the view that any supposition about the outcome of some game of chance of which you had no experience would be equally rational. On the sole evidence that a card is to be drawn from a normal pack of cards (and so one containing 13 out of 52 spades), and no other evidence about the pack and who is drawing the card, the probability that the card drawn will be a spade is surely $\frac{1}{4}$; it would be incorrect to suppose it to be $\frac{3}{4}$. Yet the judgment that it is $\frac{1}{4}$ depends essentially on it being equally probable intrinsically that any given card will be drawn. But a denial that we could ascribe prior probabilities on a priori grounds would have the consequence that the judgement could not be made. Of course, if we acquire further evidence, about who is drawing the card and whether he has a history of cheating at cards and has made a bet that a spade will be drawn, that is going to alter the probability. But the fact remains that, we almost all acknowledge, there is a correct way to ascribe a prior probability in the absence of any contingent evidence. And what goes for this example, goes for innumerable others—such as tosses of coins and results of lottery draws.

We can now take these points about the intrinsic probabilities of different scientific theories and states of affairs together, and put them in general philosophical terms, as follows. There are innumerable possible worlds, ways things might have been. They differ from each other by their explanatory hypotheses (laws and initial conditions[30] and/or personal causes), as well as by the different developments that any given explanatory hypothesis allows. (An all-embracing deterministic hypothesis will allow only one series of subsequent states, but indeterministic hypotheses will give different degrees of probability to different subsequent states.) Each would then have an intrinsic probability, depending on the intrinsic probability of its explanatory hypothesis (for example, its initial conditions and the scientific theory governing their subsequent development) and on the probability that that hypothesis will give rise to the particular development it does. The intrinsic probability of such an explanatory hypothesis will depend on its simplicity alone—since all such hypotheses have the same scope; they tell us about all the principles that explain everything. The intrinsic probability of any proposition is then the sum of the intrinsic probabilities of all the worlds to which it belongs.

I stress once again that intrinsic probabilities, like most other probabilities, have only a very rough value; and frequently all that we can say about

[30] Or, if the worlds do not have a beginning, their 'boundary conditions'—that is, those facts about the amount and distribution of matter in them that hold throughout their history, but are not consequences of their laws.

them is that that intrinsic probability is greater than this one or less than that one.

Pragmatic Arguments for the Probability Calculus

The many writers on probability who call themselves 'Bayesians' mean by this that they believe that rational ascriptions of probability should conform to the axioms of the calculus (and so to its theorem, Bayes's theorem). But they often give arguments in favour of adopting these axioms quite other than my arguments that they capture our ordinary a priori criteria of what is evidence for what. Their arguments are in essence arguments that attempt to show that there is something analogous to inconsistency in a set of beliefs about probability that violate these axioms. For, the claim is, just as a set of literally inconsistent beliefs must fail to correspond to the world in some respect—whatever the world is like—so a set of beliefs about probability that violate the axioms will for certain consistent goals of our actions lead to us performing actions designed to achieve those goals that will inevitably fail—whatever the world is like. This 'something analogous to inconsistency' is called incoherence. The prototype of such arguments is the 'Dutch book' argument.

This argument can be run in a number of different ways. I use a version due to Howson and Urbach.[31] They introduce the notion of a subject's 'fair betting' odds—that is, the betting odds on some hypothesis *h* at which a subject would regard a bet as fair; 'values above or below' would, he believes, 'confer advantage on one or other side'. 'The odds you take to be fair on *h* will clearly reflect the extent to which you believe it likely that *h* will turn out to be true.' Thus, suppose you believe that the probability that 'Red Rum will win the Grand National' (*h*) is $\frac{1}{3}$. Then fair betting odds on Red Rum are 2:1; and so a bet in which you win £2 if Red Rum wins and lose £1 if he loses is fair, and so is a bet in which you win £1 if Red Rum loses but lose £2 if he wins. Then it can be shown that, if you are prepared to take any bets that you regard as fair, unless your allocations of probabilities to hypotheses conform to the Bayesian axioms, someone can bet with you in

[31] Howson and Urbach, *Scientific Reasoning*, ch. 5. For discussion of 'Dutch book' and other arguments in favour of the axioms of the probability calculus, see, as well as Howson and Urbach, John Earman, *Bayes or Bust?* (MIT Press, 1992), ch. 2. These are both very good books that develop and criticize the consequences of the probability axioms. But none of the authors is prepared to offer objective principles for ascribing prior probabilities, which they all recognize as necessary if a full objective account of what is evidence for what in science is to be given.

such a way that you will inevitably on balance lose money, whichever hypotheses are true. To use the technical term, a 'Dutch book' can be made against you. For example, if you ascribe probabilities of $\frac{1}{3}$ to each of the horses in a two-horse race winning, then someone can bet £1 with you on each horse, so that they gain £2 if the horse wins and lose £1 if it loses. Then, whichever horse wins, you will win £1 and lose £2—a net loss of £1. The goal of not losing money is a consistent one. Yet the means (accepting bets from anyone at what you regard as fair odds), which your beliefs about probability entail, will (given that a moderately clever person bets with you in order to win money) ensure that you fail—whatever the world is like (in the respect of the feature about which you are betting, the outcome of the race).

You can avoid inevitable loss only if you allocate probabilities in such a way that the probabilities of exclusive and exhaustive alternatives sum to 1—that is, conform to Bayesian Axiom 3; and so, if you judge one horse in a two-horse race to have a probability of $\frac{1}{3}$ of winning, you must judge the other horse to have a probability of $\frac{2}{3}$ of winning. Similar arguments show the need to conform to the other Bayesian axioms. It is true that the inevitable loss does depend on someone else moderately clever seeking to bet with you so as to win money, but it does not depend on the outcome of the race, and it is that which makes the violation of the probability axioms analogous to inconsistency in a system of beliefs. The analogy may, however, be strengthened if we suppose the agent to be making bets rather than merely being willing to accept them; and then the inevitable loss will result merely from his betting certain sums of money at odds that he regards as fair when those odds do not correspond to beliefs about probability conforming to the Bayesian axioms (when betting the same amounts at odds conforming to the axioms would not lead to inevitable loss). You will inevitably lose if you bet £10 on each of three horses winning a certain race at 1:1 (that is, you win £10 if that horse wins, and lose £10 if that horse loses). Regarding 1:1 as fair odds involves believing that it is as probable that the horse will win as that it will not win. The beliefs that each of three horses (only one of which can win) has a probability of ½ of winning violates Axiom 3.

Now it might seem that this argument has little relevance to those of us who bet little and for whom the value of a gain or loss is not measured accurately in monetary terms (for example, those for whom a gain of £2 is worth only $1\frac{1}{2}$ times as much as a gain of £1, and for whom a loss of £1 is far worse a disaster than a gain of £1 is a good state). However, many writers have sought to show that an argument of this kind has more general application. We all do actions that produce gain if some hypothesis is true, and loss if that hypothesis is false. Doing such an action is analogous to betting on the truth of the hypothesis. And let us suppose the gains and losses to be measured in units of utility that reflect accurately the value to the agent, positive or negative, of the gains and losses respectively. In a situation of uncertainty about the truth of relevant hypotheses, agents seek to make overall gains. They can, therefore, be represented as doing those actions that in their view have positive expected utility. The expected utility of an action that produces a gain if some hypothesis is true and a loss if it is not is ((the gain if the hypothesis is true) multiplied by (the probability that the hypothesis is true) minus (the loss if the hypothesis is false) multiplied by (the probability that the hypothesis is false)). Then these writers seek to show that, if an agent does many actions that in his view, given his beliefs about the probabilities of hypotheses, have positive expected utility, he will inevitably make an overall loss, unless which actions he does are governed by judgements of the probabilities of the various hypotheses constrained by the Bayesian axioms (for example, he does not give to each of two incompatible hypotheses probabilities that add up to more than 1).

But the most that such arguments show is that in certain situations making your probability judgements to conform to the Bayesian axioms is a necessary condition for not making an overall loss. They do not begin to show that it is sufficient condition for this, and obviously it is not.[32]

For the Bayesian axioms are compatible with wildly different ascriptions of probabilities in almost all cases. To take but another obvious example: suppose that we know initially with respect to some coin with faces of heads and tails only that it was produced by a process that produces only two sets of coins—ones with a very high statistical probability (in an infinite sequence) of landing heads and ones with a very high statistical probability of landing tails. We toss it 100 times, and we observe that every time it comes down heads. It would surely be right to conclude that the coin has a very high statistical probability of landing heads and so that the next toss will be heads also. Let us represent by h_1 the hypothesis that the coin has a very high statistical probability of landing heads and by h_2 the hypothesis

[32] If we suppose, as does 'subjective Bayesianism', that the only constraints of reason on the allocation of probability values are that those values should at any one time conform to the Bayesian axioms, then we will not be able to justify a further plausible principle concerned with the rational ascription of probability values by an agent at different times—the Principle of Conditionalization. This objection does not hold against the 'objective Bayesianism' that I have been advocating, which holds that there are additional correct a priori principles for allocating values to probabilities. I show this in Additional Note J.

that the coin has a very high statistical probability of landing tails. *e* reports the results of tosses so far. *k* may be regarded as irrelevant. Then $P(e/h_1\&k)$ will be fairly high and $P(e/h_2\&k)$ very low indeed. But if we ascribe a very high prior probability to h_2 and a very low prior probability indeed to h_1, then Bayes's theorem will yield the result that h_2 has higher posterior probability than h_1 and so make it probable that next time the coin will come down tails. Intuitively that is an obviously incorrect result. Yet, allocating a very high prior probability to h_2 and a very low prior probability is h_1 is perfectly compatible with the Bayesian axioms: all that would be incompatible with them is to allocate high prior probabilities to both, or low prior probabilities to both hypotheses. Yet, intuitively, it is highly probable that, if, after the results of the 100 tosses have been observed, we bet on the supposition that h_2 is more probable than h_1, we shall make a loss. And a theory of probability that fails to take account of that intuition seems to me gravely deficient.

If science is really a rational enterprise in the sense that certain evidence really does make one hypothesis more probable and another hypothesis less probable, and so there are indeed correct criteria of inductive inference, of what is evidence for what and how strong particular evidence is, there must be principles of probability additional to the Bayesian axioms, and in particular a priori principles for ascribing intrinsic probabilities. I have tried to bring out in this chapter what these principles are. If I have to some extent misanalysed these principles, that will not affect the main argument of the book. Just replace my account by the correct account, whenever necessary. But, if there are no such a priori criteria, we should give up studying science, history, and every other subject of university study. For no one will be able to produce evidence that others can correctly recognize as making one hypothesis in the field more probable than any of an infinite number of rivals; and no retrodiction or prediction as any more probable than any other.

In all my claims about what our criteria are, I mean that they capture the criteria that almost all of us use most of the time when we believe that we are making correct judgements of probability, and that most of us who are able to grasp the concepts involved and understand the issues would agree are our criteria after quite a bit of reflection on many examples of what is evidence for what. There is plenty of psychological evidence that those who do not think much about these matters make different claims about what is evidence for what and that many of us sometimes operate in practice by different criteria, not merely in respect of the principles for allocating intrinsic probabilities but also in failing to conform our probability judgements to the Bayesian axioms. The work of Tversky and Kahneman shows that many people defend principles of deductive reasoning that all professional logicians hold to be manifestly invalid, as well as non-Bayesian principles of probabilistic reasoning. Some people claim, for example, that the probability of a conjunction (*p* and *q*) is sometimes greater on given evidence than the probability on the same evidence of one of its conjuncts (*p*)—which, according to the probability calculus, can never happen. Distilling from ordinary use our standards of rationality and giving them precise form is a job for an expert; and, for someone to be an expert, his expertise must be recognizable by most others who take trouble to reflect on the issues. In consequence, there is no incoherence in psychologists reporting that in certain respects many people are irrational.[33]

Testimony

Much of the information any individual gains about the world comes not from her own observation, but from the testimony of others—what other people tell us orally or in writing about what they have perceived, experienced, or done ('I saw John steal the money') or what they claim to know on good authority to be so ('Caesar invaded Britain in 55 BC'). Let us call testimony of the former kind 'direct testimony' and testimony of the latter kind 'indirect testimony'. Why should we believe the direct testimony of others? Is it probable on the evidence of the observations of each of us that normally the testimony of others is true, in virtue of principles discussed so far, or would we need a quite independent fundamental epistemic principle to infer from the testimony of others that it is probably true? I think that it is probable on the basis of observations that each of us can make that normally the testimony of others is true in virtue of principles discussed so far, and we need not invoke a special epistemic principle—though again that is not to beg the question as to whether our belief that others usually tell us what is true needs this kind of support, in order for us to be justified in using it. I will come to that issue in due course.

[33] For the work of Tversky and Kahneman, see R. Nisbett and L. Ross, 'Judgmental Heuristics and Knowledge Structures', repr. in H. Kornblith (ed.), *Naturalizing Epistemology* (2nd edn., MIT Press, 1997). For defence of the claim that it is not a presupposition of ascribing beliefs to subjects that they reason in all respects rationally, see Stephen P. Stich, 'Could Man be an Irrational Animal? Some Notes on the Epistemology of Rationality', in ibid.

Hume claimed that our 'assurance' in a case where we could not check for ourselves that the direct testimony of another is true 'is derived from no other principle than our observation of the veracity of human testimony, and of the usual conformity of facts to the reports of witnesses'.[34] But there is a major objection to this account. We have learnt to interpret what people are saying to us, on the prior assumption that people normally say what they believe to be true; and so, since, we assume, they usually have true beliefs about what they have perceived, that people usually say what is true. We learnt to understand what 'it is raining' means by hearing people say 'it is raining' when it is raining. And so generally. This is evidently the method by which investigators learn to interpret an entirely unknown language spoken by a newly discovered tribe. And plausibly it is the assumption in virtue of which we believe that we understand what speakers of our own language say now. But, if that is so, I could not discover by experience that others normally say what is true—because I have a belief about what they mean by their words only on the prior assumption that normally they are telling the truth. That assumpton could not be established by empirical investigation, the argument goes—contrary to Hume. Likewise we could not have evidence for believing a particular piece of indirect testimony on an issue that we could not check for ourselves by doing a survey and finding that most claims about what people claim to know on good authority are so. The only ways (apart from checking for ourselves) of finding out whether what people say is true is by finding out (by asking them) from whom they learnt it, and from whom their instructor learnt it . . . until we reach someone who gave direct testimony; or by checking what one person says against what another person says. To do all this requires us to understand the meaning of what we are told. And so, both in order to understand what the claim is, and in order to ascertain whether it is based on good authority, we have to assume that we know what people mean by their words. And we are entitled to make this assumption only in virtue of having made a prior assumption that normally people tell the truth. Again, it seems that whether they do or not is not to be established by experience.

Once we have made this assumption that what people tell us is normally true, and thus we become entitled to believe that we understand what they are saying, the objection continues, we can investigate whether particular individuals or kinds of individuals tell us the truth on particular occasions or kinds of occasions. If we find that they do not, we may come to a conclusion as to whether it is more probable that they are lying or are incom-

[34] D. Hume, *An Enquiry Concerning Human Understanding*, §88.

petent (misobserve, forget, and so on, the relevant facts). But, writers have claimed, this process of checking can operate only within a fundamental epistemic assumption: that people normally say what is true. This assumption yields, on this view, a fundamental principle of testimony—that someone uttering some proposition as an assertion makes it probable that it is true. Thus Reid regarded it as a 'first principle', 'that there is a certain regard due to human testimony in matters of fact, and even to human authority in matters of opinion'.[35]

However, there is no need to regard the principle of testimony as an independent epistemic principle dependent only on a fundamental assumption. We have already noted in Chapter 2 that no individual hypothesis about a belief or purpose of someone else yields any consequence about their behaviour. Only hypotheses about a set of purposes plus beliefs plus bodily powers yield a consequence about behaviour. The simplest joint hypothesis about a person's powers, beliefs, and purposes that fits with background evidence and yields with the greatest probability the data of their behaviour on a particular occasion is that most probably true, and so is the simplest hypothesis about their desires and beliefs that yields their purposes on particular occasions, and so their behaviour over time. Plausibly the simplest joint hypothesis by which to explain vast tracts of observed human verbal behaviour includes humans having a desire to tell only what they believe to be true, and having true beliefs about their surroundings acquired by the use of their senses, and beliefs about the meanings of words that are the same as the beliefs of almost all other speakers of some language about the meanings of words; their desire leads to purposes of telling the truth on particular occasions, and these purposes,

[35] Thomas Reid, *Essays on the Intellectual Powers of Man*, Essay 6 'On Judgment', ch. 5 (in R. E. Beanblossom and K. Lehrer (eds.), *Thomas Reid's Inquiry and Essays* (Hackett, 1983), 281). In his recent book *Testimony* (Clarendon Press, 1992), C. A. J. Coady takes a moderately Reidian line when he writes (p. 173) that we begin 'with an inevitable commitment to some degree' of the 'reliability' of testimony, which we then find 'strongly enforced and supported' by its cohesion with our experience. His emphasis on cohesion as an epistemic principle derives from his moderate support for Davidson's 'principle of charity'. I have argued (Chapter 2) that the principle of charity (to the extent to which it is applicable) follows from the principle of simplicity itself. It is not clear to me whether the initial 'inevitable commitment' to the reliability of testimony of which Coady writes is supposed to be a psychologically inevitable one or a logically inevitable one. In the former case, this is a simple comment that young human children initially inevitably believe that others are telling the truth. I have no quarrel with that suggestion. The philosophical issue, however, is whether children or anyone else require a separate principle of inference (from those we use in our inferences about the inanimate world) in order to make the step from the sentences that people utter to the truth of what they say. That I am denying. But I am not claiming that they normally make that step or need to do so.

together with the latter beliefs, form parts of simple joint hypotheses about why particular people utter the words they do. Any other explanation of the latter will, I suggest, normally be much more complicated—it will need to include some purpose for uttering the words other than communicating truth, and beliefs about the meanings of words varying with the speaker. It would, I suggest, require a complicated hypothesis to explain how people acquire beliefs about the meanings of words that does not represent them as learning the meanings on the assumption that yet other people desire to tell only what they believe to be true, and usually have true beliefs about their surroundings, and so on. But, if we adopt the hypothesis that they learn using the latter assumption, it follows that their beliefs about meaning will be the normal ones and so we can explain their verbal behaviour on the supposition that they themselves have the desire of truth telling. So, I suggest, it is plausible to suppose that the principle of testimony follows the simplest account of human verbal behaviour, given the ease with which we can attribute beliefs about the meanings of words to others on the assumption that they seek to tell the truth. There is no need, in order to provide justification for relying on direct testimony, to add the principle of testimony to our four criteria of correct explanation, as an additional criterion of probable truth.

We may, of course, also have evidence of observation that certain people (or kinds of people) are bad observers, or do not desire to tell the truth on certain matters, or even have a poor command of the English language. That evidence has the consequence that their testimony gives considerably less probability to that which they assert than it would do otherwise. This obvious point follows directly from the relevance criterion (p. 104). Testimony to *h*, which might quite probably be given even if *h* were not true, is not such good evidence as testimony that, it is immensely probable, will be given (if and only if) *h* is true. Indirect testimony may take the form of testimony to a specified chain of testimony about someone's experiences, perceptions, or actions—I may tell you that John said to me that Jane said to him that she saw such-and-such. Such a chain will be subject to the problem of 'diminishing probabilities'. In the absence of any other relevant evidence about whether such-and-such, if my saying *p* makes it probable to degree 0.9 that *p*, and John saying *q* makes it probable to degree 0.9 that *q*, and Jane saying *r* makes it probable to degree 0.9 that *r*, then my testimony that John said to me that Jane said to him that she saw such-and-such is only going to make it probable that such-and-such to degree $(0.9)^3$—that is, 0.729. And the longer the chain, the lower the probability of that to which it testifies. However, there may be other evidence about whether or not such-and-such. In particular, the existence of a second independent chain of testimony can greatly increase the probability of that to which it testifies. If, as well as my telling you that John said to me that Jane said to him that she saw such-and-such, George tells you that Harry told him that Judith told him that she saw such-and-such, that will enormously increase the probability that such-and-such (all of which follows from Bayesian principles).

Indirect testimony may, however, take the form not of testimony to a specified chain, but of a claim that 'everyone knows that *h*', or of a claim that *h* by some purported authority on the subject matter—where *h* may be the report of an experience, perception, or action; or anything at all (a claim about the truth of some scientific or religious theory, for example). In both of these cases, too, I think we have observed evidence that makes it in general probable that such claims (that *h*) are true. It is a fact of human experience from childhood upwards that, once we have understood the meanings of sentences (and I have outlined above one way in which we can come to understand these), normally what we are told turns out to be true, on any matter where we check it out. Eighty per cent of what we read in the newspapers about our own activities we recognize as true. Eighty per cent of instructions about how to use a microwave oven so as to cook edible food, how to use a TV set so as to get the TV news, how to get from *A* to *B*, etc. etc., turn out to be true. But we also soon learn that certain informants or kinds of informant are very trustworthy on certain kinds of matter, and that certain other ones are not very trustworthy on certain kinds of matter. One important kind of evidence that makes it much less probable that the information given by certain purported authorities in a field is true is evidence that there are two or more groups of authorities who have rival theories about the field. Before trusting one group, we need evidence that it is in a much better position than the other group to know the answers. This may take the form of direct testimony that the predictions of the former and not the latter have normally been verified by observations. Or it may take the form of the simplest theory of a wide range of evidence of the kind of experience you need to be expert in some subject—for example, that you need to be trained in a physics department of a university recognized by the government in order to be an expert on physics.[36]

[36] For some aspects of the history of the recognition of 'experts' in some area, see Douglas Walton, *Appeal to Expert Opinion* (Penn State University Press, 1997); see esp. ch. 6 for different criteria that the American legal system has used for determining what constitutes an 'expert witness'.

I emphasize that all that I have been claiming in this section is that people do or can assemble evidence in the form of observations that they have themselves made that makes it probable that direct and indirect testimony is true (subject to all sorts of qualification on the kinds and sources of this testimony). I am not claiming that the beliefs of very many people that (for example) the earth is spherical or that the sun exerts gravitational force on the earth, or that the Normans invaded Britain in AD 1066, are based on such evidence. Rather, for most people, given the account of basing that I shall develop in the next chapter, the situation must be that either these beliefs are themselves basic beliefs, or they are based on a belief that historians and scientists in our universities claim these things and the belief that these people are reliable sources of information on their subject area, which latter two beliefs are themselves basic.

5

Basicality

Being Based On

For internalist and externalist, non-basic beliefs must not merely have their content made probable by grounds, but must be 'based' on those grounds. What is it for a belief to be based on grounds that are adequate for the belief (that is, make its content probable)? On an externalist theory of grounds, when the subject needs have no access to the grounds of his belief, being 'based on' is naturally interpreted simply as being 'caused by'—that is, 'causally sustained by'. If the grounds of my present belief that there is a desk in front of me is some neural state, then my belief being based on those grounds is simply my belief being kept now in existence by them. To this we must add that the causal chain must be non-deviant (see pp. 12–13). But, given grounds of a purely externalist kind, I cannot see that non-deviance can amount to anything more than that the causal process is not of a very narrow type (concerned with just one kind of belief in very special circumstances, as illustrated by the example on p. 13). There is the same natural interpretation of basing even when grounds include mental states other than beliefs. If the grounds of my belief that I have twelve spots in my visual field are my sensations, including twelve spots in my visual field, then my belief is based on my sensations if and only if they cause the belief (via some non-deviant causal chain).

Such a simple account seems, however, to fail as an analysis of basing, when the grounds of a belief are other beliefs. For a subject's belief that *r* might cause his belief that *q* by a (non-deviant) process of which the subject was unaware. He might think the belief that *r* irrelevant to his belief that *q*; and in that case it would be odd to call his belief that *r* the basis of his belief that *q*. Ordinary usage suggests that there should be something conscious and rational about the process if one belief is to be 'based' on another. This naturally leads to an internalist requirement that, for a subject's belief that *q* to be 'based' on his belief that *r*, the subject (in so far as he thinks about it) should believe that *r* makes *q* logically probable. The subject has to think that there is this rational connection between the two beliefs. For, suppose that a detective has observed certain clues, and that by an odd neural route this causes his belief that Jones committed the murder. Even if the clues do make it probable that Jones committed the murder (in some sense of 'probable'), it would be very odd to say that the detective's belief was based on the clues, unless he thought that the clues made the belief that Jones committed the murder inductively and so (see Chapter 3 n. 15) logically probable. And it is now natural to interpret the causal requirement as requiring that the belief that *r* and the belief that *r* makes *q* (logically) probable should together (by a non-deviant route) cause the belief that *q*.

But maybe not even this is enough. For, suppose that the subject's belief that *q* is indeed caused by his belief that *r* and his belief that *r* makes *q* (logically) probable, he may still not believe that that is why he believes *q*. For he may also believe *s* and believe that *s* makes *q* probable, and believe that it is these latter beliefs that cause his belief that *q*. The detective may believe that the clues make it probable that Jones committed the murder, but he may also believe that he heard Jones say that he committed the murder and that also makes it probable that Jones did commit the murder; and the detective may believe that it was what he believed he heard (and what he believes that that makes probable) that led him to hold his belief. However, in this we may suppose, the detective is mistaken—it was his observation of the clues that led him to hold the belief. Is his belief that Jones committed the murder based on his belief that he observed the clues, or not? If we answer No, it then becomes necessary to add an additional condition that, not merely should the subject's belief that *q* be caused by his belief that *r* and his belief that *r* makes *q* probable, but that (in so far as he thinks about it) he should believe that his belief that *r* together with his belief that *r* makes *q* probable cause his belief that *q*. Non-deviance would have to be spelled out in terms of the causal process being of a sufficiently wide reliable type, and that raises all the difficulties (discussed in Chapter 1) of why a token belief-forming process should be seen as an instance of one such type rather than another. But let us suppose this done in some natural way. We then have a full mixed causal and doxastic theory of basing.[1]

I do not think that the rules for the ordinary use of 'based' give a clear enough answer as to whether both extra doxastic conditions are required as well as the main causal condition (or as to how 'non-deviance' is to be

[1] For analysis of Robert Audi's sophisticated account of believing for a reason, which is tantamount to having a belief based on another belief and which incorporates all my three conditions, see Additional Note K.

spelled out). But, can we have 'basing' without the main causal condition being satisfied? Lehrer claims that we can—that it is not necessary, in order for a belief that *q* to be based on a belief that *r*, that the latter should cause the former. To substantiate this claim, Lehrer produced his example of the gypsy lawyer.[2] The client of a certain lawyer is to all appearances guilty of a hideous crime. But the lawyer reads his cards, in whose deliverances he has total faith, and they tell him that his client is innocent. So he believes the latter; let us call the belief that his client is innocent his belief that *q*. In consequence, the lawyer re-examines the other public evidence (let us call it *r*); and he then finds a complicated but conclusive line of reasoning (from *r*) to show that the client is innocent (*q*). He believes that the line of reasoning does show that. But, were the cards to show that his client is guilty, the gypsy lawyer would believe that instead. Lehrer is assuming (explicitly) that the belief that *r* is totally justified, and that *r* entails *q*; and so that the belief that *q* has adequate grounds in the belief that *r*. Assuming that, in order for the belief to be justified, it needs to be 'based' on these grounds, he claims that the belief that *r* need not cause the belief that *q* for this basing relation to be satisfied. For 'the evidence which completely justifies [the lawyer's] belief does not explain why he believes as he does'. One reaction to this example is simply to deny that the lawyer's belief that *q* is based on his belief that *r*, and so that his belief that *q* (rendered probable—indeed entailed—by *r*) is justified. The lawyer is not justified in believing that his client is innocent—since the evidence which probabilifies this belief has no influence on whether he holds it.[3]

I read Lehrer as claiming[4] that all that is required for a belief that *q* to be based on a belief that *r* is a belief that *r* supports *q*—which I have spelled out more precisely as the belief that *r* makes *q* (logically) probable; the latter belief that *r* provides adequate grounds for the belief that *q* if in fact *r* makes *q* probable, and these two conditions taken together mean that the belief that *q* is justified. One could also require in addition or require instead the second internalist condition that the subject should believe that his belief that *q* is caused by his belief that *r* and his belief that *r* makes *q*

[2] Keith Lehrer, *Knowledge* (Clarendon Press, 1974), 124–5.

[3] See Audi's denial that the belief is justified in his 'The Causal Structure of Indirect Justification', in *The Structure of Justification* (Cambridge University Press, 1993), 221–7.

[4] Lehrer is fully explicit in claiming that all causal theories of basing are to be rejected (*Knowledge* (Clarendon Press, 1974), 123). His original discussion of this example is complicated by the fact that it occurs in the context of discussion of a theory that he rejects—foundationalism. But his discussion of a similar example in his later work (*Theory of Knowledge* (Routledge, 1990), 168–73) suggests the positive account of the 'basing' necessary for justification that I state above.

probable. But the difficulty for all purely doxastic theories of basing remains—how can someone be justified in holding a belief if he does not form it through sensitivity to the evidence, and merely believes that he is sensitive to the evidence or that the evidence probabilifies his belief? Yet the initial objection to all merely causal theories of belief also remains. It is not enough that one belief (that *r*) should cause another one (that *q*), to constitute the latter being based on the former in a sense that provides the extra condition (beside the probability relation between the two) for justification. The belief that *q* has to be formed by the subject being sensitive to *r* and forming his belief that *q* in the light of *r*. A mixed causal and doxastic account seems to provide the best analysis of the ordinary-language claim that someone's belief that *q* was 'based' on his belief that *r*. It remains, however, open to question whether having a belief that *q* that is 'justified' in the sense that it is based (in this sense) on a belief that *r* that provides adequate grounds for it is more worth having than one that is based on the belief that *r* in some other sense. I shall come to that issue in Chapter 6. Meanwhile, I shall allow for the possibility of pure causal and pure doxastic theories of basing such as I have explicated, as well as the mixed theory.[5]

A theory of the basing of a belief will be an internalist theory if the subject has privileged access to what are the grounds on which his belief is based. If basing is spelled out solely in terms of having a further belief—for example, the belief that one's belief is caused by or rendered probable by other beliefs—then in that respect clearly we have an internalist account. If it is spelled out in terms of the belief being caused—either by some other belief or by some public phenomenon—then whether we have an internalist or an externalist account depends on whether a subject has privileged access to what are the causes of her belief. On a 'regularity' theory of causation,[6] to say that an event *A* causes another event *B* is just to say that events in some way like *A* are normally followed by events in some way like *B* (the types of events being described in terms of universal properties that involve no reference to particular individuals). So, whether one's belief that *p* was caused by some other particular belief or public phenomenon is a matter of whether events like the latter are normally followed by beliefs like the belief that *p*. Since beliefs like the belief that *p* occur in people other than

[5] I am much indebted in this discussion of the literature on basing to Keith Allen Korcz, 'Recent Work on the Basing Relation', *American Philosophical Quarterly*, 34 (1997), 171–91. For discussion of Marshall Swain's modified causal account of basing, see Additional Note L.

[6] Such theories derive from the first of the two definitions of 'cause' given by David Hume, at the end of his chapter on causation (1. 3. 14) in *A Treatise of Human Nature*.

the subject of the particular token belief that *p*, the subject will have no privileged access to what kind of events normally precede beliefs like her belief that *p*. On this, subjects must defer to the results of psychological studies. Hence, on a regularity theory, a subject has no privileged access to the causes of her beliefs, and so an account of basing in terms of causing will be an externalist account. However, on a different theory of causation, which I prefer,[7] where causing is a fundamental indefinable relation between events (and regularities are evidence of causation, but do not constitute it), it becomes plausible to say that subjects have privileged access to what are the causes of their beliefs, at least in those cases where the causes are mental events. For we are often aware through introspection that we have this belief because of that belief—for example, 'that, if one did not believe the bookstore reliable, one would not believe a certain book is on order'; or that we have this belief because of that sensation, 'that one's belief that there is something white here is in part sustained by one's impression of a white surface'.[8]

Basic Beliefs

The notion of a 'basic belief' was introduced by Plantinga[9] as a belief that the subject believes 'not on the basis of' any other beliefs. As we have just seen, the notion of a belief that *q* being based on another belief that *r* can be spelled out in a number of different ways; and so there will be a corresponding number of different ways of spelling out the notion of a basic belief. There is the purely causal way—a basic belief that *q* is a belief not caused by any other beliefs. This, I suggest, is to be read as the requirement that the subject's other beliefs together are not causally sufficient for the belief that *q* (to suggest that none of them, even if they are taken together, is causally necessary would allow the possibility that a person could have just one belief, the belief that *q*. That does not seem plausible and I argued on p. 40 that no belief can be held in isolation from others.) There are then two separate purely doxastic ways of spelling out the notion of a basic belief. A belief could be said to be basic if the subject does not believe that

[7] See my 'The Irreducibility of Causation', *Dialectica*, 51 (1997), 79–92.

[8] These examples are taken from Robert Audi, 'Causalist Internalism', in his *The Structure of Justification* (Cambridge University Press, 1993), pp. 344, 347, where he defends our 'introspective access to the causal conditions of justification'.

[9] See Alvin Plantinga, 'Reason and Belief in God', in A. Plantinga and N. Wolterstorff, *Faith and Rationality* (University of Notre Dame Press, 1983), 46–55.

it was rendered probable by any of his other beliefs. Or it could be said to be basic if the subject does not believe that it was caused (that is, causally sustained) by his other beliefs in the sense that he does not believe that his other beliefs taken together are causally sufficient for his having this belief. Or one could have a mixed account, which requires satisfaction of at least one of these conditions. If the suggestion of the previous section is accepted, that we have privileged access to the causes of our beliefs (at any rate when they are mental events, including other beliefs), all of these accounts will be internalist accounts.

As we noted in Chapter 1, the notion of a basic belief plays its main epistemological role in a foundationalist internalist theory where basic beliefs form the starting points for forming other beliefs (the 'foundations' of a subject's 'noetic structure' in Plantinga's phrase). Some of these will then be 'rightly' or 'properly' basic. Now I suggest that it is not relevant to whether a belief is in fact such a starting point, whether the subject believes that it is made probable by other beliefs. The starting points of our belief-systems are sometimes beliefs that are, and that we believe to be, made probable by our other beliefs. I believe that I am seeing my desk in my room—which is where I believe it was two minutes ago. My belief about where it was, my belief that desks do not move, and that I am now in my room looking in the right direction, make it probable that I am now seeing my desk in my room. But I would believe (although less strongly) that I am now seeing my desk in my room, whether or not I had these other beliefs. The belief that I am seeing my desk in my room would be there, playing its role as a starting point, whether or not I had the belief about probability. The choice for a definition of 'basic belief' seems to be between a definition in terms of causation (a basic belief is one for holding which the subject's other beliefs are not causally sufficient), or one in terms of the subject's beliefs about causation (a basic belief is one for holding which, the subject does not believe that his other beliefs are causally sufficient), or a definition that requires one or other of these. Given that we have privileged access to the causes of our beliefs, we will not often be in error as to whether some belief *B* is caused by another belief. But privileged access is not as such infallible access; and, while, I have claimed, we have infallible access to what are our beliefs, it is not plausible to suppose that we have infallible access to what causes them. So, on the second account, if *B* is caused by another belief (in the sense that the latter is causally sufficient for the former) but the subject does not believe that it is, *B* is still a basic belief.

An internalist can choose his definition, and we get a different internalist theory according to the choice he makes. The second account (in terms of the subject's lack of beliefs about the causes of his beliefs) does, however, seem more fully internalist (in that access to whether or not it is satisfied is infallible rather than merely privileged); and for this reason I will operate with it—while allowing substitution by the first or third accounts if one of these is preferred. On the second account my basic beliefs are the beliefs that are the ones from which, as far as I am concerned, I am starting; and an internalist theory that uses this notion takes no account in assessing the justification of a belief of causal processes of which the subject is unaware. So—more formally—I shall understand by a belief being basic that it is a belief that the subject does not believe that he holds because it is causally sustained by other beliefs; and so by a belief being non-basic that it is a belief that the subject believes that he holds because it is sustained by other beliefs. This notion will need to be refined a little shortly, partly to meet an objection that may have occurred to the reader, but that is the central idea with which I shall operate.

Evidence

For an internalist (and for some externalists), the only admissible grounds for a person's belief are his 'evidence'. To be justified, a person's beliefs must be based on his 'total available evidence'. The rest of this chapter will spell out many different ways of understanding that notion; and these results will be utilized in the subsequent chapters, where I shall spell out many different kinds of justification of internalist and externalist kinds that a belief may possess.

The narrowest way to construe a subject's evidence is in terms of his other beliefs.[10] And, given the implausibility described in Chapter 1 of

[10] Richard Feldman's paper 'Having Evidence' (in D. F. Austin (ed.), *Philosophical Analysis* (Kluwer, 1988)) is concerned with the question of how the 'available evidence' is to be construed. He is clearly concerned to analyse such a notion solely in order for it to play a role in an internalist account of justification (though he does not say so explicitly). He writes (p. 100) that 'evidence can include things other than beliefs', but his examples ('the fact that one feels a certain way, or that things look a certain way') are to my mind most naturally spelled out in terms of beliefs. He wishes, however, to confine evidence to (p. 83) the things a 'person is thinking of or aware of at a time'. So long as we understand 'is aware of' as 'can readily become aware of', his account seems to me more or less an account in terms of actual beliefs. (To insist that a person's evidence at a time should consist only of beliefs that he 'is thinking of at that time', as opposed to beliefs in the background of awareness that he can readily call to mind, would give us a very narrow evidence-set indeed—a set that would provide no justification for almost any of our ordinary beliefs.) His concern is to rule out the beliefs we would have if we thought about things for a while. As Feldman comments

supposing that we think of all our beliefs as deriving their justification solely from the support given to them by all our other beliefs, that is naturally construed as the conjunction of the subject's actual (narrow content) basic beliefs. The basic beliefs will clearly include perceptual beliefs—'I see a desk in front of me', 'I hear a drill making a noise outside the window'; personal memory beliefs—'I remember having gone to London yesterday'; and beliefs about one's mental life—'I am aware of a blue image in my visual field'. And they will in most people include beliefs about what one remembers having heard other people say, or what one remembers having read—not what the words were, but what the propositions were; which puts one in a position to check out which other people normally tell the truth—in a more direct way than is possible if one starts only with beliefs about which words were uttered or written. (See above, pp. 123–8.)

But the class of our actual basic beliefs is enormously wider than these traditional kinds of example. I believe all sorts of facts about the world, because I believe that I have been told them by, or read them in, a reliable source, but what that source was I cannot now recall. I believe that I have read in or been told by a reliable source that the Normans invaded Britain in AD 1066, and that light has the same two-way velocity in all inertial frames. That I have been reliably informed of these things are basic beliefs—because I do not believe that these beliefs (that I have been reliably informed of) are now causally sustained by any other of my present beliefs. Likewise, beliefs that reliable informers have told me that this or that race are murderers, that Hitler or Stalin love all the people of the country, or that there is or that there is not a God, are typical basic beliefs. The beliefs that honest and well-informed people have told me these things then give rise to the beliefs that they are true. Among these beliefs are also those very general beliefs that Wittgenstein discusses in *On Certainty*, such as 'The Earth existed long before my birth'.[11] And there are too general beliefs about the world, describing the subject's experience of it (not what he has been told about it): that it is hotter in summer in Britain than it used to be, or that university standards have declined. Such beliefs are basic when, as is frequently the case, the believer has no other beliefs on the basis of which he holds them; he has, for example, no detailed beliefs about what percentage of which group of students in

(p. 83): 'Although theories about epistemic rationality and justification often appeal to the notion of the evidence a person has at a time, little has been written about what the conditions are under which a person "has" something as evidence.'

[11] L. Wittgenstein, *On Certainty*, ed. G. E. M Anscombe and G. H. von Wright (Blackwell, 1969), §288.

which past year answered which questions well in what way. Beliefs formerly grounded in other beliefs become basic when we forget the other beliefs.

Strictly speaking, when we are dealing with contingent matters, the basic belief is always the belief that the subject has seen or remembered or otherwise learnt by experience that such-and-such. But, as the belief which is the content of the experience ('there is a desk in front of me', or 'I went to London yesterday') is part of the content of the former belief, it is natural to speak of it as a basic belief. ('See', 'hear', 'remember', and so on are success words. 'I see that he is old' entails 'he is old'. 'I remember' (as opposed to 'I apparently remember') 'going to London' entails 'I went to London'.) When the mode or fact of experience is unimportant, I too shall write in this loose way, equivocating between the experience and its content as basic beliefs. But occasionally it is all important to make this distinction (the evidential force of the content may be very different from the evidential force of the experience), and then I shall be careful to emphasize that—strictly speaking—the basic belief is that one is seeing something, or that one remembers something, or whatever.

It is most natural for an internalist to confine 'evidence' to (narrow content) basic beliefs. For all other states, including our own mental states, are accessible to us only as factors having in a natural sense an evidential role in virtue of our beliefs about them; we have no other such access to them. If those beliefs are false, those states including the mental states are in an important sense ones of which we are unaware. My evidence for my belief that the number of spots in my visual field is the cube root of 1,000 is my belief that I have ten spots in my visual field, not the ten spots themselves (if there are ten spots—I may have misobserved). My basic beliefs are the rock bottom. My beliefs about which beliefs I have are, I claimed in Chapter 2, infallible; and, if I am honest with myself, my beliefs are what I admit to myself to be my beliefs. Infallible evidence that provides the gateway to all other things that might be called evidence is a natural kind of evidence to which the internalist may confine himself. Put in propositional form, one's evidence is a conjunction of propositions reporting, not the things that the subject believes, but that he believes them.

But the internalist may wish to include all internal states to which the subject has privileged access as among his evidence—not merely the subject's beliefs about his mental states, but those mental states themselves (the spots in the visual field, the patterns of colour produced when we look at the world, or the noises we hear whether produced by the outside world or from within our heads).[12] Put in propositional form: our evidence will include the true descriptions of our mental states, as well as our possibly false beliefs about them.

Given that we confine evidence to beliefs, we could construe it in terms not only of our actual beliefs but rather in terms also of the basic beliefs that we would have if we 'looked around' in some way—for example, beliefs about the medium-sized objects that surround us. Ordinary language certainly allows us to talk of 'evidence' that someone had, although she did not notice it. And then one could construe it more widely as the beliefs someone would have if she took five minutes' trouble to investigate some issue. And so on and so on.

In non-philosophical discussions, a person's 'evidence' is more normally supposed to include states of affairs in the world to which there is public access—not merely his beliefs about them. And, if an externalist thinks of a subject's grounds as being or including his evidence, it will be evidence in this more natural sense that he has in mind. Most narrowly, within this wider class, a person's evidence is those states of affairs that he actually observed to be the case—the detective's evidence are the footprints and bloodstains that he actually saw. Slightly less narrowly, it includes also those states of affairs that he saw (in the sense that they caused images in his visual field) (or otherwise perceived)—that 'stared him in the face'—but that he did not notice. Less narrowly still, it includes those states of affairs that he would have perceived if he had 'looked about' a bit in various ways. And there are many kinds of 'various ways'. It includes the fingerprints on the chair that he did not bother to have examined, and what the witness was clamouring to tell him when he decided that he had done enough work that day. Most widely of all, a person's evidence may be construed so as to include those facts generally believed in the community,

[12] That 'epistemic rationality' involves a correct response to non-doxastic mental states (e.g. sensory states) as well as to beliefs, is a thesis of (among others) Pollock. (See John L. Pollock, *Contemporary Theories of Knowledge* (Rowman & Littlefield, 1986), 87- 92.) For Moser, only 'the non-conceptual component of an experience can be an unconditional probability maker' (see Paul K. Moser, *Knowledge and Evidence* (Cambridge University Press, 1989), 88). Moser objects to beliefs themselves being the foundation for the probability of other beliefs, because this would involve believed propositions having a 'self-probability', i.e. being 'evidentially probable just in virtue of themselves' (his p. 55), and he does not see how that can be. I have argued in Chapter 4 that every proposition and so every believed proposition must have an intrinsic probability—i.e. a prior probability arising from its content alone and independent of all evidence. But, as I am going on to argue, as well as having an intrinsic probability, those contingent propositions that report what the subject believes that he has learnt through experience gain a further increment of probability merely in virtue of being believed. Beliefs do, I am arguing, have a 'self-probability'.

even though the person concerned had not heard of them. A physicist's evidence may be construed as what is reported in the physics journals, even if he has not read some of them. When the evidence in any of these senses is put into propositional form, the propositions are the ones that truly state how things are in these respects in the public world.

Doxastic Foundationalism

Returning to the most natural internalist understanding of a subject's evidence as his basic beliefs—the view called 'doxastic foundationalism'—we must now tidy it up a little further. I am operating with an understanding of a basic belief as one that the subject does not believe that he holds merely because it is causally sustained by other beliefs, and so does not believe that he holds merely because he believes that it is made probable by other beliefs. But beliefs differ in the degree to which—it seems to the believer—they are rendered probable by other beliefs; and so in the degree to which—it seems to the believer—they are held because they are rendered probable by other beliefs. It is plausible to suppose that the vast majority of our beliefs are held in part because—it seems to us—they get some degree of probability from other beliefs; and thus are in part—we believe—causally sustained by the beliefs that they do get this probability. Our most ordinary perceptual beliefs are held in part because they fit in with—that is, get some degree of probability from—our general world view. I believe that I am seeing a desk in my room. But, as I noted earlier, I also believe that it was there two minutes ago, that desks do not move, and that I am looking at where it was. Although I would have the belief that I am seeing a desk even if I did not have these other beliefs, it would not be as strong without them. My belief that I am seeing a desk is strong because it fits in with my other beliefs that support the belief that there is a desk in front of me, and so make it probable that what I am seeing is indeed a desk and not a table or even a hologram. Without these other beliefs, my perceptual belief would not be as strong; and it would be even weaker if I believed that the world is full of holograms, and that there are at most three real desks in the world. We need a more nuanced amount of 'basic belief' to take this point on board. So many of our beliefs, that is to say, are partly basic—they arise partly from a conviction seemingly formed by perception or memory or logical intuition that things are so in the world, and partly because we believe that they fit in with our other beliefs. A more nuanced notion must also take account of the fact that among beliefs some are a lot stronger than others, and of very few are we maximally confident . My belief that there is a desk in front of me is a lot stronger than my belief that I was in London last week, and that is a lot stronger than my belief that $14^2=196$.

We also start with beliefs that there is quite a probability that something is so, but with a probability less than $\frac{1}{2}$, so that it does not constitute a belief that it is so. There is quite a probability (but less than $\frac{1}{2}$), I tell the policeman, that the car number plate of the car that I saw this morning had a five in it. Let us call such attitudes towards propositions that something is so basic 'semi-beliefs'. We also find ourselves with inclinations to believe certain propositions, which would lead to belief but for other beliefs that suggest that the inclinations mislead. I find myself inclined to believe that I am flying through the air like a bird (it seems to me that I am flying), but I strongly believe also that I cannot do such things and so must be dreaming. The internalist who claims that our beliefs must be grounded on basic beliefs will naturally also include such basic inclinations to belief among the foundations of our noetic structures; they are beliefs that I would have but for my belief that they are made improbable by other beliefs.[13] They too come with different strengths. So, our noetic structures have as their foundations beliefs, semi-beliefs, and inclinations to believe, with different degrees of basicality. (That is, they have different strengths additional to the strength that they gain—in the subject's view—from being made probable by other of the subject's beliefs.) When we have a belief, I argued in Chapter 2, we think of it as sensitive to how things are in the world. If we think about it, we believe that our beliefs, to the extent to which they are basic (that is, do not arise from our other beliefs) are forced upon us directly (that is, not through a chain of inference) by the world. This 'world' may be either the public world of tables and chairs, or the private world of our sensations and desires, or the world of necessary truths, such as the truths of logic. The stronger a basic belief, the stronger (if he thinks about it) is the subject's belief that it is forced upon him by the world. And the same goes for basic semi-beliefs and inclinations to believe.

Now, it is plausible to suppose that the very fact of my believing that some proposition being forced upon me by my experience or by the deliverance of reason is as such reason for me to believe it to be true. And the stronger the conviction that it is so forced, the stronger the reason for me to believe

[13] I distinguish these 'inclinations' to believe that are states of affairs of which the subject is aware, from propositions that the subject is 'disposed' to believe in the sense that he would believe them if they were 'put to' him. (See Chapter 2.) What prevents the subject from believing the latter is simply that he has not thought about the matter. What prevents the subject from believing the former is that he has other beliefs that count against their truth.

it to be true. If that were not so, I would never have good reason (in the sense of a reason of which I am aware) for believing anything. Consider, for example, among my basic beliefs, my personal memory beliefs—about what I did and what happened to me at various stages of my past life. Apparent memory is essentially belief about what I did in the past (which I do not believe that I hold merely because it is made probable by other of my beliefs)—it may sometimes be accompanied by images of me doing things; but it needs a belief about what the images are images of before they can constitute evidence about the past. And so often I have no images at all that accompany my memory beliefs about what I did in the past. The same goes for factual memory—as I noted earlier, I believe all sorts of facts about the world (for example, that China has more than one million inhabitants) because I believe that I have been told them by others (but cannot recall when I was told or by whom). I believe truths of logic and arithmetic ('2+2=4') because (metaphorically) they seem to stare me in the face. And so too (in a less metaphorical sense) do the states of affairs that I believe that I am perceiving. If having, or being inclined to have, beliefs of these kinds is no reason for believing them true, there is no other reason (in the sense of a reason of which I am aware) that can be provided. Certainly, additional reasons can be given for some of these beliefs in terms of other beliefs that we have. But either merely having (or finding ourselves inclined to have) these other beliefs as a result of apparent experience or reason is good reason for having them (in which case why should not the same apply to all basic beliefs?), or it is not—and then there is no reason (of which the subject is aware) for believing anything. If we carry these thoughts a little further and suppose that, not merely is having a basic belief (or a semi-belief or inclination to believe) a reason for having it, but it is the only reason for having a basic belief, if, that is, we confine reasons to ones of which the subject is aware—we then arrive at a principle that I call the Principle of Credulity.[14] This principle claims that every proposition that a subject believes or is inclined to believe has (in so far as it is basic) in his noetic structure a probability corresponding to the strength of the belief or semi-belief or inclination to believe. Understanding 'seems' in the epistemic sense—that is, saying that something 'seems' such-and-such being saying that one is inclined to

[14] I retain this name for the stated principle, because it has gained a certain currency since I first used it for a less precise form of this principle in 1979 (see my *The Existence of God* (Clarendon Press, 1979), 254). However, I regret having used this name in this way, since Thomas Reid has the priority in having given the name to the different principle, which I have called the Principle of Testimony (this book, p. 125). See Reid's *An Inquiry into the Human Mind*, ch. 6, §24.

believe that it is such-and-such—then, put more aphoristically, the Principle says: things are probably as they seem to be. This Principle leads on to the view that the person with justified beliefs, the rational person, is the credulous person; she believes everything until she has reason not to do so.[15] The opposite, the sceptical person, believes nothing until she has reason to do so; but as 'reason' can consist in this narrowest internalist picture only of other beliefs, she will have no reason to believe the latter beliefs, and so can never get started. (In the next few pages, when talking about basic beliefs, I include semi-beliefs and inclinations to believe; but, for the sake of simplicity of exposition, I do not always mention them explicitly.)

Once we have a set of beliefs of varying strengths (in respect of the extent to which they are apparently forced upon us by the world), these beliefs then sustain other beliefs that in turn increase or diminish the strengths of the basic beliefs, and may eliminate some. I believe that I have observed many iron balls placed in the swimming pool sinking to the bottom. My beliefs that propositions p_1, p_2 . . . (this iron ball sank, that iron ball sank, and so on) are true sustain a belief that all iron balls sink (L). This is incompatible with a belief that on one occasion I saw an iron ball not sink (p_n). Either p_n or L must be false. (Varying with their strengths and number) the beliefs that p_1, p_2 . . . will give a certain strength to L. The stronger is L, the more likely it is that p_n will be eliminated; and, conversely, the stronger p_n, the more likely it is that L will be eliminated. I believe that I am seeing a desk, but, in the light of my stronger belief that there are many holograms around, I cease to believe that I am seeing a desk—but I still have a semi-belief (a belief that there is a small probability that I am seeing a desk),

[15] Gilbert Harman, among many others, has supported a principle that beliefs should be abandoned only when one has positive reason for doing so. To continue to hold a belief, it is not necessary that that belief should be justified by a special sub-class of beliefs (e.g. beliefs about what one has observed or been told on particular occasions). Harman seems to regard this as a criticism, not of a particular form of foundationalism, but of the fundamental idea of foundationalism. This latter view, however—in my terminology—is the view that some (but not all) beliefs start with degrees of prior probability different from their intrinsic probability (that is, different from that confered upon them by mere a priori considerations) or from what the subject believes to be their intrinsic probability. This may be because the subject believes that he observed what is believed, or because the subject believes that he used to have a justification in observation but cannot now recall what it is, or for many other reasons. Harman's point seems to support, and not oppose, this general view. Harman points out that, if we could recall all the observational beliefs on which our more general beliefs were originally based (e.g. could recall who told us when that 'the earth existed long before my birth'), we would have serious difficulties in assessing the present evidential force of those beliefs in view of all the subsequent evidence that we would have acquired. Humans need to forget quite a lot in order to be able to assess the evidential force of their beliefs. See his *Change in View* (MIT Press, 1986), ch. 4.

which could reacquire the status of a belief if (because I have been so told) I acquire the belief that there are no holograms in this building.

Among the other beliefs (the background evidence) themselves dependent on basic beliefs that will quickly eliminate some of the beliefs from which we begin will be beliefs to the effect that it is statistically very improbable that beliefs of a certain kind are true, unless rendered probable by basic beliefs of some other kind. We may, for example, have a belief *B* that beliefs about the future are (in the statistical sense) unlikely to be true unless rendered probable by beliefs about the past. Belief *B* will then lead to my dismissing a basic belief (a sudden conviction with which I find myself) that (very probably) I will die tomorrow. Similarly, we may believe that scientific theories are unlikely to be true unless rendered (logically) probable by evidence of observation of particular phenomena. So, even if I think that I have 'seen' that Quantum Theory is true, I'd still need it to be supported by apparent observations of particular phenomena before my total evidence would render it probable. Among the other beliefs may also be beliefs about the reliability of certain kinds of basic belief. Quite a bit of psychological work has been done on the reliability of different kinds of memory. There is, for example, the work of Johnson and Raye showing that veridical personal memories typically have 'more contextual attributes' (that is, more information about time and place), 'more sensory attributes', and 'more semantic detail'[16] than non-veridical memories. If I have a basic belief that I have read about this work and that the psychologists who did it are reputable psychologists, then that will greatly reduce my confidence in some memory belief not characterized by any of these three characteristics. It will perhaps reduce it from being a basic belief to being a semi-belief.

We acquire new basic beliefs all the time—we see new things, people tell us new things. As children grow up, they often become exposed to a wider culture where people tell them things quite contrary to what their parents have told them. They have to weigh their basic beliefs that parents are honest and well informed against new basic beliefs that at any rate some of their current informants are honest and well informed. That will often lead to children investigating things for themselves, by processes that I shall consider in Chapter 7. Very few people, in my view, have basic beliefs of sufficient strength to withstand the pressure of large numbers of basic beliefs that seem to them to render the former probably false. If enough people tell you that your parents were mistaken when they told you that such-and-

[16] Marcia K. Johnson and Carol L. Raye, 'Reality Monitoring', *Psychological Review*, 88 (1981), 67–85.

such and show you things apparently incompatible with such-and-such, then you need more basic beliefs that render it probable that such-and-such, if you are to continue to believe that such-and-such.

So far I have described the diversity and role of basic beliefs rather loosely in words. It is now appropriate to represent this in more formal terms. I suggest that, in formalizing doxastic internalism, the philosophical analyst should regard as the foundation of our noetic structure, not 'basic beliefs', but 'basic-propositions' in this sense. I understand by a 'basic-proposition', not an ordinary or first-order belief (for example, that I saw a table in front of me, or that there is a table in front of me, or that 2+2=4), but a proposition that ascribes to such a belief a prior probability proportional to the strength that it has (that is, the degree of conviction the subject has of its truth), quite apart from the strength that it gets (in the subject's view) from or loses in virtue of others of the subject's beliefs. If we accept the Principle of Credulity, then prior probabilities will be logical probabilites. (Otherwise they will be merely subjective probabilities. The probabilities are 'prior' because they are the probabilities of propositions from which they start before other evidence increases or decreaes their probability.) For what the Principle of Credulity affirms is that the very having of a basic belief, semi-belief, or inclination to believe is itself evidence of the truth of that belief, in proportion to its strength. Each person at each time has a conjunction of such basic-propositions, which form the foundation of his noetic structure. The subject's different degrees of conviction of the truth of these propositions will then interact causally to produce various other beliefs and reduce the strengths of others. But, as well as such an actual route of belief interaction, there is the route the subject should follow. It is a major theme of this book, yet to be explored more fully, that such a 'should' may be interpreted in a variety of ways. But, if the subject should, for example, be guided by logical probability, it is the route whereby beliefs (semi-beliefs and inclinations to believe) with various prior probabilities make other propositions logically probable and thereby increase or reduce the probabilities of the basic beliefs themselves above and below their prior probability—by correct criteria of logical probability; and the subject adjusts the strength of his beliefs to the new probabilities.

Rightly Basic Beliefs

So an internalist who confines evidence to beliefs (semi-beliefs and inclinations to belief) will naturally construe a subject's 'total available evidence' as the conjunction of such basic-propositions—for our evidence is where we start from. But the question arises whether the basic-propositions from which a subject starts are the ones from which (in an objective sense) she 'should' start; whether, that is, the Principle of Credulity that seems so plausible is correct. It has often been urged that certain kinds of belief alone can form correct starting points on which to build noetic structures. Plantinga characterized a view that he called 'classical foundationalism' as follows:

> Here we have a further characteristic of foundationalism: the claim that not just any proposition is properly basic. Ancient and medieval foundationalists tended to hold that a proposition is properly basic for a person only if it is either self-evident [for example, '2+2=4'] or evident to the senses [for example, 'I see a desk'], modern foundationalists—Descartes, Locke, Leibniz, and the like—tended to hold that a proposition is properly basic for *S* only if either self-evident or incorrigible [for example, 'I seem to see a desk'] for *S*. Of course this is a historical generalization and is thus perilous; but perhaps it is worth the risk. And now let us say that a *classical foundationalist* is any one who is either an ancient and medieval or a modern foundationalist.[17]

I introduced in Chapter 1 the term 'rightly basic beliefs' to designate those basic beliefs that the subject is 'right' to hold as basic, his rightly basic beliefs (because intrinsically or merely in virtue of our having them they are probably true);[18] and, in line with my use of the notion of basic-proposition, I shall call the subject's 'rightly basic-propositions' the conjunction of propositions ascribing probabilities to propositions that measure the strength of belief in those propositions that she is 'right' (in this sense) to have, independently of the support or undermining they gain from other propositions. Then an alternative plausible way for an internalist to understand a subject's 'total available evidence' is as the conjunction of her rightly basic-propositions (so understood). For—plausibly—if there is some basic belief from which she is not 'right' to start, it cannot confer

[17] Plantinga, 'Reason and Belief in God', in A. Plantinga and N. Wolterstorff, *Faith and Rationality* (University of Notre Dame Press, 1983), 58–9.

[18] Plantinga (*Faith and Rationality*, 46, 48) used the phrase 'properly basic beliefs'. I use a different phrase—'rightly basic-propositions'—for two reasons. I include in the 'foundation of our noetic structure' the different strengths which our different beliefs ought to have, and hence I talk of 'propositions' that report these. As I explained in Chapter 1, I use the adverb 'rightly', to contrast with Plantinga's 'properly', because while for Plantinga a properly basic belief is one that the subject is justified in holding without that justification being provided by other beliefs, he does, however, hold that such beliefs may need grounding in non-doxastic states. In attempting to spell out as pure an internalist account of evidence as can be had, I am assuming that there is never any need for such grounding.

justification on other beliefs; and, if it has the wrong degree of strength to start with, it will confer the wrong degree of justification on other beliefs.

The reason why the subject is not justified in starting from certain beliefs (or, more precisely, starting from certain basic-propositions) may be a posteriori or a priori. If it is an a posteriori reason, but not another belief of the subject, we are operating with a conception of 'evidence' wider than that of belief. If, for example, it is claimed that I am not justified in starting from a belief that there are ten spots in my visual field, because as a matter of fact there are only nine spots in my visual field; or that I am not justified in starting from a belief that there is blood on the carpet, because the red stain on the carpet is made not by blood but by red ink, a wider conception of evidence is constraining the beliefs from which we ought to begin. So too, if it is urged that beliefs that result from taking LSD are not rightly basic, because such beliefs are often false. In attempting to develop as purely internalist an account of evidence as can be had, I ignore such constraints. Nor can the a posteriori reason be simply another belief of the subject—for example, his belief that beliefs that result from taking LSD are often false—for that will not affect the justification for having some belief as a basic belief, since that is a matter of whether one should start from the latter before one takes other beliefs into account.

There may, however, be a priori reasons affecting the probability that the believer is right to ascribe to a proposition additional to the reason of the strength of his basic belief in it. For, even given my argument that having a basic belief or inclination to believe some proposition is a reason for believing it, there may still be a priori reasons (of which the subject is not aware, but of which he can become aware) for not believing it or not believing it so strongly. And there may be a priori reasons why some semi-belief should be a basic belief. And there may be a priori reasons why some proposition not believed should be a basic belief or semi-belief. If one thinks of such a priori reasons as part of one's 'evidence', then again we are operating with a concept of evidence wider than that of belief, although still a fully internalist conception (for a priori reasons are internalist reasons). But it is natural to think of a priori considerations not as evidence but as rules for operating with evidence, rules for doctoring the set of basic-propositions, and in that case we are still within the spirit of doxastic foundationalism. The claim that basic beliefs alone form our 'evidence' must then be understood as the claim that they alone form our contingent evidence, the evidence that one investigator may have and another investigator may not. The Principle of Credulity must then be understood more narrowly as the claim that having a basic belief (or semi-belief, or inclination to believe) is *a* reason for having a belief; but it will not rule out a priori reasons for taking beliefs as basic or for not taking them as basic.

I argued in the last chapter for the view that all propositions have intrinsic probabilities, prior logical probabilities determined solely by the a priori criteria of scope and simplicity. Hence, in the absence of other evidence, those intrinsic probabilities are the ones that (objectively, whether they realize it or not) people ought initially to ascribe to propositions—for in such a situation those are the logical probabilities of those propositions. So, to start with, all truths of logic, being truths that hold in all worlds, will have intrinsic logical probabilities of 1. And so we must distinguish between the prior probability that some logically incompetent individual ascribes to them (in virtue of the strength of his belief in them), and their true prior probability, the one that a priori considerations suggest should be ascribed to them. And all logically impossible propositions will have true intrinsic probabilities of 0, even if someone has a basic belief that one such is true. Further, all contingent propositions, of whose truth or falsity the subject has not had apparent experience, should have their intrinsic probability as their prior probability. As I emphasized all along, most propositions have only very rough intrinsic probabilities. But the criteria of scope and simplicity that I developed in Chapter 4 do often give clear verdicts on the relative intrinsic probabilities of different propositions. A subject who violates these rules starts with a set of basic-propositions different from the set of rightly basic-propositions from which he ought to start.

Now, given my earlier argument that having a basic belief (or semi-belief or inclination to believe) is a reason for having it, how much of a reason is it, given the a priori considerations? With regard to logically necessary or impossible propositions, whatever our basic beliefs about them, a priori considerations clearly dictate that the former have prior probabilities of 1 and the latter have prior probabilities of 0 in the set of rightly basic-propositions. Our beliefs about these propositions may indeed constitute a reason of which a subject is aware for believing or not believing them, but it is a reason totally overwhelmed by the a priori reasons (of which the subject may be unaware).

But for contingent propositions, whose truth or falsity is not totally fixed by a priori considerations, then, when a basic belief (or semi-belief or inclination to believe) about their truth or falsity is an apparent deliverance of experience, then that belief must have weight. (By a belief being an 'apparent deliverance of experience', I mean that either it is, or is the content of, a belief about experience—either 'I saw the desk in front of me'; or 'the desk is in front of me', when I have also a belief of the former kind.) Having the belief then provides a reason for having the belief, not overwhelmed by the a priori considerations, but additional to them. To the extent to which one believes that one has perceived some state of affairs, then the prior probability of a basic belief that it has occurred will be higher than its intrinsic probability. And, to the extent to which one believes that one has perceived that some state did not occur, then the prior probability of a basic belief that it did occur will be lower than its intrinsic probability. For, although the arguments of p. 141 are now qualified by allowing a priori reasons of which the subject is unaware (although he can become aware), clearly a priori reasons are not going to get us very far with respect to the empirical world. Simplicity and scope will make some propositions more probable than others. But so many particular contingent propositions will have equal scope and simplicity to each other; and virtually all propositions will be intrinsically very improbable. Only if apparently seeing the desk, or remembering having seen it, or believing that desks normally stay where they are put, provides good reason for believing that the desk is there or was there or that desks normally stay where they are put, can we have any belief with any substantial logical probability of truth about the position of the desk or anything else contingent.

I wrote above that a belief that is an 'apparent deliverance of experience' has this effect on probability. If a belief about a contingent matter represents itself only as a deliverance of reason, as a belief on a priori grounds about the logical probability of some proposition, then, if our concern is with rightly basic beliefs, such a belief will not affect the logical probability of the proposition believed; for that will be determined by the correct a priori considerations, not by the subject's (possibly false) beliefs about these.

So, if we allow a priori considerations (of which the subject is unaware) to affect the logical probabilities of his beliefs, we have a new but still fundamentally doxastic understanding of a subject's 'total available evidence' as the conjunction of propositions ascribing prior probabilities to all possible propositions—these probabilities being intrinsic probabilities increased or decreased by an amount representing the subject's degree of confidence that he has perceived that they are or that they are not true. Believing that it was marginally more likely that one saw that there was a five on a certain seven-numeral car number plate, than that one saw that there was no five, will raise the prior probability of there being a five on the number plate a bit above the intrinsic probability. If we have no evidence about which numerals occur on car number plates, we must ascribe the same intrinsic probability to every combination of seven numerals. It will follow that there is already an itnrinsic probability of 0.52 that any car number plate will contain a five, and only an intrinsic probability of 0.48 that a car number plate does not contain a five. So, although I may be only marginally more confident that I saw a five on the car number plate, than that I saw that the number plate contained no five, I must ascribe a prior probability greater than 0.52 to it containing a five. But a very strong conviction that one has perceived some state of affairs must raise the prior probability of the belief close to 1 (but only to 1 in the case of those few states of affairs about which one's experientally acquired beliefs are infallible, including one's beliefs themselves). And I suggest that the considerations that lead to a qualified form of the Principle of Credulity have the consequence that a strong conviction that one has observed some state of affairs must give that state a fairly high prior probability—only a posteriori considerations (for example, that one believes that everyone says that states of affairs of this kind never happen) can reduce it below 0.5. If one does not say something like that, one will not get the result that most of our ordinary mundane beliefs are probable on our evidence: and I am analysing our criteria of probability on the assumption that the most obvious judgements of probability that we make are more-or-less correct. If, for example, propositions about our past experiences were in no way more probable for being purportedly remembered, no belief about the past would be in the least probable. And, unless propositions about our past experiences were significantly more probable than not for being purportedly remembered, very few beliefs about the past would be very probable.

'Classical Foundationalism', as expounded by Plantinga (who is in no way committed to it), thus needs much qualification before we can accept it as an account of 'right' basicality. If we allow a priori considerations, the most sophisticated theorems of mathematics have as much claim to the status of being rightly basic as the 'self-evident' ones (for both will have logical probabilities of 1). 'Incorrigible' propositions in the sense of those propositions about the mental life that are infallible (for example, about one's own beliefs) will also have prior probabilities of 1. Propositions 'evident to the senses' will have lower prior probabilities. They may have very low prior probabilities (we may be very unconfident of having observed them); but nevertheless, as very unconfident reports of what we have observed, they may form right starting points for our belief-system—even unconfident reports have some evidential force. I can see no mere a priori reason for disbelieving any apparent deliverance of experience about a contingent matter (for example, 'I seem to see an elephant in the garden' or 'I seem to hear the voice of omnipotent God'); only a posteriori considerations (that is, many and various apparent experiences) can show which kinds of experience should be trusted, which apparent senses are real senses.[19]

So I have developed a distinction between the basic beliefs from which an individual who knew all a priori truths—that is, a logically omniscient individual—would start—that is, those formed by adding or subtracting amounts to the intrinsic probabilities of propositions, in virtue of the strength of his inclinations to believe them arising apparently from experience; and the basic beliefs with which a particular logically incompetent individual finds himself in consequence of his apparent experiences and the apparent deliverances of reason. We could also distinguish the basic beliefs that different individuals with different degrees of logical competence ought to begin in the light of their experiences and apparent deliverances of reason. But, for simplicity's sake, let's just distinguish between the rightly basic beliefs (as those from which a logically omniscient individual who doctored his inclinations to believe by a priori considerations would begin) and someone's actual basic beliefs. Rightly-basic-propositions are propositions ascribing right prior probabilities to basic beliefs (either actual basic beliefs or ones that for the stated reasons the subject ought to have). Basic-propositions ascribe probabilities to basic beliefs (semi-beliefs and inclinations to believe) in accord with the subject's actual strength of belief in them (apart from the strength they get from or lose in virtue of other believed propositions).

The conclusion of this chapter is that a person's 'total available evidence' may be understood in very many different ways—as the conjunction of his actual basic beliefs (with their different strengths), of his rightly basic beliefs, of the basic beliefs he would have if he 'looked around' a bit, of all his mental states, of the public phenomena that he has correctly observed or could 'readily' have observed, or of the public facts known in the community. Understood in terms of public evidence (or non-doxastic mental states), it is to be represented propositionaly as the conjunction of true propositions that report that evidence. Understood in terms of basic beliefs (or rightly basic beliefs), it is represented propositionally as a conjunction of propositions ascribing prior probabilities to the propositions believed—either prior probabilities that reflect the subject's degree of conviction, or ones in which those values are doctored in the light of a priori considerations.

[19] See Additional Note M both for how the process of the change of probability of a proposition in the light of new uncertain evidence can be represented in the probability calculus; and for exceptions to the rule that an apparent perception of a state of affairs increases the prior probability of its occurrence.

As I have noted earlier in the book, it may be useful in various contexts to make a distinction within one's evidence (in any of the senses that I have distinguished) between one's 'evidence' in a narrower sense and one's 'background evidence'. There are various ways of doing this, and not a great deal turns on whether or how it is done. But, loosely, the narrower kind of evidence will be the evidence most directly relevant to the hypothesis at stake, typically evidence of immediate particular observations; background evidence will be evidence that certain sorts of observations were made in the past, or that a certain general theory is true.

When expounding in subsequent chapters internalist theories in which the evidence is the subject's basic beliefs or rightly basic beliefs of certain strengths, I shall normally omit the phrase about their strengths and I shall not—until I come to the end of the exposition—re-express the theories in terms of the evidence being the subject's basic or rightly basic 'propositions'. This is solely to aid the reader in following the main lines of the argument. I shall bring in at important stages the relevance of the beliefs being of certain strengths.

6

The Value of Synchronic Justification

Fully Internalist Accounts

A belief is justified if it is based on adequate grounds (or if it is (rightly) basic). Grounds are adequate if they make the belief probable. A fully internalist account of justification will understand grounds as total available 'evidence', and evidence as evidence to which the subject has privileged access. That means understanding it as beliefs, or more widely as all mental states—for example, as including sensory states. A fully internalist account of probability will understand it as inductive probability—either logical, epistemic (of the kind relevant to the subject's capacities), or subjective (by the subject's own inductive criteria). All these kinds of probability are ones to which either a subject has privileged access or are a priori. Logical probability is a relation knowable a priori. Epistemic probability (of the kind relevant to the subject) is logical probability watered down in the light of the subject's logical knowledge and capacities—to which clearly he has privileged access. Subjective probability for a given subject is probability on that subject's own criteria of what makes what logically probable—again something to which he has privileged access.

So—leaving aside for the moment the 'basing' requirement—in which senses of 'evidence' and 'probability' is it good that a subject shall have beliefs that are truth-indicative in the sense of being probable on his total available evidence? I argued in Chapter 2 that it is good to have true beliefs. It follows that, even if having true beliefs is the only point in having beliefs probable on their evidence, the answer for *all* internalist understandings of 'evidence' is that it is as such good that a subject should have beliefs rendered logically probable by her total available evidence. For that fact on its own (that is, if we do not take into account anything else we know about the world) makes the belief (logically) probably true. If my beliefs are rendered logically probable by my rightly basic beliefs, or by all my mental states, then that fact on its own makes it logically probable that the belief is true. And the same applies if my beliefs are rendered logically probable by the public evidence (however widely or narrowly construed). But what about the cases when a belief is rendered logically probable by my basic beliefs where these are not the same as my rightly basic beliefs? Then the a priori reasons that dictate that some basic belief is not rightly basic form part of our criteria for what makes what probable; and so ensure that basic beliefs that are not rightly basic do not give a degree of probability to some other belief that it would not get from rightly basic beliefs. Differences between what is rendered probable by basic beliefs and what is rendered probable by rightly basic beliefs emerge only when we are dealing with some kind of probability other than logical probability. So, on any understanding of 'total available evidence', if anyone has a belief rendered logically probable by his total available evidence, that is as such a good thing, because that by itself renders the belief probably true by correct evidential criteria.

But the subject can only consciously respond to evidence of which he is aware—that is, in virtue of his beliefs about it. To the extent to which his awareness of his evidence is fallible, to that extent he is unable consciously to respond to it. Only of his beliefs can his awareness be infallible. And even here a subject can have relevant beliefs, about which his awareness would be infallible if they occurred to him, but which simply do not occur to him. All the same, if evidence is confined to beliefs, a subject can have the fullest awareness of the quality of his conscious response to it that is possible; and it is this quality (by a priori reflection on his standards of probability and how to apply them) over which in the long run he has the greatest power of control. In this sense a belief rendered logically probable by rightly basic beliefs has the kind of internal rationality to which the subject has best access, and by which he can (with best prospect of success) seek to be guided in the future. But only a logically omniscient person who calls to mind all his relevant beliefs will automatically have all and only beliefs rendered logically probable by his rightly basic beliefs. For others of us it is a goal to be aimed at, and in the long run we can improve the quality of our beliefs in this respect by reflecting on what are the correct criteria of logical probability (and so the factors by which basic beliefs should be doctored to make them rightly basic). Any belief rendered logically probable by evidence is good to have, but that most accessible to the subject is the belief being rendered probable by his rightly basic beliefs.

Whether it is good for someone to have beliefs rendered epistemically or subjectively probable by basic or rightly basic beliefs depends on how much his basic beliefs diverge from rightly basic beliefs, and how much in error are the assessments of logical probability to which epistemic probability and subjective probability lead. *p* renders *q* epistemically probable (by *S*'s standards) in so far as to the extent that can be calculated from *S*'s limited logical knowledge and with *S*'s power of calculation, *p* renders *q* logically probable. Differences between logical probability and epistemic probability (by the standards of some investigator *S*) will arise only in so far as *S* does not fully apply the criteria of logical probability described in Chapter 4—because of incompetence. Thus suppose *S* is a detective investigating a murder. Let *p* be the very large number of pieces of evidence in the form of rightly basic beliefs with high prior probabilities that *S* acquires. *p* includes evidence that the nephew *N* of the victim of a murder will inherit half the victim's wealth, was heavily in debt, and was in the vicinity of the crime when it was committed. *q* is the hypothesis that *N* committed the murder. *S* considers *q* logically probable because, as far as he knows, *N* is the only person in the vicinity of the crime with a motive—he will inherit half the victim's wealth and is heavily in debt. *q* makes it probable that *N* has a motive. There were a number of other people in the vicinity at the time, but *S* has no evidence of their motives and no other evidence made probable by the hypothesis that one of these did the murder—he thinks. However, among the evidence *p* is evidence from which it follows deductively by a complicated line of argument that the knife entered the victim's body at an angle that could be made only by a left-handed person, and evidence that the detective had seen *N* do many one-handed tasks with his right hand. On this evidence it is in fact very improbable (logically) that *N* did the murder—because the evidence *p* includes evidence that is very improbable if *q* (that is, if *N* did the murder). But the detective is overwhelmed by the sheer quantity of his evidence and has not seen the relevance of this piece of evidence. And, given that he is a simple detective constable, we may think that he could not be expected to realize this. So (by *S*'s standards) it is epistemically probable on his evidence that *N* did the crime—but it is not logically probable.

And when we are concerned with epistemic or subjective probability, rather than logical probability, there may occasionally be a great difference between what is probable on the subject's basic beliefs, and what is probable on his rightly basic beliefs. For someone may have a basic belief in a necessarily false proposition—for example, that $7 \times 12 = 86$, which, of course, will not be rightly basic. He may not have the competence to see that other of basic beliefs entail that 7×12 does not equal 86. So he will believe many propositions entailed by $7 \times 12 = 86$, which—as far as he can see—are entailed by that proposition, and so rendered probable by it.

It will be a good thing to have a belief epistemically probable (on the subject's standards of epistemic probability and his evidence—with the qualification that his basic beliefs must be rightly basic) if that belief is true. If the epistemically probable coincides with the logically probable, it is logically probable that the belief is true, and so logically probable that it is a good belief to have. To the extent to which the epistemically probable does not coincide with the logically probable (and to the extent to which the subject's basic beliefs are not rightly basic), it is (logically probably) not a good belief to have. Differences between logical probability and subjective probability (by the standards of some investigator *S*) will not, however, arise solely from *S*'s failure to recognize logical truths or deductive consequences. In such a case *S* may have different views from the true ones about the criteria of logical probability themselves. So he may think, for example, that the fact that a coin has landed heads upward ten times makes it probable that it will land tails next time; or the fact that the horse's name is the same as his own makes it probable that, if he bets on that horse, he will win. To the extent to which *S*'s criteria differ from the correct ones (and his basic beliefs diverge from rightly basic ones), to that extent it is not logically probable—on *S*'s evidence—that his belief will be true. If the subjectively probable belief does not coincide with the logically probable, it is not (logically probably) a good belief to have. In my view very few adults in developed societies of the twenty-first century form very many of their enormous number of beliefs in accord with criteria other than the correct logical ones (newspaper stories about the prevalence of astrology notwithstanding). If that view is correct, it follows that, while the best beliefs to have are those that are logically probable on our rightly basic beliefs, beliefs that are merely epistemically or subjectively probable on these (or epistemically or subjectively probable on actual basic beliefs) are not likely to be greatly in error.

Throughout this chapter I have written of beliefs being rendered probable by basic or rightly basic beliefs. To speak strictly, however, as I noted earlier, one's evidence in the form of beliefs consists of both beliefs, semi-beliefs, and inclinations to believe and their respective strengths; and so the phrase 'semi-belief or inclination to believe of given strength' should be inserted after 'basic belief', and the phrase 'semi-belief or inclination to believe of the right strength' should be inserted after 'rightly basic belief' throughout the chapter. In the terminology of Chapter 5, the evidence is basic- or rightly-basic-propositions.

But in what sense—if any—of basing is it good that our beliefs (rendered probable by our evidence) should in fact be based upon them? A theory of basing, we saw in Chapter 5, may be a purely causal theory, one of two purely doxastic theories, or a mixed theory. We saw in Chapter 5 that, while purely doxastic theories of basing are internalist, whether a pure causal theory or a mixed theory involving the causal element is internalist or externalist depends on one's theory of causation. I suggest that in none of these senses is there any epistemic advantage (that is, advantage from the point of view of getting a true belief) in having beliefs based on their evidential grounds. Consider to start with some causal-type theory of basing. So long as a given belief has adequate grounds, it is no more likely to be true if it is caused by those grounds than otherwise. However, unless there is causation or some sort of indirect causal connection between people's beliefs and grounds that are adequate for their truth, it will be statistically very improbable that people will have beliefs that do have adequate grounds. For, if there are no causal connections between the grounds of people's beliefs—and for simplicity's sake we will suppose that these are their basic (or rightly basic) beliefs—and the resulting beliefs, it would be a coincidence that when, say, someone has a basic belief that renders it (logically, epistemically, or subjectively) probable that *p* rather than the belief that not-*p*, that person then also had the belief that *p*. Yet, if the basic beliefs cause the resulting beliefs, there is a mechanism that (to the extent to which it is of the right kind) could ensure that the resulting beliefs are those rendered probable by the basic beliefs. The mechanism that ensures this need not be direct causation. If my resulting beliefs and my basic beliefs have a common cause, then again there is a mechanism that (to the extent to which it is of the right kind) could ensure that it always produced simultaneously with basic beliefs only beliefs rendered probable by them. Where there is a causal connection of either of these two kinds, it is only to the extent to which the mechanism is of the right kind that the resulting beliefs will have adequate grounds (for example, will be rendered logically probable by basic beliefs). If many kinds of resulting beliefs are covered by this mechanism, it cannot be a mechanism of the narrow type of a deviant causal chain (illustrated on p. 13); non-deviant causality is thus more valuable than deviant causality in its capacity to bring about more beliefs that have adequate grounds. (For the sake of simplicity of exposition, and because of its value for the reason just stated, I shall assume in future that the causation of beliefs is of a non-deviant kind.) But, if there is no mechanism connecting our grounds and our other beliefs, it will be statistically improbable that our grounds will be adequate for the other beliefs—in other words, a coincidence.

On the first purely doxastic theory a belief is based on its grounds—that is, the subject's basic beliefs—if the subject believes that the latter make the former logically probable. But again, satisfaction of the basing condition thus understood will not add to the probability of a belief rendered probable by the basic beliefs. However, in so far as believers consciously apply their criteria of what is evidence for what in forming their beliefs, then—in so far as their criteria are correct ones—it is probable that his non-basic beliefs will be those rendered probable by a believer's basic beliefs . We saw in Chapter 2 that, in so far as I have beliefs about this, I must believe of myself that my criteria are correct and correctly applied, and, since most others clearly in general have the same criteria and apply them in the same way, I must believe that of them too. But we cannot conclude that this is a necessary condition for a subject to have adequately grounded beliefs in this sense. For maybe I am not sufficiently sophisticated to have a belief about what makes what probable, but yet there is some causal mechanism in place that ensures that those of my basic beliefs (of the right strength) that in fact render some other belief probable but that I consider irrelevant do cause me to have the latter belief.

Similarly, if 'basing' is understood on the alternative doxastic understanding—that the subject believes that his belief is caused by his basic beliefs that in fact render it probable—the resulting belief is no more likely to be true for the subject having this additional belief about it. But, in so far as the subject has true beliefs about which of his beliefs are caused by which basic beliefs, then that, of course, entails that there is such a causal mechanism in place that could ensure that the basic beliefs that cause a resulting belief are ones adequate for its truth (for example, render it logically probable)—though it does not guarantee that the causal mechanism will have this character. But people may not have true beliefs about the causes of their beliefs, and yet (by a regular mechanism) their beliefs might be caused by basic beliefs adequate for their truth—of which causal facts the subject is unaware.

For a belief to be justified in an internalist sense, it has to be based on evidence that renders it probable. We have seen that, taking 'evidence', 'based', and 'probable' in different senses, we can generate many different senses. For future use, I wish to distinguish two of them. The first I shall call (synchronic) subjective justification. In this sense a belief is justified if it is rendered subjectively probable (that is, probable by the subject's own criteria) by the subject's actual basic beliefs (semi-beliefs, and inclinations to believe of given strengths), and the subject believes that it is caused and rendered subjectively probable by those beliefs. (Since a subject's criteria of inductive probability just are the ones that he believes correct, if he believes that a belief is rendered subjectively probable, he will also believe—subject to the qualification in Chapter 3 n. 15—that it is rendered logically probable.) This is a fully internalist sense. If a subject has a belief justified in this sense, he has lived up to his own standards in the way in which he has responded to his evidence in the form of basic beliefs, and he believes that he has done this (and he has no evidence about the world except that which comes to him via his beliefs). As I argued in Chapter 2, a subject's response to his evidence as he forms a belief is a passive one. Yet we can pass judgement on the process as to whether it forms a belief coherent by the subject's own criteria with his other beliefs. If it does so, the resulting belief is (synchronically) subjectively justified.

The other kind of internalist justification to which I shall give a name is (synchronic) objective internalist justification. A belief is justified in this sense if it is rendered logically probable by the subject's rightly basic beliefs, semi-beliefs, and inclinations to believe (of the right strength) and based on the latter, both in the sense of being caused by them and in the senses that the subject believes it is caused by them and renders them (logically) probable. A belief justified in this sense is the consciously rational response to evidence in the form of basic beliefs that would be made by a logically omniscient being. Note that, on my preferred definition of 'basic belief', there exists a distinction between a subject's basic beliefs and her non-basic beliefs only where she makes a distinction between those which she believes to be caused by other beliefs and those about which she does not hold this belief. Very young children will not make such a distinction, and so their beliefs cannot be assessed as 'justified' or 'not justified' if we have a definition of justification in terms of how their non-basic beliefs are related, or believed to be related, causally and probabilistically to their basic beliefs. Their beliefs do not have that kind of internal coherence of which they are conscious, and so will be neither subjectively nor objectively (synchronically) justified. They may still be justified in many other internalist and externalist senses, in terms of the actual (as opposed to believed) relations of causation and probability to their other beliefs or to public or private non-doxastic events.

Externalist Accounts

We saw in Chapter 1 that most externalist accounts of justification are reliabilist accounts. A belief is justified if it is based on adequate grounds. The grounds are some internal or external state; and a belief being based on those grounds is naturally understood by the externalist in causal terms. The adequacy of the grounds is a matter of similar processes (that is, any process of production of beliefs by similar grounds) producing mostly true beliefs. Adequacy is then statistical probability; there must be a high statistical probability of a process of belief production from similar grounds producing a true belief. We then get innumerable different theories according to how the 'similarity' is spelled out. How general (how deep or how wide) is the type (to which the token process belongs) to be understood? And is it the proportion of true beliefs produced in our world, or in worlds in which various circumstances are allowed to alter, or in normal worlds?

However, if the only point in having justified belief is to get true beliefs, it really does not matter. Take any reliabilist account at all. The fact that the token process belongs to a type, members of which have a high statistical probability of being true, by itself (that is, in the absence of other evidence, such as that the token process is also a token of some unreliable process) makes it logically probable that the belief is true—by the Principal Principle as developed in Chapter 4. If 90 per cent of beliefs produced by processes of a certain type are true, that gives a logical probability of 0.9 to a token belief produced by a token of that process being true. This will be so whether the processes are the processes in the actual world, or in close possible worlds, or in normal worlds. In consequence it is good that we shall have beliefs that have adequate grounds—whether or not they are based on (in the sense of caused by) grounds adequate for their truth, and whether the grounds or their adequacy are accessible or not. There could be a statistically high correlation between kinds of belief and states of affairs that make those beliefs true, without there being any (direct or indirect) normal causal connection between them. But only if there is some kind of normal causal connection will it be other than an unlikely chance that the statistically high correlation holds. That is, it will be (logically) very improbable that there is a statistically high correlation. The normally operative causal connection between states like *S* and beliefs that a state like *S* holds may be either direct—the former cause the latter—or indirect—there is a common cause (let us call it a state of type *R*)—both of states like *S* and of beliefs that a state like *S* holds. If there are such causal connections, then there is a mechanism in place that ensures the reliability of the connection. Where the causal connection is direct, then the belief will normally occur only when it is caused by the state of affairs believed to hold. Beliefs about our perceptions are like this—they normally occur only when caused by what we believe we are perceiving. (I normally have a belief that I am perceiving a desk in front of me, only when a desk causes me to hold this belief by reflecting light rays of a certain kind onto my eyes.) So the belief will be based on, in the sense of caused by, grounds adequate for its truth—that is, by a type of process that reliably produces true beliefs. (Beliefs about perceiving desks being normally caused by desks are normally true.) If the causal connection is indirect, then the belief that *S* holds will normally occur only when it is caused by a state of type *R*, and when the latter occurs normally it causes *S*. And so then also the belief will be based on, in the sense of caused by, grounds adequate for its truth; it will be caused by the state of type *R*, which is reliably connected with states of type *S*. If my belief that you are now in London was caused by your promise to go to London, and normally I believe what you say and you do what you promise, then my belief will be based on grounds adequate for its truth. So, normally, beliefs are produced by a reliable process only if they are based on, in the sense of caused by, grounds adequate for their truth.

Yet, while every belief that has adequate grounds of any reliabilist (and no doubt any other externalist) kind is—as such—probably true, there may be counter-considerations. In particular, there may be adequate grounds of some other externalist kind for its falsity. These two sets of grounds have to be weighed against each other to see if on balance—given both sets of grounds—the belief is or is not probably true. In particular, the token process of belief production may belong to two different types, one of which may reliably produce true beliefs and one of which may not (or which may produce beliefs with a different degree of reliability). We can then no longer immediately apply the Principal Principle. We need to weigh against each other these two considerations in order to calculate the logical probability of the resulting belief being true. The rules for calculating the logical probability of some individual *a* having a property *M* (for example, some belief being true) on evidence *e* that *a* has various properties *Q*, *R*, *S*, and so on, and that the statistical probabilities of an individual that has one or more of these properties having property *M* are such-and-such, are those outlined in Chapter 4.[1]

[1] There are various oversimple proposals in the philosophical literature for how such a calculation should be made, exemplified by Reichenbach's proposal that we use only 'the narrowest class for which reliable statistics can be compiled' (H. Reichenbach, *The Theory of Probability* (University of California Press, 1949), 374). Suppose we have 'reliable statistics' for the proportion of individuals that are both *Q* and *R* that are *M*, but no reliable statistics for individuals that are both *Q* and *R* and *S* that are *M*, then on this proposal we should take the probability of *a* being *M* to be given by the former—(in the terminology of p.161) $Pr\,(M|Q\&R)$. But reliability is a matter of degree, no statistics are perfectly reliable, and all statistics provide some relevant evidence that we would be foolish to ignore. And anyway, this rule gives us no guidance at all as to what to say if we have equally 'reliable' statistics for two different classes to which *a* belongs—e.g. for both $Pr\,(M|Q\&R)$ and for $Pr\,(M|Q\&S)$—but for no narrower class. For more detailed discussion of these over-simple proposals, see my *An Introduction to Confirmation Theory* (Methuen, 1973), 138–40.

Although complicated in practice, the basic idea is simple. We must consider the logical probability given by this evidence to all possible theories *Tn* about how *M*, *Q*, *R*, *S*, and so on interact (for example, whether an individual having *Q* makes it statistically more probable that it has *M* and by how much; and how much this influence is increased or decreased by the individual being *R* as well). Such theories will have high logical probability to the extent to which they satisfy the criteria described in Chapter 4. We then calculate what is the logical probability on these different theories of *a* that is *Q*, *R*, *S* being *M*. The probability of *a* that is *Q*, *R*, *S* being *M* is the sum of the probability of this on each of the theories *Tn*, each multiplied by the probability on the evidence *e* of that theory.

$$P(Ma \mid Qa \,\&\, Ra \,\&\, Sa \,\&\, e) = \sum_{n=1}^{n=\infty} P(Ma \mid Qa \,\&\, Ra \,\&\, Sa \,\&\, Tn)P(Tn \mid e)$$

Clearly we cannot in practice work this value out exactly, by taking into account all possible theories of how *M*, *Q*, *R*, *S* interact. For there is no end of conceivable mathematical relationships that might hold between these variables (forming a non-denumerable infinity). But we can get a rough result by considering the theories that are most probable. Let me illustrate these principles at work in very rough terms in two very simple examples. Suppose that our evidence concerns statistical probabilities in infinite classes, and we represent the statistical probability of an *A* being *B* by $Pr(B|A)$. Let our evidence be $Pr(M|Q)=0.5$, $Pr(M|Q\&R)=0.75$. We have no evidence about individuals that are *S*. So (barring some known odd feature of *S*), theories that postulate that *S* increases the statistical probability of an individual (whatever other properties it might have) being *M* are as probable a priori as ones that postulate that *S* decreases that probability. So theories that give higher values than 0.75 to $Pr(M|Q\&R\&S)$ are as probable on the evidence as ones that give lower values; and the a priori most probable (because the simplest theory) is to suppose that *S* has no influence: $Pr(M|Q\&R\&S)=0.75$. (At this stage it is irrelevant that $Pr(M|Q)=0.5$, since we have the more detailed evidence that $Pr(M|Q\&R)=0.75$.) Hence we may conclude that $P(Ma/Qa\&Ra\&Sa)=0.75$.

Suppose now that we get a further piece of evidence: $Pr(M|Q\&S)=0.25$. Then an obvious theory of how the properties interact is that *R* increases by a half the statistical probability of any *Q* being *M*, and *S* decreases by a half that probability; and so (since $Pr(M|Q\&R)=0.75$) that $Pr(M|Q\&R\&S)=0.375$; and on that theory the logical probability of *a* (that is *Q* and *R* and *S*) being *M* is 0.375. But there are other theories less probable (because yielding the data less accurately) that will yield higher values for

Pr (M|Q&R&S) and others that will yield lower values. Plausibly, the influence of the two kinds of theory (because each theory of one kind is as probable as some theory of the other kind) cancels out, and so we may conclude that P (Ma|Qa&Ra&Sa) = 0.375.

Suppose, more plausibly, that our evidence concerns only statistical probabilities in finite classes—that is, actual collections of data about proportions of individuals that are Q and also M and so on. Again, we must use these data to construct theories of how properties interact that make the data probable. In this case the 'weight' of the evidence will be important—that is, the size of the finite classes. For, if our evidence is that the proportion of Qs that are M is 0.5 when the class studied is very small, that evidence will not be very improbable logically on theories of the value of Pr (M|Q) in an infinite class greatly different from 0.5. Whereas if the class studied is large, that evidence will be very improbable indeed if Pr (M|Q) diverges greatly from 0.5 in the infinite class. These simple examples illustrate how different statistical probabilities of different type processes (processes having properties Q, or Q-and-R, or whatever) producing beliefs that have the property of truth (M) should be weighed against each other to yield the logical probability of a belief that is a token of several types being true.

It should be evident that, although all beliefs that have adequate grounds of any externalist kind are—as such—probably true, as we take into account other pieces of evidence about the type to which the token process belongs, and any other evidence we can get, the logical probability of the belief being true will continually change. Clearly it is good, as such, to have any belief whose grounds thus enlarged make it logically probable that it is true. If—impossibly—we could take into account all possible evidence (apart from evidence simply stating that the belief was true, or that it was false), then almost every belief would have a probability of 1 or 0 (or very close thereto) of being true. Yet none of these interesting facts can be of any use to us unless we have access to them. I can be guided in my belief formation by these facts about externalist grounds only if I am aware of them—in the sense that among my basic beliefs is a belief (of a certain strength) that these facts hold—or if the latter beliefs are rendered subjectively probable by my basic beliefs (including, for example, the belief that someone else has told me certain statistical facts). Any finite human, such as myself, will have only a limited number of pieces of evidence about statistical probabilities, but we can weigh them against each other in the way described above and add them to any other evidence we may have to reach the subjective probability on our total available evidence that a resulting belief is true.

The Intrinsic Value of Objective Internalist Justification

So far I have been assuming that the only point of having beliefs that are epistemically justified is that it is good to have true beliefs; epistemically justified beliefs are only of instrumental value. They are valuable only in so far as what they indicate (that the belief is true) is so. A true belief (about the future, say) is none the better for being epistemically justified (now). Nor, I have been assuming, is there any value in having a false belief that is nevertheless epistemically justified. Now, while epistemic justification is, of course, valuable primarily for that reason, I wish to suggest that one kind of synchronic epistemic justification is intrinsically valuable. It is good to have epistemically justified beliefs of this kind, even if they are not true; and true beliefs of this kind are better for being epistemically justified.

The kind of justification is for the belief to be logically probable on the subject's (rightly) basic beliefs, and to be based on the latter—both in the sense of being caused by them, and in the senses that the subject believes that they are caused by them and render them probable. This kind of justification is what I called earlier one having synchronic objective internalist justification. To see that we do value such internal justification for its own sake, compare the person who believes, let us suppose truly, that earthly life originated in outer space because he dreamed it one night and liked the thought, with the great scientist who has the same true belief because he assesses much evidence in the right way, and sees that the evidence supports that belief. We value the scientist for having a belief that is not merely true, but results from consciously responding to all the evidence of which he is currently aware in the right way. We value our scientist because he shows a grasp on those a priori truths that I described in Chapter 4, and is consciously guided by them in his belief formation; he does not believe things just because he likes to believe them or slips into the habit of believing them. If true belief is intrinsically important—as surely it is—conscious truth seeking is a virtue, and doing it in the right way is exemplifying that virtue paradigmatically. To the extent to which his belief is formed by an incorrect process, although perhaps it has some merit because it is the result of an intentional truth-seeking process, in so far as the criteria used are not suited for the job (for example, the epistemic probability or subjective probability diverges from the logical), to that extent it lacks intrinsic merit.

On the other hand, I can see no intrinsic merit in having a belief justified by externalist criteria of a reliabilist kind. The only value that has is that

that makes it logically probable that the belief is true. But, if a belief is true, it is none the better for being produced by a process of a type that usually produces true beliefs—any more than a chair that is comfortable is any the better for coming from a factory that usually produces comfortable chairs.[2]

[2] See Additional Note N on Naturalized Epistemology.

7

The Value of Diachronic Justification

A belief is often said to be a justified one, in the sense that not merely is it justified synchronically (in one of the senses discussed so far) but it has been based on adequate investigation. To the extent to which this holds, the belief will be diachronically justified.

Brainwashing

While we cannot change our beliefs at an instant, what we can do is to do things over time that may lead to a change of belief. One way in which we can do this is to have in mind some proposition *h* that we want to get ourselves to believe and try to brainwash ourselves into believing it. I claimed in Chapter 2 that belief is a contrastive attitude—it consists in believing this as against that, which involves a vague and primitive form of a belief about relative probability. To the extent to which one has the concept of probability, and thinks about the matter, in believing *h*, one believes *h* to be more probable than not-*h* on the evidence of one's basic beliefs. It follows that, in order to try to brainwash ourselves into believing *h*, when we did not initially believe it, while our evidence remains the same, we need to brainwash ourselves into having different criteria for assessing evidence from the ones we had originally. One way of achieving this result might be to concentrate attention on the evidence favouring some belief and to try not to think of the initially apparently stronger evidence against it, and then we might come to think the former evidentially more important than we originally supposed. But, as we begin this operation, we must think of it as a procedure for acquiring a belief that, as we look at it at that time, is probably false. (For we must think of the criteria we use for assessing evidence as the correct criteria and so as ones that yield (with subjective probability) true beliefs.) Or we might just try to forget about the negative evidence. We would also need to forget that we had forgotten it; for, if we remembered that there was strong negative evidence against some possible belief (although we could not remember what that evidence was), that very item of knowledge—that there was such evidence—would make it (logically) improbable that the belief was true. But again we would have to think of this as a procedure for getting ourselves to believe what on our present evidence was probably false. Or we might try to persuade ourselves that we had observed or experienced *h* or some strong positive evidence in favour of *h*—that is, try to force ourselves to have a new basic belief. For this process to work, we would need to forget that we had forced ourselves to acquire the belief (because, for the reasons argued in Chapter 2, what we believe that we have acquired through choice cannot be a belief). But once again, as we begin this operation, we must think of it as a procedure for acquiring a belief that, as we look at it at that time, is probably false.

There might occasionally be a good reason for pursuing such policies of self-deceit. We might be able to bear to go on living, or be able to attempt some difficult task, only if we had some belief that our evidence indicates to be false. But the good reason would not be an epistemic reason; it would not be the reason of trying to get a true belief. So no person can think about himself that, by trying to acquire a particular belief that *h*, he will get another true belief. Of course, it may be true all the same with respect to a particular individual *S* and a particular belief that *h*, that, if he tries to acquire *h*, he will get another true belief. But I know of no evidence that makes it logically probable that this is a method that will generally be truth conducive even in other people.

Inquiry

But what we can do if we are aiming at truth is, without having a particular belief in mind that we seek to reach in advance, to investigate some matter in order to improve the quality of our belief on the matter. What I mean by improving the quality of our belief is acquiring a belief on the matter that is better justified synchronically—that is, more probably true than the initial belief (which may be the initial belief itself rendered more probable, or a different one). Since true belief is a good thing, and so for that reason—in the ways that we have discussed—is synchronically justified belief of most kinds, it follows that it is good that we should seek to get beliefs as well justified synchronically as we can, and that our efforts should be efficacious. A belief will be what I shall call diachronically justified to the extent to which it is synchronically justified and its acquisition (or, in the case of a continuing belief, its maintenance) has been based on adequate investigation of its truth. Although philosophers have often mentioned the importance of adequate investigation of our beliefs and claimed that, to be justified, a belief should have been adequately investigated, they have not always distinguished sharply between synchronic and diachronic justification. And, because philosophers have given a lot less consideration to diachronic justification, there are no ready patterns for classifying theories of this. So I am simply going to ask the question head-on of what are the factors that determine whether investigation of the truth of some belief has been adequate and how the notion of a belief being 'based on' such investigation is to be understood. We shall see that our answers come in terms of probability, and that this can be spelled out in many of the various ways that we have discussed so far.

The most an investigator can do towards getting a true belief on some issue is to try to get a belief with as high a logical probability as possible on its evidence. So investigation will involve, first looking for more evidence as a result of which he may come across evidence that renders some belief on the issue (either the one he originally held or a different one) very probable. But it may also involve checking that his criteria of probability are correct (that is, that his subjective criteria are logical criteria); and that he has applied them correctly. In this activity an investigator can operate only on his own standards—using actual basic beliefs and subjective probability; but, to the extent to which his standards are close to the correct ones, he will use rightly basic beliefs and logical probability.

The obvious form that investigating takes is looking for more evidence. We do this by making observations in the laboratory, reading books, listening to people; that leads to us acquiring new basic beliefs (not through trying to get these particular beliefs, but through acquiring whatever beliefs are forced upon us through observation, and so on). This is a good thing to do—from the point of view of getting at the truth—if our basic beliefs are rightly basic and our criteria are those of logical probability (as I shall assume up to p. 172), because it is logically probable that having a belief formed in the light of more evidence will mean having a belief that is more probably true. Most probably, that belief will be the original belief, call it the belief that *h*. We can see this as follows. Suppose that on our present evidence it is (logically) probable that *h*, and so we believe. This evidence in making our belief that *h* probable makes it probable that new evidence will be as our belief predicts and so increase the probability of that belief. But, of course, the new evidence may (though improbably) lead to *h* being less probable or even improbable; and (though highly improbably) it may even lead to not-*h* being made more probable than *h* was originally (for example, if some evidence incompatible with *h* is found). (For a less loose demonstration, that it is probable that more evidence will lead to a belief more probable on its evidence, see the reference in n.5.)

Three factors determine whether it is worthwhile to investigate some belief. The first is how probable it is that investigation will make a crucial difference to the degree of synchronic objective internalist justification possessed by the belief—that is, to its logical probability on rightly basic beliefs. There is no point in investigating the truth of some belief if there is no chance that investigation will make any crucial difference. If our concern with having a true belief arises solely from the intrinsic value thereof, a crucial difference to the degree of synchronic objective justification is one that moves it from being justified to being unjustified or conversely—that is, lowers its probability below $\frac{1}{2}$ or raises it above $\frac{1}{2}$. If our concern with having true beliefs is to guide our actions, a crucial difference in the synchronic justification—that is, the probability of a belief—is one that makes a difference to which actions we should do. As we saw in Chapter 2, which actions we should do will depend on just how probable some belief is, given that achieving different outcomes by our actions have certain values. Thus a doctor may believe that some drug will not kill a patient, but he needs to be very confident of this before he will inject it. Which action he ought to do (that is, inject or not inject) will depend on the values of the different possible outcomes; in terms of Bayesian decision theory (in its second use described in Additional Note B) that means their utilities. (I assume, as most of us do in our non-philosophical moments, that there are truths about values—about what matters more and what matters less. If that is not so, replace talk about correct values of utilities with talk about the utilities the subject ascribes to outcomes.) Suppose that, if the drug does not kill, it will mildly improve the patient's well-being, and that the drug killing has a utility of -1, and that a mild improvement has a utility of $+0.05$. Then the expected utility of administering the drug is $(-1) \times$ (the probability that it will kill) $+ 0.05 \times$ (the probability that it will mildly improve well-being); and the expected utility of not administering the drug is 0. So the doctor should inject if (and only if) the probability of the drug being safe on that occasion is no less than $\frac{20}{21}$ (approximately 0.95). So the value of further investigation of a belief that the drug is safe will depend on how probable it is that the probability of the drug being safe will be lowered below or raised above the crucial threshold that makes all the difference to behaviour. As argued in Additional Note B, it may be more obvious what that threshold is than what are the utilities of the different outcomes that enable us to use Bayesian decision theory to calculate what that threshold is. But the use of the latter in my example should bring out what it is for a threshold to be crucial.

How probable it is that investigation will make a crucial difference to the probability of the belief (lowering it above or below $\frac{1}{2}$, or above or below the threshold crucial for action), can be spelled out in any of the different senses of probability that we have discussed. But, if we are concerned with logical probability, and there is no contingent evidence relevant to whether investigation will make a crucial difference, then there is an a priori consideration that is a more general form of the one that I mentioned earlier. It is more probable (logically) that it will make a difference to whether the belief is logically probable on total subsequent evidence, the closer the belief's initial logical probability on its evidence is to $\frac{1}{2}$. For, if the initial probability of the belief h is close to 1, it is very probable indeed that the belief is true and so very probable that any new evidence will be as h predicts and so not lower the probability of h, let alone make it improbable. The closer is the initial probability of h to $\frac{1}{2}$, the greater is the probability that evidence that renders the belief improbable will appear.[1] So, if the only point of investigation is to get a true belief for its own sake, beliefs require investigation in so far as their probability is not close to 1. But, if the point is to get a belief to guide action, the issue turns on how probable it is that investigation will affect the probability of the belief in such a way that it crosses the crucial threshold. The worthwhileness of further investigation into the effects of the drug turns on how (logically) probable it is that the probability of the drug being safe on that occasion will be lowered below or raised above the crucial threshold that makes all the difference to behaviour. That will depend on how close to the threshold to start with is the initial probability of the belief. For you are more likely to find evidence that alters the probability at least a bit than to find evidence that alters it a lot.

[1] More formally—Bayes's theorem tells us that:

$$P(h|e\&k) = \frac{P(e|h\&k)P(h|k)}{P(e|k)}$$

Let $P(h|k)$ denote the initial probability of h. Suppose that investigation has a number of possible outcomes—e_1, e_2, e_3, and so on. Some of these will be confirmatory, i.e. such that $P(h|e\&k) > P(h|k)$, which will hold iff $P(e|h\&k) > P(e|k)$ or—equivalently—$P(e|h\&k) > P(e|{\sim}h\&k)$. Others will be disconfirmatory, i.e. such that $P(h|e\&k) < P(h|k)$ and so equivalently $P(e|h\&k) < P(e|{\sim}h\&k)$. Now $P(e|k) = P(e|h\&k)\ P(h|k) + P(e|{\sim}h\&k)\ P({\sim}h|k)$ (where $(P{\sim}h|k) = 1 - P(h|k)$). It follows from the argument in the text that, the greater is $P(h|k)$, the more probable it is that e will be confirmatory; and as $P(h|k)$ falls, the more probable it becomes that a disconfirmatory e will occur. If there is an e for which $P(h|e\&k) < \frac{1}{2}$, the lower is $P(h|k)$ the greater the probability that that will occur.

While the initial logical probability of a belief thus affects the logical probability that investigation will make a crucial difference to the probability of the belief, it is not the only factor that does. The kind and quantity of evidence that has determined the initial probability—what has sometimes been called 'the weight of evidence'—affect the issue of how much new evidence will make any difference. If my evidence that the probability of a crucial future toss being heads is 0.7 derives solely from the fact that 7 out of 10 tosses so far have been heads, then (given the equal prior probability of any permutation before any tosses are made) it is quite (logically) probable that, if the coin is tossed 100 more times, there will be a significantly different value (greater or less) of the probability that the crucial toss will be heads. But, if the evidence to date comes from 1,000 past tosses, the (logical) probability that 100 more tosses will make much difference is small.[2]

Also, we may have (among our rightly basic beliefs) empirical evidence of the success or failure of past investigations on the topic in question to discover relevant evidence. If you have spent half the morning looking through half the reference books in the library to find the source of some quotation and not found it, that makes it less likely that spending the rest of the morning in the same way will yield any useful result. We may also have more general empirical evidence of the difference that investigations like the one being considered make to the logical probability of a belief of this kind. That too may affect the logical probability that the particular investigation will make a difference to the logical probability of the belief. Education in an experimental science will include instruction about which kinds of experimental technique have yielded useful results in the past (that is, results that make quite a difference to the probability of the hypothesis under investigation). Education in how to conduct an opinion survey will include instruction about what has been found in the past about which groups have opinions representative of the population (for example, groups in which different sexes, age groups, racial groups, and income groups are represented in proportion to their numbers in the total population). This evidence will affect the logical probability that a particular kind of investigation will make a crucial difference to the probability of a

[2] For the importance of not enshrining probability estimates based on little evidence, about whether chemicals are safe, see e.g. Ellen K. Silbergeld, 'Risk Assessment and Risk Management: An Uneasy Divorce', in Deborah G. Mayo and Rachelle D. Hollander (eds.), *Acceptable Evidence*. See especially pp. 108–10 on 'Weight of Evidence'. Thus, p. 109: 'Chemicals with less weighty evidence, but still some evidence of risk, may be controlled on an interim basis, with the opportunity for review mandated to a reasonable schedule of expected testing.'

hypothesis under investigation (for example, it may show that, probably, in order to make a crucial difference to that probability, you would need to use a much larger sample selected by some 'random' method than if you use a sample of a kind found representative of the population in earlier investigations). And evidence may include evidence of the differences made by different kinds of investigation of a sample in the past. It is one of the roles of the 'pilot study' normally undertaken before any large-scale statistical investigation to discover which kinds of investigation will give the best results—that is, will make crucial differences to probabilities. For example, before issuing a questionnaire, studies may be undertaken to discover whether particular features of the form of the questionnaire such as the colour of its paper and the typeface affect the response rate (and so the utility of a particular form of questionnaire in yielding crucial evidence).[3] Evidence may also include evidence of the difference made by investigations of different lengths. To take a recent example of the latter—in 1999 British government scientists assured the British public as a result of their investigations that genetically modified food licensed for sale in British shops is safe. But the British public felt that it had had such reassurances as a result of their investigations from scientists before (especially in the case of the danger to health from eating beef from cattle carrying the disease BSE), and the scientists were subsequently proved mistaken—that is, longer and more thorough investigations (in the BSE case, ones that took account of human deaths from CJD much later) made a significant difference to the logical probability on evidence of food being safe. There was, that is to say, empirical evidence that investigations by government scientists of only moderate length and thoroughness into food safety would have their results overthrown by discoveries made in the course of longer investigations. That increases the probability that further investigation into the safety of GM foods will make a significant difference to the probability of their safety.[4]

While the logical probability that investigation will make a crucial difference to the logical probability of a belief depends on the initial probability, the evidence relative to which it was determined, and empirical evidence about the results of similar investigations, what is, however,

[3] On how pilot studies yield results about the value of evidence produced by investigations of different kinds, see A. N. Oppenheim, *Questionnaire Design, Interviewing and Attitude Measurement* (new edn., Pinter Publishers, 1992), ch. 4.

[4] Thus the leader of the British Conservative Party, William Hague, said: 'we have learnt not to take at face value medical advice that says everything is fine' (*Daily Telegraph*, 18 Feb. 1999).

always the case is that the expected utility of actions guided by probabilities relative to more evidence is greater than that of actions guided by probabilities relative to less evidence—except in the case when no outcome of investigation can affect which action is the one that maximizes utility—that is, where the evidence is irrelevant.[5] This will apply also to the case where the alternative 'actions' are believing or not believing a proposition, and true belief has a positive utility that false belief lacks. That is to say, investigation as such is never a bad thing, and virtually always a good one.

In considering the probability that investigation will make a crucial difference to the logical probability on our evidence of some belief, I have been considering only the logical probability of this. But there will also be epistemic and subjective probabilities, a physical probability, and statistical probabilities of all the many kinds that I have analysed. Maybe as a matter of fact, after a certain determinate amount of investigation, investigations into drugs have so far never made any further difference to the logical probability of their safety—which fact (of which the investigator may be ignorant) makes it logically probable that this one (already investigated up to the determinate amount) will not make any difference.

So far I have been assuming that investigation into the truth of our beliefs takes the form of seeking more evidence—for example, more rightly basic beliefs, which can affect the probability of the former—by correct criteria or by our own criteria of probability. But can we also investigate the correctness of our criteria of inductive probability or our judgements about what are the necessary moral truths concerning which issues it matters to have true beliefs about? Clearly, total investigation is not possible—the investigation would require the use of those very criteria of inductive probability and those purported moral truths themselves. But what we can do—on the assumption that our criteria are on the whole correct—is to 'sort them out'; to use some criteria (for example, the criterion of simplicity) and our judgements about particular cases[6] (of what makes what prob-

[5] This is shown by a theorem, the first published version of which was in I. J. Good, 'On the Principle of Total Evidence', *British Journal for the Philosophy of Science*, 17 (1967), 319–21. The theorem was proved earlier by F. P. Ramsey, but his proof was not published until 1990: F. P. Ramsey, 'Weight or the Value of Evidence', *British Journal for the Philosophy of Science*, 41 (1990), 1–4. There is a simple form of the proof in Helen Beebee and David Papineau, 'Probability as a Guide to Life', *Journal of Philosophy*, 94 (1997), 217–43; see 238–41.

[6] The method of seeking 'reflective equilibrium' between initially plausible general principles and initial plausible judgements about particular cases was, of course, advocated as the correct method of reaching correct principles of morality by John Rawls. See his *A Theory of Justice* (Oxford University Press, 1972), 20.

able) as criteria for whether others of our criteria are correct. If it is one of my (subjective) criteria of inductive probability that lottery numbers are more likely to be drawn if they are somewhat similar to the birthday dates of the gambler (or that horses are more likely to win races if their names are similar to those of the gambler or events in her life), I can come to believe that this criterion is mistaken because another criterion supported by very many judgements about particular cases shows it false. For I can be shown that in the past all other gamblers who have bet on the lottery numbers that represent their dates of birth have been successful no more frequently than gamblers who have not so bet. That would be very improbable, given a theory that there is always a causal influence of the one on the other. Of course, it would not be very improbable, given a theory that this causal influence operates except over the range of the past data studied. But this theory is less simple than the previous theory of universal causal influence. If I deny that simplicity is evidence of truth, that will conflict with very many judgements that I make about particular cases in other areas of enquiry (as we saw in Chapter 4). So the improbability of the data (given an inductive criterion supported by very many particular judgements about what makes what probable), on the supposition of a connection between birth date and lottery success, may make it subjectively improbable (by my criteria) that birth dates make probable lottery success, and so lead to the abandonment of the latter criterion. Again, there can be statistical probabilities of various sorts that such investigations into the correctness of criteria lead to improvement. And someone could have evidence that on a particular occasion investigation would lead to improvement—for example, in the form of actual or rightly basic beliefs about what happened on other occasions on which he or others investigated the correctness of their criteria. Investigation of criteria will also include investigation of which basic-propositions are rightly-basic-propositions.

Note, however, that all such investigations into criteria and judgements about necessary truths can affect only the subjective or epistemic probability of a belief on its evidence. They cannot affect whether a belief is rendered logically probable by its evidence (which will be what it is, whether or not the believer recognizes it), and so cannot affect the synchronic internalist objective justification of a given belief. Nor can they, of course, affect the justification of a belief in any reliabilist sense. But the investigation can affect whether the investigator comes to hold the belief that is rendered logically probable on its evidence.

It is plausible to suppose that getting more personal experience of some subject area will often lead to improvement of one's moral views about it;

and that improving one's moral character (by making oneself naturally inclined to do what one believes good) will improve one's moral perceptions (help one better to see what is good). Both of these plausible hunches require some statistical evidence to make them probable, yet in advance of that they have some plausibility, perhaps because many of us have basic beliefs that someone has told us that there is evidence of this. Surely one is in a better position to have a correct moral view about, say, euthanasia if one has some experience of people who seek help to commit suicide (as well as people who do not wish to commit suicide but might feel an obligation to do so if society encouraged suicide). And is not someone who has made himself tell the truth sometimes in cases where it is more obviously obligatory better able than the inveterate liar to understand the extent of the sacredness of truth and whether there is a duty to tell the truth virtually always? In so far as someone believes that there are such statistical probabilities, he will have evidence about how to improve his moral beliefs, and so his beliefs about which necessary moral truths it matters to have true beliefs about.

As part of the process of trying to ensure that he does hold the belief rendered logically probable by the evidence, a subject can check whether he has taken into account all his relevant beliefs, and has applied his criteria of probability correctly. This investigation will include such mundane operations as checking whether his arithmetical calculations are correct. Here there is no guarantee that it is probable that such investigation will improve quality—some investigators get their calculations right first time more often than they get them right second time; as may be shown by their third, fourth, etc. calculations and the testimony of others. But there are statistical probabilities of various kinds giving various values of the probability that such investigations lead to improvement. And a subject can have evidence of various kinds (in the form of basic beliefs) about what others say about when our calculations are most often correct, or about what usually happens when we do calculations many times, which will give a probability to the proposition that rechecking our application of criteria will lead to improvement.

The second factor determining whether it is worthwhile to investigate some belief is the probable importance of true belief on the subject in question; or, to put it more accurately, the probable importance of holding the opposite belief to the one you currently hold (that is, the negation of your current belief), if that opposite belief were true. For investigating is opening yourself to changing your belief, and that will be worthwhile only in so far as it would matter to hold the opposite belief if it were true. Or, where not holding some belief but holding it with sufficient strength is what matters (because it makes the difference to action, as in the drug example), the crucial factor is the probable importance of holding the belief (if true) with a degree of strength that leads to a different action from the one that you should be doing otherwise. From now onward up to p. 182, I shall often write of 'probable' importance, cost, or whatever, or of the 'probability' of truth without specifying the kind of probability. Everything I write can be interpreted in terms of the different kinds of probabilities, and I draw attention to that at the end of the discussion.

As I wrote earlier, I am assuming that there are truths about values—about what matters more and what matters less—that I shall call here simply moral truths. (If someone thinks that there are no moral truths, then replace talk about 'moral truths' by a subject's beliefs about moral truths, or—less misleadingly—the utilities the subject ascribes to certain kinds of state of affairs.) I suggest that, among moral truths, while all true beliefs have value, true beliefs on big matters and matters central to our lives have greater intrinsic values. It matters more that we should have a belief about whether the universe is spatially infinite or whether the earth is the centre of a small universe than about the proportion of nitrogen in the atmosphere of Jupiter. And it matters more that we should have a true belief about who are our parents and what our children are doing than that we should have a true belief about exactly how many undergraduates there are at a certain distant university. These examples concern the intrinsic worth of the relevant beliefs. But beliefs matter also for practical purposes. And the value of true beliefs of sufficient strength to lead to some action depends on the value of doing the action if the belief is true as opposed to the disvalue of doing it if the belief is false. If our belief is such as to lead us to give the patient the drug, true belief about whether it will kill or cure matters a lot.

If there are moral truths, there will be fundamental necessary moral truths. Any contingent moral truths—that is, ones that hold only under certain circumstances—will hold because those circumstances hold and so there will be a necessary truth that, if those circumstances hold, the contingent moral truth holds. It can be true that I ought to pay you £10 (unless—implausibly—it is a necessary truth by itself that I ought to do so), only if there are some contingent circumstances in virtue of which I have this obligation. Whether the circumstances are easy to describe (that I promised to pay you £10) or more complicated (that I promised to pay you £10, and that I have lots of money, and it is simple to give some to you), unless there are circumstances such that it is in virtue of my being in these circumstances that I have this obligation, it cannot be true that I have this obligation. And so anyone situated in circumstances the same in all the specified respects (for example, that she promised to pay you £10, and has lots of money, and it is simple to give some to you), would have a similar obligation (to pay you £10). This connection between the circumstances that give rise to the obligation, and the obligation, must be a necessary one. For, if it were merely a contingent matter that I have some obligation in some circumstances, however fully those circumstances were described, there would be a possible world differing from the actual world solely in moral respects (for example, a world in all respects including people's beliefs and social conventions the same as ours except that there paying debts is in fact not obligatory, whatever people believe about it, while here it is obligatory. Or that there genocide is right whereas here it is wrong). But that is absurd. Hence, there must be a necessary moral truth (be it simple or complicated) of the form that anyone in such-and-such circumstances has such-and-such obligations (for example, to pay money).

The importance of true belief on some matter will generally depend on both necessary and contingent matters. The importance of a true belief about whether Mount Vesuvius will erupt soon depends on whether saving human life is of very great moral importance; and on whether, if Mount Vesuvius does erupt soon, people will be killed. The probability of the belief being of moral importance will depend on the probability of the two latter factors. The probable importance of a true belief about whether Mount Vesuvius will erupt soon depends both on the probability of saving human life being of very great moral importance and on the probability that, if Mount Vesuvius does erupt soon, people will be killed. I have already drawn attention to the different ways in which the probability of propositions like the latter may be understood. Purported necessary moral truths, like any purported necessary truths, will have logical probabilities of either 1 or 0 on any evidence. But their epistemic or subjective probabilities may be very different, and so may the statistical probability of moral propositions similar to the one at stake being true.

When holding a true belief that *p* is important for intrinsic reasons, it is plausible (though not obviously correct) to suppose that it is just as important to believe *p* if *p* is true, as to believe not-*p* if not-*p* is true. It is just as important to believe that the earth is the centre of the universe if it is, as to believe that the earth is not the centre of the universe if it is not. But, where true belief is important for practical reasons, because of the actions to which it leads, what is important may be—as we have seen in the drug example—not which belief one holds, but whether one holds it strongly enough to lead to this action (for example, administering the drug) rather than that one (for example, withholding it). The importance of holding a belief strongly enough, if it is true, may differ from the importance of holding the belief less strongly, if it is true (or the negation of the belief, if the negation is true). Suppose, as before, that, if the drug is safe, it will cause only a mild improvement to the patient's well-being, but that, if it is not safe, it will kill; and that in consequence the doctor will administer the drug if (and only if) the probability of it being safe is no less than 0.95, otherwise he will not do so. Then it is surely more important to have the belief that the drug is safe with sufficient strength (that is, that the probability of its being safe is 0.95 or above) if the drug is safe, than to have that belief with lower strength or the negation of the belief, whether or not the drug is safe. Given our earlier figures, a true belief of the former kind leading to the corresponding action will have a positive utility of 0.05, whereas the latter belief (true or false) will lead to no action—and so have a utility of zero. Hence there is more reason for investigating whether the drug is safe if you initially believe this with insufficient strength or do not believe it at all (because there is the possibility of benefit to a patient), than if you initially believe it with sufficient strength. In the latter case, there is no reason for investigating at all—you already have such strong evidence that the drug is safe that the doctor is justified in administering it. But, of course, the moment any evidence (unsought) appears lowering the probability of safety below 0.95, the doctors must stop administering until more investigation raises the probability above the crucial value.

The final factor relevant to the adequacy of the investigation is the probable 'cost' of obtaining new relevant evidence. The more trouble and expense required to obtain new evidence, the less investigation is required; because taking trouble and spending money on other things will give relatively better value. By the 'probable cost' of an investigation, I mean its 'expected cost'—that is, the sum of the possible costs each weighted by the probability that that will be the actual cost, when 'costs' are measured in terms of the probable values of different expenditures of money and effort and bad side effects. But, again, the probabilities of the various costs may be logical, epistemic, or subjective probabilities on evidence of different kinds available to the subject; or statistical probabilities of the costs of similar investigations, and so on. One of the roles of a 'pilot study' undertaken before a large-scale statistical investigation is to get evidence about the probable cost of large-scale investigations of various kinds—for example, the time needed to get necessary permissions, and to conduct interviews.[7]

[7] See again Oppenheim, *Questionnaire Design*, ch. 4.

New drugs are tested on animals before they are tested on humans. Drug-testers have a rough and ready rule to give to humans being tested a dose that is from $\frac{1}{10}$ to $\frac{1}{100}$ of the 'no-effect' animal dose (that is, the maximum dose at which no toxic side effect is observed in any animal tested).[8] This rule is presumably meant to take account both of the small probability on the evidence that a smaller dose that the animal no-effect dose would have a toxic effect on a human, and the very high disutility of it doing so—in my terminology, that element of the probable cost of the drug test on humans arising from the risk of a toxic side effect.

An investigation may be of various kinds and lengths. If there is only one reason for the importance of a true belief—its intrinsic value, or its value for one particular practical consequence—then there will be only one 'crucial difference' to its probability that investigation could achieve—for example, making it more or less probable than $\frac{1}{2}$, or making it more or less probable than some other particular probability threshold. But, if a true belief is of importance for more than one reason, there may be more than one crucial probability threshold. I may seek a true belief about whether John stole the money both for intrinsic reasons (I need to know how to regard him) and also for various practical reasons (for example, to determine whether to sack him, or to continue to trust him with money in the future). I may need my belief that he stole the money to have very high probability before I sack him (because of the great disutility of sacking an innocent man, in comparison to the utility of sacking a guilty man). But I may need my belief to have only a fairly low probability before I cease to trust him with money (because of the great disutility of having money stolen, in comparison to the utility of having an innocent John do the money-carrying work). So, we need to calculate separately, for each reason for which a true belief of sufficient strength is important, the probable positive utility of investigation; and take the sum of these terms to yield the overall probable positive utility of the investigation. The disutility (negative utility) of any investigation is its probable cost. So, for an investigation of a given kind and length, the overall expected utility will be the sum of ((the probability that it will make a crucial difference) multiplied by (the probable importance of a resulting true belief of a certain strength different from your current belief)) for each crucial difference *minus* the probable cost of the investigation. However, for the sake of simplicity of exposition, I shall assume in future that a true belief is of importance only

[8] See Barry A. Berkowitz and Bertram G. Katzung, 'Basic and Clinical Evaluation of New Drugs', in B. G. Katzung (ed.), *Basic and Clinical Pharmacology* (Lange, 1998), 65–6.

for one reason, theoretical or practical. The expected or probable utility of an investigation of a given kind and length will then be the ((the probability that it will make a crucial difference) multiplied by (the probable importance of a resulting true belief (of sufficient strength) different from your current belief), minus the probable cost of the investigation). The corrections necessary for what I say to take account of a more complicated situation should be clear. I have used the words 'utility', 'worth', 'value', and 'importance' interchangeably; and 'cost' to designate negative utility. Since what concerns us in this context is whether an investigation of a certain kind and length is worthwhile at all, what matters is whether the probable utility of undertaking it is positive or negative; we can use any scale we like to measure probable importance against probable cost—so long as importance and cost are both measured on a common scale. The issue covers (loosely) how much time it is worth using and how much money it is worth spending in order to get a more probably true belief on the issue. It is indeed artificial to suppose that such things could be measured in exact quantities. But, supposing that they could, and exhibiting in a formula what kind of relative strengths they would need to have, helps us to see what is at stake when we consider whether an investigation is worthwhile. That enables us to judge in many particular cases that this investigation would, and that one would not, be worthwhile—because to suppose otherwise would involve assessing the importance of true belief or the time-and-money cost of investigation too high or too low.

Clearly investigating a belief by an investigation of a certain kind and length may be worthwhile, while pursuing a longer or different investigation is not worthwhile. A belief held at a time *t* has, we might suppose, been adequately investigated if (and only if) it has been investigated at any earlier time when it would have been worthwhile to investigate it. But to take 'any' literally might seem to put the standard for a belief being diachronically justified very high. Does failure to have investigated some belief long ago when it was worthwhile to investigate it, although it has not been worthwhile to investigate it recently, really remove the diachronic justification of a present belief? It may be that (in one of the ways analysed) it would have been good in 1998 for me to investigate some belief because the strength of my belief could make all the difference to whether or not I did some action that I would have to choose whether or not to do very shortly; yet I did not then investigate it. In 1999 maybe no such crucial choice depended on whether I held the belief, but for theoretical reasons it would still have been good to have a true belief on the subject; yet the probable cost of investigating this belief has greatly increased, in such a way that it would no longer be worthwhile to investigate the belief. That, let us suppose, remains the case up to the present. Has the present belief really not been adequately investigated? We might try to deal with this kind of case by replacing the earlier suggested definition of adequate investigation by the following: a belief held at a time *t* has been adequately investigated if (and only if) it has been investigated during some period of time terminating at *t* when it would have been worthwhile to investigate it. This has the consequence that a belief has been inadequately investigated only if there is no period of time terminating at the present during which the believer should be investigating his belief but is not. But that too seems to lead to counterintuitive consequences. Consider a belief that required investigating an hour ago when I had the leisure to investigate it but failed to do so. For the last five minutes I have had some urgent task to do, which prevents me investigating it. So I have not failed in my investigative duties for the last five minutes. Is that really enough to make my present belief adequately investigated?

What these examples suggest to me is that the notion of a present belief having been adequately investigated is—like almost all the notions that I have sought to analyse in this book—extremely vague and susceptible of many different precise explications. But I suggest that, if we are to capture the vague ordinary-language understanding of 'adequately investigated', we should explicate a belief having been adequately investigated, as it having been investigated by such investigation as would have been worthwhile during any *recent* earlier period of time. 'Recent' can be understood in various ways, or dropped from the definition. For almost all of our beliefs, it is not worthwhile to investigate them. I have innumerable beliefs about the positions of objects in my room and what I did yesterday, about history and geography, which it would not be profitable to investigate. Did I really see John in the street yesterday, or was it the day before that? To look in my diary, to try to recall mentally the details of what I did yesterday, to ask those with whom I was walking whether they saw John in order to get a synchronically better justified belief about whether I saw John yesterday or the day before that, would normally be a total waste of time. But occasionally it could be of great importance which belief I held—if, say, the day on which I saw John in the street formed a crucial piece of evidence in a murder trial. And then quite a bit of investigation would be needed before my belief had been adequately investigated.

For a belief to be diachronically justified, a belief must not merely be synchronically justified and have been adequately investigated; the belief must have been based on that investigation. If no investigation was required, this requirement is redundant—synchronic justification suffices for diachronic justification. But, if investigation was required, the 'basing' requirement insists not merely that the belief should have been adequate, but that the belief shall have been based on that investigation. The point of some sort of 'basing' requirement is that adequate investigation is useless unless it affects what we believe.

There are available to us two of the three ways of understanding 'basing' that were available to us when we considered synchronic justification. A belief being 'based' on adequate investigation may be understood as it being caused by that investigation; the present belief, that is, is held because the investigation caused it to be held—either caused a previous belief to be maintained or a new belief to come into existence. But, alternatively, we can understand a belief being based on adequate investigation as the subject believing that it was caused by the investigation. (There does not seem to be scope to understand a belief being based on investigation as believing that it is rendered probable by the investigation; because an investigation does not make a belief probable, only the results of the investigation do so.)

If basing is understood in causal terms, then a diachronically justified belief is one that is caused by adequate investigation. If basing is understood as believing that the synchronically justified resulting belief was caused by adequate investigation, then the subject must believe that he did investigate adequately, and that it is (causally) because of that that he now believes what he does to be made probable by his evidence. As also with the basing of synchronic justification, this is perhaps a less natural ordinary-language spelling-out of 'basing', but it may be the kind of substitute for causation that a certain kind of purely internalist theory requires. A believer may well believe that, although his present belief is well justified synchronically, he really ought to have checked it out more thoroughly at an earlier stage. If he does not believe that he has done this (even if, in fact, he has done this, but forgotten), then he must think of himself of having a belief inadequately justified by his own standards.

So—in summary—a belief is diachronically justified if (and only if) it is synchronically justified and it has been based on adequate investigation. A belief has been adequately investigated if it has been investigated by such investigation as would have been worthwhile during any recent earlier period of time. An investigation of a given kind and length is worthwhile if its probable utility is positive. The probable utility of an investigation is ((the probability that it will make a crucial difference to which belief is held or how strongly) multiplied by (the probable importance of a resulting true belief different from the current belief of sufficient strength) minus the probable cost of the investigation). A crucial difference is, in the case of a belief valuable for intrinsic reasons, it is one that affects whether the original belief or its negation is held subsequently; in the case of a belief valuable for a practical reason, it is one that leads to a different action. All of these terms may be understood in the variety of different ways, which I have been analysing in this book. To start with, there are different senses of synchronic justification. Then there are different senses of 'probability', and each of them itself spawns a variety of different interpretations of all the terms used in explication of the definition of diachronic justification. For example, if the probability that particular investigation of a certain kind and length will make a crucial difference is to be taken as the statistical probability that an investigation like this will make a difference, then there are many different ways of understanding 'like this'—that is, many different types of which the token process of investigation can be taken as a token that have different probabilities of making crucial differences. And, if the probability is of some inductive kind, then it is relative to evidence, and again—as we have seen—there are many different ways in which 'evidence' can be understood. 'Basing' too can be understood in two different ways. So, the issue becomes—in which senses of 'diachronic justification' is diachronic justification worth having?

Extrinsic Value of Diachronic Justification

Let us answer that question on the initial assumption that synchronically justified beliefs are valuable only in so far as what they indicate (that the belief is true) is so. Clearly a synchronically justified belief is no better an indication of truth if it has resulted from adequate investigation in some sense than if it has not. The goodness of investigating a belief is the goodness for the subject in an initial situation to take steps towards improving the quality of the belief. So the question in effect is—when is it a good thing to investigate one's beliefs in order to obtain more probably true beliefs? I have claimed that an investigation is good or worthwhile if its probable utility is positive—the probable utility of an investigation being ((the probability that it will make a crucial difference) multiplied by (the probable importance of a resulting true belief different from the current belief of sufficient strength) minus the probable cost of the investigation). But I reached this intuitively appealing result without considering whether it held for all kinds of probability. So let us ask—in which senses of 'probable' is it good to investigate, where it is probable that investigation will make a crucial difference and the cost will probably not be excessive, given the probable value of having a true belief?

On all the possible understandings of statistical probability, it is good to investigate a belief at any time in so far as it is probable at that time that investigation will lead to a more probably true belief, unless it will—for its probable importance—probably cost too much. If, for example, it is statistically probable that investigation of beliefs like this token one (in some specified respect) will lead to a belief that has a greater probability of truth, then it is good to investigate this token belief. This is because the cited statistical probability by itself makes it logically probable that investigating the token belief will lead to a belief with a greater logical probability of truth. But, if it is statistically probable that the cost of gaining new evidence relevant to beliefs of this sort is high, then that makes it logically probable that investigating this token belief will be expensive and so decreases the logical probability that the utility of investigation will be positive. As with synchronic justification, so also with diachronic justification, statistical probabilities are valuable because of what they make logically probable. But statistical probabilities can affect an investigator's conduct only if they become part of his evidence.

Although we could discuss the worth of each of the very large number of other possible kinds of diachronic justification that result according to the different senses we give to 'probability', 'evidence', and so on, it will, I suggest, suffice to consider further only two crucial kinds of internalist diachronic justification, parallel to the two kinds of synchronic justification that we considered in the previous chapter. The results for the other possible kinds of diachronic justification will be evident from the results for these kinds. The first kind is the kind of justification available to the logically omniscient investigator who takes account of his investigation. The best a logically omniscient investigator can do at any time is to investigate for as long as and in such a way as, it is logically probable, given his initial rightly basic beliefs, that the utility of investigation will be positive. He must devote to investigation what he believes to be the correct amount of time (given the logical probability on his evidence that investigation will lead to beliefs with a greater logical probability on his subsequent evidence, the cost of investigation as estimated by him on logically correct standards, and the logically probable importance of a true belief about that matter). Let us call a belief objectively internally diachronically justified if it is objectively internally synchronically justified and is based on (in the sense of both 'caused by' and 'believed to be caused by') investigation that is adequate in the above sense (at each recent earlier time). From the point of view of getting at true beliefs, it is good that the subject should have investigated his beliefs adequately by the correct standards of adequacy, and acquired the belief rendered logically probable as a result of the investigation. That again is because all this makes it logically probable that the utility of investigation will be positive.

But subjects of course do not normally form their beliefs in quite such a rational way. They must make their judgements of whether investigation is worthwhile starting from their actual basic beliefs (including their beliefs about moral importance) and using their own criteria of inductive probability (that is, subjective probability). And so the best a subject can achieve is a synchronically subjectively justified belief based on adequate investigation (at each recent earlier time), adequate by the subject's own criteria of right basicality, probability, and moral importance, and 'based on' it in the sense of 'believed by the subject to be caused by' it. Such a belief I shall call a diachronically subjectively justified belief. A subject's initial views about basicality, probability, and importance may lead him to investigate those views, in so far as he regards them as less than certainly true; and that investigation—for example, of his criteria of probability—may lead to his adopting different criteria from those from which he began. But he will, of course, begin from where he stands.[9]

Whether it is a good thing from the point of view of their getting true beliefs that subjects should have diachronically subjectively justified beliefs depends on how much in error their criteria are. Sometimes doing the best by their own lights will lead subjects further away from the truth. Some subjects might be so prone to misassess evidence of certain kinds that getting more evidence would lead only to greater confidence in false beliefs. Or they might be so inept at working out the consequences of statistical evidence about the costs of investigations that they misassess badly the probability that investigation would be too expensive. I myself am an optimist about these matters. My view is that almost all people will improve the quality of their beliefs by following their own criteria. (This will sometimes involve their 'sorting out' their own criteria, with the consequence that those criteria are more nearly the correct ones.) However, the point remains that subjective diachronic justification is worth having (to the extent to which it does not coincide with an objective internalist one) only in so far as it is logically probable that investigation by the subject's

[9] A person whose beliefs are subjectively diachronically justified is one whom Foley has called 'egocentrically rational'. For his development and advocacy of the importance of egocentric rationality, see Richard Foley, *Working without the Net* (Oxford University Press, 1993), ch. 3.

own criteria will have a positive utility; and whether it is or not depends on how much in error the subject's criteria are—all this so long as the only point of having justified beliefs is to have true beliefs.

Intrinsic Value of Diachronic Justification

I claimed in the previous chapter that a belief being synchronically justified by externalist criteria is not intrinsically valuable—it is valuable only in virtue of the truth of the belief of which having such justification is evidence. The same, I suggest, goes for diachronic externalist justification. There is no intrinsic value in a subject pursuing a course of investigation that as a matter of fact usually leads to better justified beliefs, unless the subject believes that this kind of investigation usually does have this result and is pursuing it for that reason. Maybe there is a high statistical probability that, if you ask a psychic, she will tell you where to find a missing corpse. Suppose a detective investigating a murder does consult a psychic in order to discover the corpse. The only value in his doing so is in the consequence that (in view of the statistical probability) will probably follow. But only in so far as the detective believes or has reason to believe that psychics can tell you where to find a corpse is there any intrinsic merit in his asking the psychic.

I suggested, however, in the previous chapter that we value synchronic objective internalist justification for its own sake (and not merely for the sake of the truth that it will probably yield). It is, I think, more obvious that we value diachronic objective internalist justification for its own sake. We value the scientist who is rational not merely in his response to the evidence he has at a time, but who looks for more evidence for and against his theory, checks his calculations thoroughly, and tries to think of alternative theories—so long as (it is logically probable that) the theory concerns an important enough matter in view of the amount of time and money that the scientist will need to put into his investigation. We value the scientist for spending many nights looking through his telescope, checking his calculations, seeking to get a very well-established theory (whether that is the current theory, or some quite new theory)—especially if the issue is an important one for science. We value him for seeking to get a (logically) highly probable theory. For he has, at any rate at a subconscious level, and sees the ramifications of, some very important beliefs—a priori beliefs about what is evidence for what—and is guided by them. He sees some of the deepest necessities that there are and they influence his conduct.

We value this kind of objective response to the evidence for its own sake; and, I suggest, in the case of diachronic justification we also value for their own sake beliefs that are subjectively justified. We value a person having a belief that is rendered probable by his own criteria by his actual basic beliefs, when it has (in the subject's view) resulted from an adequate investigation—by the subject's own criteria of how important is a true belief in this matter and, given his own criteria of probability, the likely cost of investigation and the probability of it making a difference. We value people who try to get true beliefs, to the extent to which they think it matters. For we value people living up to their own standards (even if they are not the correct ones) in this all-important respect. And it is only in respect of whether they do or do not live up to their own standards that they are a proper subject of moral praise or blame.

Synchronic justification (in all senses) is a matter of how a subject forms beliefs at a given time; and, since the subject cannot help which beliefs she forms, being justified cannot involve being praiseworthy nor can being unjustified involve being blameworthy—on the reasonable view that praise and blame belong to agents only in respect of actions that they choose to do, and not in respect of states in which they cannot help being. Praise and blame may, however, belong to an agent in respect of whether their beliefs are subjectively diachronically justified—that is, in respect of whether they have taken proper steps by their own standards. For, I reasonably suggest, someone is morally praiseworthy only for doing what they believe to be morally good (not for doing what is in fact morally good, if they do not believe it to be). Someone is morally praiseworthy only for investigating an issue to the extent to which they think it matters morally. Likewise, moral blameworthiness belongs only to someone who fails to investigate an issue to the extent to which they think it matters.[10] There is no moral merit in someone spending more time than they think it deserves in investigating an issue that they themselves believe to be a trivial one. But someone whose beliefs are subjectively diachronically justified has done what is morally right; and that is a very good thing, quite apart from whether those beliefs are true.

[10] I have argued elsewhere more precisely that (with exceptions) praise belongs to and only to someone who does more than (they think) duty requires, and blame belongs to and only to someone who fails to do what (they think) duty requires. Someone is not praiseworthy for doing (what they believe to be) their duty, nor blameworthy for failing to do (what they believe to be) supererogatory. See my *Responsibility and Atonement* (Clarendon Press, 1989), ch. 2.

John Locke

The central ideas about the value of synchronic and diachronic internalist justification that I have developed so far in this book, culminating in this chapter, were recognized in a vague way by John Locke. In his recent book *John Locke and the Ethics of Belief*, Nicholas Wolterstorff sees Locke with his development of such themes as the narrow range of what we can really know, the need for probable opinion on most matters, the need to acquire new evidence and test it and not depend on past authority, and the need to guide our belief-forming mechanisms thereby, as articulating 'a prominent component in the mentality of Western modernity'.[11]

I have already cited Locke's view that we cannot help having the belief we do at a given time. Yet he also held that we have an obligation to seek true beliefs, and to seek to hold them with the right level of confidence. To do this we must (if we do not have it already) collect evidence and assess it; and then hold the belief rendered probable by the evidence; and, even if we forget the details of the evidence that we collected, it suffices if we can recall that our present belief was founded on proper investigation:

> It suffices, that [men] have once with care and fairness, sifted the matter as far as they could; and that they have searched into all the particulars, that they could imagine to give any light to the question; and with the best of their skill, cast up the account upon the whole evidence: and thus having once found on which side the probability appeared to them, after as full and exact an enquiry as they can make, they lay up the conclusion in their memories, as a truth they have discovered.[12]

Locke recognized that the obligation on each of us to investigate concerns only matters of 'concernment'—that is, fundamental moral and religious matters and certain 'practical matters' (presumably what I have called contingent moral matters) that concern the particular individual. For some of these, and in particular the religious matters, according to Locke, all of us have time:

> Besides his particular calling for the support of this life, everyone has a concern in a future life, which he is bound to look after. This engages his thoughts in religion; and here it mightily lies upon him to understand and reason right. Men, therefore, cannot be excused from understanding the words, and framing the general

[11] Nicholas Wolterstorff, *John Locke and the Ethics of Belief* (Cambridge University Press, 1996), 226. I am indebted to Wolterstorff for all the references to Locke, and the discussion thereof.

[12] John Locke, *An Essay Concerning Human Understanding*, 4.16.1.

notions relating to religion, right. The one day of seven, besides other days of rest, allows in the Christian world time enough for this (had they no other idle hours) if they would but make use of these vacancies from their daily labour, and apply themselves to an improvement of knowledge with as much diligence as they often do to a great many other things that are useless.[13]

Yet we can be held to account only for acting or not acting in accord with our own conscience (in my terminology, for our diachronically subjectively justified beliefs):

It is impossible for you, or me, or any man, to know, whether another has done his duty in examining the evidence on both sides, when he embraces that side of the question, which we, perhaps upon other views, judge false: and therefore we can have no right to punish or persecute him for it. In this, whether and how far any one is faulty, must be left to the Searcher of hearts, the great and righteous Judge of all men, who knows all their circumstances, all the powers and workings of their minds; where it is they sincerely follow, and by what default they at any time miss truth: and He, we are sure, will judge uprightly.[14]

Of course Locke missed a lot. He thought that our evidence must consist of things we know, and he was not sensitive to the fallibility of knowledge and its corrigibility in the light of well-established (that is, very probable) world views, nor did he have much of a doctrine of probability. But his general approach was, I suggest, the correct one.

Virtue Epistemology

In her book *Virtues of the Mind* Linda Zagzebski has urged that terms of epistemic appraisal—calling a belief 'justified' or saying that it amounts to 'knowledge'—apply to beliefs in so far as they result from the exercise of intellectual virtue. She has sought to develop a 'virtue epistemology' paralleling the 'virtue ethics' that various recent writers have sought to develop. The basic idea of the latter, deriving from Aristotle, is that human acts are good in so far as they constitute the exercise of a virtue.[15] Virtues are dispositions to act in certain ways for certain reasons. An act of feeding a hungry person because he is hungry is good, according to virtue ethics, because it is an act of a kind that a person having the virtue of benevolence would

[13] John Locke, *Conduct of the Understanding*, §8.

[14] John Locke, *Third Letter Concerning Toleration.*

[15] For a full-length recent defence of virtue ethics, taking account of all the recent writings in this tradition, see Rosalind Hursthouse, *On Virtue Ethics* (Oxford University Press, 1999).

do. My natural reaction to virtue ethics is that it gets things the wrong way round. An act of feeding a hungry person because he is hungry is a good act, for the reason that the person is hungry—not because it is the exercise of the virtue of benevolence. Acts are good either intrinsically or because they consist in bringing about good states of affairs for the right reason. Dispositions constitute virtues just because they are dispositions to do acts of a certain good kind for the right reason. So, of course, if an act is good, it will be an act that a person with the disposition to do acts of that good kind for the right reason will do. But that is not *why* it is good.[16] It is good *because* it is intrinsically good or because it consists in bringing about a good state of affairs for the right reason. That is not to deny that a disposition to do good acts of a certain kind is a good thing to have—both because it is likely to lead to further good acts in future, and because it is an intrinsic good—it is good to be benevolently inclined, even if you never have the opportunity to exercise that benevolence.

Her virtue epistemology leads Zagzebski to the following definition of a justified belief: 'A justified belief is what a person who is motivated by intellectual virtue, and who has the understanding of his cognitive situation a virtuous person would have, might believe in like circumstances.'[17] She mentions as among the intellectual virtues: 'fairness in the evaluation of evidence, thoroughness, reliance on the most knowledgeable members of the community', 'intellectual courage, carefulness, autonomy, perseverance, humility', 'boldness, creativity, inventiveness, insight'.[18] She sees these as virtues because of their truth-conduciveness; and she sees them as bound together by the virtue of *phronesis* (judgement), which is a disposition to balance them against each other (for example, it guides us when to rely on the authority of others, and when to exercise 'autonomy'), and to balance them against the moral virtues in the right way.

[16] We can see that from the fact that humans might have no settled dispositions to do good acts of a certain kind, and so no concept of such a disposition. It could be that each time any human had an opportunity to feed the hungry or meet similar human needs, they had an agonizing choice of whether or not to do so, and how they would act could not be predicted; the past performance of such acts would not make future performance any more likely. (Fortunately, humans are not made like that. Doing a good act of some kind one day makes it easier to do it the next day. But they could have been made like that in some respect.) In such a case, humans could still recognize that it would be good to feed the hungry, without their having any concept of doing so being the manifestation of a disposition of benevolence.

[17] Linda Trinkaus Zagzebski, *Virtues of the Mind* (Cambridge University Press, 1996), 241.

[18] See her pp. 223, 220, and 225 for these lists.

The first point to make about virtue epistemology parallels that which I have just made about virtue ethics. A certain belief being at a time or over time justified is not justified because it exhibits a virtue. It is justified because the evidence supports it, or it has been adequately investigated; but, if (for example) the evidence supports it, then it would be the belief that someone who is disposed to believe what the evidence supports would believe.

However, Zagzebski is surely correct that we do think that the characteristics that she lists are ones that it is good that people should exercise because they are truth conducive. But it is important to distinguish those that do so by contributing to synchronic justification (for example, 'fairness in the evaluation of evidence'—making the objectively correct response to the existing evidence) from those that contribute to diachronic justification (for example, 'perseverance'). It is important to distinguish 'truth conduciveness' of an externalist kind, from truth conduciveness of an objective internalist kind. For some of these virtues are only contingently truth conducive (and hence exercising them is a virtue because they reliably lead to truth). One such virtue is 'intellectual courage'. There are worlds in which unfashionable beliefs will always turn out false (for example, worlds in which science has achieved as much as it can); although in our world much progress is made by people who show intellectual courage. Some virtues are necessarily truth productive. A virtue would not be a virtue of 'insight' unless it reveals how things really are. (The problem, of course, is to know whether someone has exhibited insight, and that is to be shown by the criteria I have discovered.) Other virtues are necessarily truth conducive (though not guaranteed to attain truth)—for example, again 'fairness in assessing evidence'. Only if you assess evidence in the right way will you get a belief that is probably true—by objective logical criteria.[19]

Justification: Overall Conclusion

My conclusion about justification is that the many different internalist and externalist theories of justification are not rival theories of the same con-

[19] Virtue epistemology as a theory of knowledge, but not of justification, was introduced into recent epistemology by Ernest Sosa. He sees knowledge as true belief resulting from the exercise of intellectual virtue. He spells out having an intellectual virtue in terms of having a reliable tendency to produce a true belief from a source of a certain kind, of which the subject is aware. See his *Knowledge in Perspective* (Cambridge University Press, 1991), *passim*; and especially his final summary on pp. 290–3. Plantinga's 'proper functionalist' account of knowledge is in effect a virtue theory, which I discuss in Chapter 8.

cept, but accounts of different concepts; and the externalist concepts can be applied in different ways according to the type to which we refer the token process of belief production. It is important to distinguish a belief being synchronically justified—that is, constituting the right response by way of belief to the situation in which the believer finds herself at a given time, from a belief being diachronically justified—that is, being both synchronically justified and based on adequate investigation. Internalist theories of both synchronic and diachronic justification may be either subjective (the justification is in terms of the believer's own criteria) or objective (the justification is in terms of correct a priori criteria). At any one time people cannot help having the beliefs they do, but they can get beliefs better justified (internally) synchronically as a result of investigation. At any one time people can use only their own criteria (the ones that seem right to them), but over time they can improve their criteria, so that their later beliefs are not merely better justified subjectively but also better justified (internally) objectively. While a belief being justified in most senses (internalist and externalist) is a good thing to have, because it is probable by correct criteria that such a belief is true, it is only in so far as externalist justification becomes internally accessible that people can be guided by it and consciously seek to improve their beliefs and achieve their goals in the light of it.

8

Knowledge

Knowledge (of propositions) is supposed to be something of the same kind as, but superior to, mere (synchronically) justified belief. I argued in the Introduction that knowledge involves true belief—knowing that William the Conqueror invaded Britain in 1066 involves believing that he did, and that belief being true. And plausibly the belief has to be a strong one. If on the whole you believe that William invaded in 1066, but have considerable doubt about it, it is doubtful whether you can be said to know this. Conviction is needed for knowledge. But clearly something else is needed if a (strong) true belief is to amount to knowledge; and for this something else (as explained in the Introduction, n.2) I am using the technical name of 'warrant'. Knowledge is warranted true (strong) belief.

Philosophers have given many different accounts of warrant that—on the assumption that knowledge is a clear concept—they have represented as alternative accounts, at most one of which can be the true account of warrant. But I suggest that knowledge and so warrant are not clear concepts. The situation rather is that, as with the case of justification, the philosopher is faced with a vast number of actual and possible cases where we all say that someone knows something, and a vast number of actual and possible cases where we all say that someone believes (strongly) some true proposition, although he does not know it. The philosopher seeks a general formula for warrant that will yield the answer that we all give in these agreed cases for whether or not someone knows something. There are, however, many different formulae that will yield the answers we all give for these cases, but disagree in their verdicts about the answers to other possible cases about which we differ in our intuitive judgements. Although there is this range of disputed cases (examples of which will be provided in this chapter), it is a much smaller range than the range of disputed cases of whether a belief is 'justified'; and I shall seek to explain why this is so—why the different formulae so often yield the same result as to whether some true belief amounts to 'knowledge'. The accounts available divide naturally into largely internalist ones, and totally externalist ones. In the former, the primary component of warrant is (strong) justification in a (synchronic) objective internalist sense.

Largely Internalist Theories

The account of warrant fashionable in the 1950s simply equated it with such strong internalist justification. A belief being warranted was its being rendered logically (very) probable by the subject's basic beliefs; and, either implicitly or explicitly, there was usually the requirement that the resulting belief should be 'based' on the basic beliefs. Since those early theories hardly considered some of these matters in any detail, let us tighten them up a bit, by understanding the 'basing' in the sense defined for objective internalist justification on p. 158 and insist that the basic beliefs be rightly basic beliefs. These details are plausible fillings out of any largely internalist account of knowledge, and are not relevant to the subsequent criticisms of it. Hence I will assume them throughout this section.

To such an account the Gettier counter-examples proved fatal.[1] The paradigm counter-examples concern cases where *S* believes *h* because he infers it (explicitly) from another proposition *q*. *S* is justified in believing *q* for some reason (for example, *q* may be a rightly basic belief), *q* makes *h* logically probable (it may even entail it), and so *S* is justified in believing *h*; *h* is true. And so *S* has a justified true belief that *h*. But if *q* is false, the claim goes, surely *S* does not know that *h*. Examples bring this out. S, let us suppose, is justified in believing that Jones owns a Ford (*q*) (he has at all times kept a Ford in his garage, and so on). This entails (*h*) 'either Jones owns a Ford or Brown is in Barcelona'. *S* believes *h*, although he has no justification for believing that Brown is in Barcelona, and does not in fact believe that. But, suppose that Jones does not own a Ford, but Brown is in Barcelona. In that case *S*'s justified belief that *h* is true—but he cannot be said to know *h* under these circumstances. And this is because it is a matter of luck that his inferential procedures yield a true belief.

We can deal with paradigm Gettier examples by adding another clause to the definition of knowledge that rules out any true proposition *h* based on a false proposition *q* via an explicit inference (deductive or inductive). But there is a wider class of Gettier counter-examples where *S* believes *h* in a way that 'depends on' a false proposition *q*—where there is no explicit inference, but where *S* would not be justified in believing *h* if he did not

[1] Edmund L. Gettier, 'Is Justified True Belief Knowledge?', *Analysis*, 23 (1963), 121–3.

believe q. There are, to start with, the cases where the inference is not explicit, but *S*'s belief that h is still based on his belief that q. Take this example of Chisholm:

A person *takes* there to be a sheep in the field and does so under conditions which are such that, when under those conditions a person takes there to be a sheep in the field, then it is *evident* for that person that there is a sheep in the field. The person, however, has mistaken a dog for a sheep and so what he sees is not a sheep at all. Nevertheless it happens that there is a sheep in another part of the field. Hence, the proposition that there is a sheep in the field will be one that is both true and evident and it will also be one that the person accepts. But the situation does not warrant our saying that the person *knows* that there is a sheep in the field.[2]

Here the person's belief that 'there is a sheep in the field' (true) is still based on his belief that 'this' (in front of him) 'is a sheep' (false), even though there is no explicit inference from the latter to the former.

Further away still from paradigm Gettier cases are ones where the true belief is not based on any actual false belief, but rather there is some false proposition q that the subject believes, and which is such that, if he were apprised of its falsity, he would not justifiably believe h. We may construe Goldman's barn example as of this type. Henry is driving through the countryside and sees what looks to him like a barn and indeed is a barn. So he has a justified true belief that he sees a barn. However:

unknown to Henry, the district he has entered is full of papier-mâché facsimiles of barns. These facsimiles look from the road exactly like barns, but are really just façades, without back walls or interiors, quite incapable of being used as barns. Having just entered the district, Henry has not encountered any facsimiles; the object he sees is a genuine barn. But if the object on that site were a facsimile, Henry would mistake it for a barn.[3]

Let us construe this example, so that Henry actually has the false belief q, 'most barn-looking objects in this district are barns' (as opposed to merely not having the true belief t, 'most barn-looking objects in this district are not barns'). In that case it is plausible to suppose that Henry does not know that he sees a barn. But we need not suppose that his belief that q plays any causal role in sustaining his belief that he sees a barn. He would believe that he sees a barn whether or not he had even thought about what proportion of barn-looking objects are barns. Rather q plays no role unless Henry is apprised of its falsity.

[2] Roderick M. Chisholm, *Theory of Knowledge* (3rd edn., Prentice Hall, 1989), 93.

[3] Alvin I. Goldman, 'Discrimination and Perceptual Knowledge', *Journal of Philosophy*, 73 (1976), 771–91; see pp. 772–3.

In all these cases it is the involvement (in some way) of a false proposition *q* (believed to be true) in the justification of the true belief that makes the subject having a true belief on the subject a matter of luck. A solution of the type proposed by Lehrer[4] can deal with all these cases. The basic idea is that, for *S* to know that *p* we need, as well as 'personal justification' (that is, justification in our objective internalist sense), also what Lehrer calls 'complete justification'. Call the system of *S*'s beliefs *X*. You are allowed to eliminate any false belief from *X*, and (if you wish) replace it by its negation. If *S* would still be justified in believing *p*, whatever such changes you make, then *S* is completely justified in believing *p*. Such belief amounts to knowledge. In the first example, therefore, you are allowed to eliminate the false proposition 'Jones owns a Ford'. If you do, there is no justification for believing 'either Jones owns a Ford or Brown is in Barcelona'. In the barn example, you are allowed to eliminate 'most barn-looking objects in this district are barns' and replace it by its negation. Henry will then believe 'most barn-looking objects in this district are not barns', and so be left with no justification for believing that he sees a barn. So in neither of these cases does the critical true belief amount to knowledge.

The trickiest cases are those where the subject does not have any actual false beliefs (involved in the justification of his true belief), but there is a true proposition *t* (which is such that he believes neither it nor its negation) such that, were he to come to believe it, he would no longer justifiably believe the such true proposition *h*. The problem is to distinguish those true propositions that have this debilitating effect from those that do not. Compare two cases much discussed in the literature.

Suppose I see a man walk into the library and remove a book from the library by concealing it beneath his coat. Since I am sure the man is Tom Grabit, whom I have often seen before when he attended my classes, I report that I know that Tom Grabit has removed the book. However, suppose further that Mrs Grabit, the mother of Tom, has averred that on the day in question Tom was not in the library, indeed was thousands of miles away, and that Tom's identical twin brother, John Grabit, was in the library. Imagine, moreover, that I am entirely ignorant of the fact that Mrs Grabit has said these things. The statement that she has said these things would defeat any justification I have for believing that Tom Grabit removed the book, according to our present definition of defeasibility . . . The preceding might seem acceptable until we finish the story by adding that Mrs Grabit is a compulsive and pathological liar, that John Grabit is a fiction of her demented mind,

[4] Keith Lehrer, *Theory of Knowledge* (Routledge, 1990), ch. 7.

and Tom Grabit took the book as I believed. Once this is added, it should be apparent that I did know that Tom Grabit removed the book.[5]

And:

A political leader is assassinated. His associates, fearing a coup, decide to pretend that the bullet hit someone else. On nation-wide television they announce that an assassination attempt has failed to kill the leader but has killed a secret service man by mistake. However, before the announcement is made, an enterprising reporter on the scene telephones the real story to his newspaper, which has included the story in its final edition. Jill buys a copy of that paper and reads the story of the assassination. What she reads is true and so are her assumptions about how the story came to be in the paper. The reporter, whose by-line appears, saw the assassination and dictated his report, which is now printed just as he dictated it. Jill has justified true belief and, it would seem, all her intermediate conclusions are true. But she does not know that the political leader has been assassinated. For everyone else has heard about the televised announcement. They may also have seen the story in the paper and, perhaps, do not know what to believe; and it is highly implausible that Jill should know simply because she lacks evidence everyone else has. Jill does not know. Her knowledge is undermined by evidence she does not possess.[6]

The common wisdom among philosophers (as illustrated by the comments of the inventors of the stories) is that the first example is a case of knowledge (Mrs Grabit's announcement does not debar knowledge), whereas the second is not. (Jill's knowledge is undermined by the evidence she does not possess). In both cases, however, there is a true proposition *t* that, if the subject ('I', 'Jill') were to come to believe it, she would no longer believe the true proposition that she does believe *h* ('Tom Grabit took the book'; 'the leader is assassinated'). *t* is that Mrs Grabit said what she did; and that the TV anounced what it did.

Wherein lies the difference? I concur with Pollock[7] that the difference lies in what 'we are socially expected to be aware of'. 'We are expected to know what is announced on television', but not perhaps what Mrs Grabit said to one acquaintance (if in fact she is a compulsive liar).[8] Hence, if *S*'s

[5] Keith Lehrer and Thomas Paxson, 'Knowledge: Undefeated Justified True Belief', *Journal of Philosophy*, 66 (1966), 225–37; see p. 228.

[6] Gilbert Harman, *Thought* (Princeton University Press, 1973), 143–4.

[7] John L. Pollock, *Contemporary Theories of Knowledge* (Hutchinson 1987), 192.

[8] Lehrer (using a Grabit case, altered from the original in an irrelevant respect that I ignore) finds the difference in another place. He claims that Jill's belief in the assassination case depends on an actual false belief of hers that others 'accept the story' in the newspaper, whereas the belief about Tom Grabit does not depend on an actual belief about what his mother did or did not say. The former seems unnecessary—Jill need not have had an actual

justified true belief that *p* would not be justified if *S* had the justified true belief that *r*, which she is socially expected to believe, then *S* does not know that *p*. (I have replaced Pollock's phrase 'expected to know', question-begging in this context, by 'expected to believe'.) But, of course, such expectations vary with the society, and give rise to large border areas with respect to which experts may well differ about what is socially expected or about which they agree that expectations are diverse.[9] There may well be societies in which everyone consults a suspect's mother before reaching judgements about guilt. And how 'nationwide' would the television coverage need to be, in order to undermine Jill's claim to knowledge?[10]

Many philosophers who have written about knowledge have done so in the contexts of discussions of global-type scepticism—scepticism about whether there is an external world of public objects (perhaps we are just solitary minds) or whether there was a world more than five minutes ago. A few of these have defended a position called contextualism, that what counts as 'knowledge' varies with the context of discourse, and that it might be true to say in the context of such a discussion 'I do not know that there is a desk in front of me', even though it would not be true to say that in more ordinary contexts (when, we would ordinarily say, 'it is obvious that there is a desk in front of me').[11] One writer who has claimed this

belief that others accept the story, though she would have believed this if it was put to her. And, more importantly, if we expand the Grabit example, so that quite a number of otherwise reliable people say what Mrs Grabit said (although the believer is ignorant of this), we would be inclined to say that 'I' did not know that Tom Grabit had stolen the book.

[9] Peter D. Klein ('Misleading Evidence and the Restoration of Justification', *Philosophical Studies*, 37 (1980), 81–9) seeks to make the distinction between those non-believed true propositions that undermine knowledge and those that do not in a more objective way. He holds that *S*'s justified true belief that *p* amounts to knowledge if (and only if) all the defeaters of *S*'s justification are misleading ones. A defeater is a proposition *q* that, if added to *S*'s evidence, would render his belief that *p* no longer justified. *q* is a misleading defeater, if *q* being added to *S*'s evidence has the effect that *S* no longer justifiably believes that *p* in consequence of *q* making 'plausible' a false proposition. ('Plausible' is presumably to be interpreted in my terminology as meaning something like 'fairly probable'.) But this does not make the required distinction between the Grabit case and the assassination case. In both cases someone (Mrs Grabit, the television announcer) says something that makes plausible a false proposition ('Tom was thousands of miles away and has an identical twin who was in the library', 'the assassination attempt failed').

[10] Roderick Chisholm has attempted to deal with Gettier examples within a fundamentally 'justified true belief' account of knowledge without allowing that justified true belief can fail to amount to knowledge in virtue of some true proposition that the subject does not believe. I discuss other difficulties in Chisholm's account in Additional Note P.

[11] I call contextualism the position that holds that, while sentences of the form 'I know that *p*' have a truth value (that is, are true or false), what that truth value is depends on the context of utterance. I distinguish this position from the position that holds that sometimes, or perhaps always, such sentences are simply ways of affirming *p* more

recently is David Lewis.[12] He claims that '*S* knows that *p*' is true if (and only if) *p* holds 'in every possibility left uneliminated by *S*'s evidence'—except those properly ignored; and there then follows a list of kinds of possibility properly ignored. He then claims that one of the factors that determines which possibilities are properly ignored is the context of utterance, which delimits the kind of possibilities open for consideration. Hence wildly sceptical possibilities are properly ignored in everyday contexts but not in discussions of epistemology. ' "I know that I have hands" [spoken, it is assumed, by a typical two-handed person] is true in an everyday context, where the possibility of deceiving demons was properly ignored', but not—he implies—in the context of a discussion of epistemology. But—given that there are no deceiving demons (and that not many people say that there are)—'I know that I have hands' is surely true in all contexts; certainly on an account of knowledge as involving justified true belief (in any internalist sense), it is a strongly justified strong true belief, the justification for which does not depend in any way on any false belief. (Any account of justification that held that the cited proposition was not justified in any of the internalist senses of 'justified' as 'probably true' that I have considered would have something wrong with it—for example, it might be assuming that a belief being justified always involves it being justified by something else. (Lewis seems to assume this—see his p. 551.) For obviously it is virtually certain that I have hands.) The fact that the issue of whether 'I know I have hands' is being discussed by epistemologists should not affect its truth criteria in any way. For what epistemologists are considering when they consider whether 'I know that I have hands' is true is whether, when a typical person says that in a normal context (that is, a context other than that of epistemological discussion), what he says is true.[13]

vigorously. They are performative utterances. 'I know that *p*', like 'I swear that *p*', gives the hearer the right to rely on the speaker in respect of *p*; it does not say that the speaker has a particular kind of mental access to *p*. J. L. Austin advocates this latter position as the correct account of many utterances of 'I know' in his 'Other Minds' (republished in his *Philosophical Papers* (2nd edn., Oxford University Press, 1970)). I do not think that this account of knowledge can be generally correct even for first-person uses ('I know that *p*'), let alone for other uses ('He knows that *p*'). In most cases there is a further factual issue beyond whether *p* is true, whether a certain person knows that it is true; and the various theories discussed in this chapter seek to give an account of the criteria for this.

[12] David Lewis, 'Elusive Knowledge', *Australasian Journal of Philosophy*, 74 (1996), 549–67; see pp. 551, 564.

[13] For another defence of contextualism, see Stewart Cohen, 'Contextualism, Scepticism, and the Structure of Reasons', in James E. Tomberlin (ed.), *Philosophical Perspectives 3* (Blackwell Publishers, 1999). See also the articles in the same volume, by Feldman, Heller, Lehrer, Sosa, and Vogel discussing contextualism

The only way in which (on a largely internalist account of knowledge) context could come in is if there was a true proposition of which the subject was ignorant that is such that, if he believed it, it would make his beliefs about his hands unjustified. Such a proposition might be that there are deceiving demons often at work making it seem that ordinary things are very different from the way these really are (or even the proposition that many people say that there are such deceiving demons at work). There could be contexts in which we were in a position to discover this, and it was 'socially expected' that we should; and other contexts where that was not so. In that case, in the former type of context, even if the belief that 'I have hands' was true (that is, deceiving demons did not produce this belief), strongly held, and strongly justified, it would not amount to knowledge because it would be held only with justification through ignorance that deceiving demons are often at work (or that many people say that they are). But I cannot see that the mere fact of the context being one of epistemological discussion puts the belief that I have hands in the category of one for which we ought to take seriously the possibility of deceiving demons. The proposition that there are such demons would need to be true, or many people would need to say that it is, before ignorance of such facts by some members of the society could defeat a claim to knowledge. Although Lewis does not endorse (or reject) the view that a belief being justified is necessary for it being knowledge, I suggest that, if any of the normal externalist accounts of knowledge are adopted, it will again turn out that context will also affect what counts as knowledge only by affecting which true propositions of which the believer is unaware are ones of which he is expected to be aware.

All the theories of knowledge discussed so far (apart from that of Lewis, which was discussed to illustrate a different point) are largely internalist theories, in that they have as a component a largely internalist notion of 'justification'—that is, of a belief having 'adequate' grounds. The belief has to be true; and the justification must not proceed through a false proposition or depend on ignorance of a true one that one is socially expected to believe. These latter are externalist elements (being matters of whether certain propositions—normally about matters outside the subject—are true or false, or ones that others expect one to believe). The extra elements that turn a strongly justified strong true belief into knowledge all make for the justified belief being true not being a matter of 'luck' or 'accident'. If with justification you infer some belief that *p* from a justifiably believed false belief, then it will be a matter of luck if your belief turns out to be true. Or, if your holding the belief that *p* with justification depends on your being ignorant of something others expect you to believe, then again you are lucky if your belief turns out to be true. *S*'s true belief having warrant, and so amounting to knowledge, involves *S* not merely being now justified in holding it, but that *S* would still be justified in holding it if his other relevant beliefs were true and he had also all the relevant true socially expected beliefs. Under these circumstances, *S*'s belief being true would not be a matter of luck.

Reliabilist Theories

Externalist theories do not use an internalist notion of justification, but they too require that one's true belief shall not be a matter of 'luck'. They differ, however, from internalism and (according to how they are spelled out) from each other as to the kind of luck it is not a matter of. Most externalist theories of knowledge are reliabilist theories. On such a theory, a belief has warrant if (and only if) it is based on adequate grounds. 'Being based on' is normally understood as 'being caused by'. The grounds need not be accessible. They are adequate if they cause the belief by a token process that reliably (and perhaps with a higher degree of reliability than is required for justification) produces true beliefs. Like reliabilist theories of justification, reliabilist theories of knowledge differ from each other in respect of how general (in depth and width) is the type to which the token belief-forming process is seen as belonging, and whether its reliability is measured by the proportion of true beliefs it produces in the actual world or in some class of possible worlds. (On these distinctions, see Chapter 1).

Nozick's 'truth-tracking' theory,[14] expressed in terms of counterfactual conditions (conditionals 'if *p*, then *q*', in which it is implied that the antecedent, *p*, is false), is expressible as a reliabilist theory in which it is required that two separate processes in close possible worlds should both be reliable. For Nozick the warrant of a belief depends on whether the token causal process that produces it is 'tracking the truth' on the particular occasion of its production. The 'luck' that is ruled out if we are to have knowledge will then be the token causal process that produced the belief not being a truth-tracking one, but nevertheless producing on that occasion a true belief. On this theory, *S* knows that *p* if (and only if) (1) *p* is true, (2) *S* believes that *p*, and:

(3) if *p* were false, *S* would not believe that *p*,

[14] Robert Nozick, *Philosophical Explanations* (Clarendon Press, 1981), ch. 3.

(4) if *p* were true, *S* would believe that *p*.

For those who find talk of closeness of possible worlds helpful, these latter are to be read as (3) 'In the closest worlds to the actual world in which *p* is false, *S* does not believe *p*', and (4) 'In close worlds to the actual world in which *p* is true, *S* believes *p*'. This basic account is then complicated in various ways to deal with cases where there is more than one method by which *S* does or might acquire a belief that *p*; and to deal with cases where the belief concerns what is either a necessary truth or a necessary falsehood, and cases where the belief is acquired by probabilistic inference. But what the basic account amounts to depends on what else has to be the case 'if *p* were false', and 'if *p* were true'; or, in possible-worlds terms—which worlds are the 'close worlds' referred to. I think that both (3) and (4) assume that the same laws of nature hold as in our world. In that case, what (3) amounts to might initially seem clear enough. We alter *p* to not-*p*, and then make all the changes that this would cause in accord with our laws of nature. If, in consequence, *S* no longer believes that *p*, then (3) is true; otherwise it is false. But what will be the effect on *S*'s belief of altering *p* to not-*p* will depend on whether any other changes are allowed. If we suppose that none are allowed, the token process will belong to a very narrow type 'production of any belief about *p* at the time in question in worlds identical to the actual world except for not-*p* and any effects thereof'. Since nature is virtually deterministic, it would seem that this process would normally be either nearly 100 per cent reliable or nearly 0 per cent reliable. None of the ambiguities that we detected in Chapter 1 in connection with reliabilist theories of justification would seem to arise.

However, they clearly do arise in conection with (4). For (4) to be true, it is not merely required that both *p* and '*S* believes that *p*' (for that is ensured anyway by conditions (1) and (2)), but that that would (normally) continue to hold 'in the "close" worlds where *p* is true'[15]—that is, if you allow conditions to vary in the proportions in which they do in the actual world within a narrow spatio-temporal region. But whether (4) is true or not will depend on just how narrow (and in what way) that is. Suppose that, if *p* is true and *S* had taken LSD, he would not believe that *p*; but on the occasion in question he did not take LSD. Suppose, however, that on most days of that year, *S* did take LSD. Suppose, too, that until that year *S* has not taken LSD, nor is taking LSD common in *S*'s city over recent years. If you take a very narrow spatio-temporal region (the very close worlds varying from the actual world only in the respect that *S* takes LSD

[15] Ibid. 176.

on this occasion in the same proportion of them as he did on days of the past year) and consider the consequences of *p*'s being true in it, *S* would not believe it—(4) is false. But if you take a bit wider region (the close worlds varying from the actual world only in the respect that *S* takes LSD on this occasion in the same proportion of them as people did in his city on days of recent years), (4) is true. Put in terms of reliability of processes, what (4) requires is that the very narrow type 'production of any belief about *p* in *S* at the time in question in close possible worlds where *p*' should be reliable—normally, when *p*, *S* believes that *p*; and everything can turn on how close that is. Further, how deep is the type supposed to be—within how long a period of time before the production of the belief are conditions allowed to vary in the way they do vary in the actual world?

How deep we take the process of production to be can causally affect the truth of the initially unambiguous (3). For suppose that *p* describes a state of affairs that has no causal role in producing the belief that *p*; but that both *p* and *S*'s belief that *p* have a common cause: *p* may be that *R* will go to London, and the common cause of *p* and *S*'s belief that *p* may be *R* telling *S* that he plans to go to London. In that case, if we follow our recipe for interpreting (3)—alter *p* to not-*p* and make only the changes this would cause in accord with our laws of nature—(3) would automatically become false; since *p* has no causal influence on whether *S* believes *p*. That does not seem a natural way to interpret (3), but, if we do so interpret (3), (3) will never be satisfied and so no one will ever have warrant for beliefs of this kind.

The obvious way to interpret (3) to take account of beliefs of this kind is to change *p* to not-*p*, and then, allowing conditions to vary in the proportion in which they do in the actual world (in some relevant narrow spatio-temporal region), consider what, under most conditions in which not-*p* was caused at the later time, would have to have been the case at an earlier time. If this earlier time includes the time at which *R* told *S* that he plans to go to London, then, if *R* is normally a reliable informant, in most conditions he would not have told *S* that he planned to go to London unless subsequently he went to London. So, for most conditions, if we delete *R* going to London, we must delete *R* having told *S* that he planned to go to London, and, if the laws of nature are such that *S* normally believes what he is told, that involves deleting *S* believing that *R* will go to London. For nothing will have occurred to cause *S* to believe that *R* will go to London and (3) will remain true. But, if we do not trace the process of belief-production back as far as any common cause, changing *R*-going-to-London to *R*-not-going-to-London and amending the causal sequence for a certain distance backwards will make no difference to *S*'s belief and so (3) will be false. Put in terms of reliability of processes—what is required for the truth value of (3) is the reliability, not of the type suggested on p. 201, but of the type 'production of any belief about *p* at the time in question by a process of considerable length in close possible worlds in which *p* is false' (just how considerable a length, being unclear). As before, 'close possible worlds' are ones in which conditions vary in the proportions in which they do within a narrow region of space and time surrounding the actual process of belief-production (just how narrow, being unclear).

So, in effect, for the satisfaction of his two conditions (3) and (4) Nozick requires that two separate very narrow type processes of belief-production be reliable. The process types are very narrow, for they are both types of process that produce a particular belief (that-*p*) at a particular time in a particular person; and very little is allowed to vary from the actual process by which the actual belief that *p* is produced. Even so, we have noted, all the ambiguities of a reliabilist account of justification described in Chapter 1 re-emerge in this account of warrant. It may also seem that too specific a type will not yield an account of warrant that will fit too well with our ordinary concept of knowledge. Suppose that normally I am virtually blind, but that, over a small range of typical variations of the lighting, positions of objects in the room, and so on, if there is a desk in front of me, I have a true belief that there is a desk in front of me; and, if there is no desk in front of me, I do not have such a belief; yet this connection between how things are and my beliefs about them does not hold for anything else except the desk. For my belief about the desk to be warranted and so constitute knowledge, it might seem that we need the connection between how things are and my beliefs about them to hold for a wider range of beliefs. The requirement for knowledge that the belief being true should not be a matter of luck suggests that connections that are so nearly 'one off' are lucky connections. But intuitions about this may differ. Suppose I cannot normally make out words on a page two feet away without glasses. One day, because of some unusual and quite unpredictable event in my optic nerve, for ten seconds my eyes work very well. Looking at a page, I suddenly acquire the true belief that the page says such-and-such. Some speakers might call this a lucky case of knowledge, rather than a lucky case of true belief that did not amount to knowledge.

Still, it is doubt about the knowledge status of beliefs produced by such (nearly) one-off causal processes that moves some writers in the direction of a more general (because wider) form of reliabilism. On a more general form of reliabilism, there is no need to require the reliability of two separate types of process of belief production. This is because we do not specify the particular belief produced (that *p*), and require that most beliefs concerned with a certain subject matter (including the belief that *p*, or the belief that not-*p*) produced by a certain type of process be true, for the process to be reliable. These more general theories normally come with various qualifications about the absence of defeaters, to the effect that the subject must not have another belief that results from an equally reliable process that in some way counts against *p*.[16] These qualifications, like the similar ones in Nozick's theory, are important; but for present purposes we can ignore them. So, in essence, my true belief *B* that there is a desk in front of me amounts to knowledge if it is produced by some process of visual perception of a general type that yields true beliefs most of the time. But once again, with more general as with narrow forms of theories of knowledge, and as with reliabilist theories of justification, there arises the problem of the reference class. My belief *B* was produced by a particular token process on a particular occasion. But the token is a token of many different types (some deeper and some wider than others)—visual perception, visual perception by me, apparent visual perception in a dark room, and so on. Some type processes to which the token belongs are reliable and some not. As with the similar problem for theories of justification, it remains the case that there are many different types, no one of which is the obviously relevant one, even if we confine the types to those picked out by factors involved in the process of belief-production—that is, factors that affect which belief is produced; for example, the type 'apparent visual perception in a dark room' and not the type 'visual perception on a Thursday'. And, for each of these types, there is the issue of whether its reliability is to be assessed by reliability in the actual world, close possible worlds, 'normal' worlds, or what.

However, on a more general form of reliabilism in so far as there seems to be a natural type to which to refer the token process, the belief's being true not being a matter of luck is a matter of its not being a one-off connection, but being a connection typical of the general type. But even some

[16] Pure general reliabilist theories of knowledge are hard to find. Perhaps the purest is that of David Armstrong, *Belief Truth and Knowledge* (Cambridge University Press, 1973). Most general reliabilist theories tend to come with various qualifications and amplifications, not merely of a reliabilist kind as indicated in the text, but of a non-reliabilist kind as well. But the most fully developed example of a theory that includes a very general form of reliabilism is Alvin I. Goldman, *Epistemology and Cognition* (Harvard University Press, 1986). The account in his chapter 3 requires both a local counterfactual condition (like Nozick's theory) and that the belief is produced by a very general reliable process, if a belief is to be warranted (in our terminology).

more general types seem so untypical of processes of belief-formation in humans as not to be general enough. For example:

> Suppose (contrary to what most of us believe) the *National Enquirer* is in fact extremely reliable in its accounts of extraterrestrial events. One day it carries screaming headlines: STATUE OF ELVIS FOUND ON MARS!! Due to cognitive malfunction (including the 'epistemic incontinence' Alston speaks of elsewhere), I am extremely gullible, in particular with respect to the *National Enquirer*, always trusting it implicitly on the topic of extraterrestrials. (And due to the same malfunction, I don't believe anything that would override the belief in question.) Then my belief that a statue of Elvis was found in Mars is in fact based on a reliable indicator which is appropriately accessible to me; and I don't know or believe anything overriding this belief. But surely the belief has little by way of warrant.[17]

This process operating only in me and some other gullible people with respect to reports in the *National Enquirer* about extraterrestrial events seems untypical of the processes that produce true beliefs in most humans. So my having a true belief as a result of it was a matter of luck—not in the sense that the token process is truth conducive only if it is thought of as belonging to a very narrow type, but in the sense that the moderately general reliable type to which it belongs is untypical of types operative in most humans. Perhaps we would be more confident in counting the belief that the statue of Elvis was found on Mars as knowledge if the reports of most newspapers (not just the *National Enquirer*) about extraterrestrial events were true, and produced true beliefs in most people.

The Gettier problems that so plague largely internalist theories of warrant, need not arise with reliabilist and other externalist theories. This is because, where a subject comes to hold a true belief through inference from (or taking for granted) some false belief, or through ignorance of some relevant fact, the token process can be thought of as belonging to a type individuated in part by the kind of inference or ignorance involved, and so as belonging to a type that does not reliably yield true beliefs. The process of inference from false propositions (a very general type) will not reliably yield true ones. So, if it does yield the true belief 'either Jones owns a Ford or Brown is in Barcelona', this is not knowledge on this very general reliabilist theory. And, if we consider the inference in question as belonging to the precise type of inference from 'Jones owns a Ford', the type is still not reliable. The trouble is, however, that, for many examples of Gettier

[17] Alvin Plantinga, *Warrant: The Current Debate* (Oxford University Press, 1993), 191. Plantinga claims, with respect to this example, that 'under these conditions, I may be justified in accepting these beliefs, but none of them has any warrant for me'. The claim that I am justified could hold only on a subjective internalist theory of justification.

problems, while plausible understandings of the relevant type process can always be adduced, which rule out Gettier cases as cases of knowledge without the need for an extra clause to do so, equally plausible understandings of the relevant type process will count them in as cases of knowledge. In the barn case discussed on p. 194, for example, if we think of the token process that leads to the belief 'this is a barn' as belonging to the type 'observing barn façade in this neighbourhood leading to belief that there is a barn', then the process will not belong to a reliable type. But, if we think of it as belonging to the type 'observing barn façade (anywhere in the world) leading to belief that there is a barn', then the token process will belong to a reliable type—because almost always (except in this particular neighbourhood) barn façades are the walls of barns. On this understanding of what is happening, the token belief that there is a barn is then produced by a token of a reliable process, and so is warranted and—being true—amounts to knowledge.

'Luck' and 'accident' are relative to what counts as the norm; and, because there are so many different possible (internalist and externalist) understandings of that, there is a large range of borderline cases for what counts as knowledge.

Proper Functioning

Alvin Plantinga has developed a somewhat different and highly complicated externalist theory of warrant that may be regarded as an attempt to separate the right from the wrong sort of reliable processes. Central to his account is the concept of a cognitive faculty 'functioning properly'. A cognitive faculty is a faculty such as memory or inference that produces or utilizes beliefs. We often speak of bodily organs—stomach, liver, eye, or whatever—'functioning properly'. What is meant by this? The stomach functions properly if it breaks down the food we ingest into smaller components in certain kinds of way. The eye functions properly if it enables us to see and distinguish various kinds of object at certain distances. There is a level at which human stomachs are expected to perform; they are expected to break down certain kinds of substances into certain other kinds of substance within a certain time. There is a level too at which human eyes are expected to perform. They are expected to enable us to read numbers 6 inches tall at a distance of 25 yards, but not the page of a normal-sized book 100 yards away. They are expected to enable us to distinguish red from green objects, but not to recognize shades of infra-red. And, similarly for other bodily organs—they are expected to do or enable us to do certain jobs to a certain standard. And what they are expected to do or enable us to do varies with the age of the human—the eye of a 1-year old baby is not expected to enable its owner to do the same things as the eye of a 30 year old, nor the latter the same things as the eye of a 70 year old. And, similarly for other bodily organs, there is a level of performance. If that is reached, the organ is functioning properly.

What features of an organ's performance makes the notion of proper functioning applicable to it, and what determines the level? I suggest that, if an organism has an organ that, if it performs in a certain way, contributes towards the survival (or well-being) of the organism (or its species), in the kind of environment in which the organism is currently situated; and that does perform in that way in many organisms that are so situated for a significant period of time, then the notion of proper functioning is applicable to the organ. The level is set by the performance of the organ in most organisms of its species (in the environment in which the organisms are situated—let us call it a 'normal environment'). What counts as an environment of the same 'kind', as 'many' or 'most' organisms, and a 'significant' period of time can be brought out by examples. The eye, giving the organism the power of sight, contributes towards its ability to survive. The eye functions properly if it makes the contribution it makes in most organisms of its species.

By analogy, since cognitive faculties contribute towards the survival (and well-being) of organisms, they too can function properly. They do so if they function at the level typical of the species. Our memory contributes to our survival. Our memory functions properly if we are as good at remembering as most humans (and that means, given our age, as good as most humans of that age).

Does the notion of proper functioning apply to an organ only in so far as it contributes to the organism's survival, or are other contributions relevant—for example, do sexual organs have a proper function only in virtue of contributing to that organism's survival, or also in virtue of contributing to the survival of the species, or to the happiness of the organism? And does a cognitive faculty function properly in so far as it provides for us true beliefs even if those beliefs are quite irrelevant to our survival (for example, because they are beliefs about remote history or distant astronomy)? I do not think usage is very clear here; we need to stipulate . So let us think of proper functioning as contributing to the well-being of that organism and of its species in a wide sense.

Now Plantinga has a different understanding of 'proper functioning' from an understanding of the kind that I have just described and that I believe to be that of ordinary usage. He believes that he is merely describing our ordinary understanding; I believe that Plantinga is not describing but reforming that understanding. For Plantinga an organ functions properly if it functions the way the organism's creator intended it to function. Its creator may be God, and in that case 'functioning properly' is functioning the way God intended it to function. The main alternative to God having created us is that there is no God and that 'evolution' is our creator, and so 'proper functioning' is functioning the way evolution intended us to function. The problem here is that God is an agent who has intentions, and functioning 'the way he intended us to function' is a clear notion. But evolution has no intentions in any literal sense, and for myself I cannot see that there is any clear meaning in supposing that it has intentions in any sense at all. Plantinga is entitled to point out that many Darwinian theorists do sometimes attribute intentions and even 'design plans' to evolution; but I suggest that all that is meant by an organism having a 'design plan' is that it is so made that its organs have a way of functioning properly—in the sense that I have described earlier. That is, these organs are such that the corresponding organs of other members of the species often contribute to the well-being of those members in the environment in which they are often found. We cannot understand by evolution's design plan any more than that, because evolution notoriously is blind. It brings about the existence of faculties and causes them to function in certain environments. Sometimes they function so as to help organisms to survive and flourish, including by means of holding true beliefs; and sometimes they do not. When an organ functions at a level typical of the level at which such organs function generally in organisms of the species so as to contribute to well-being in the kind of environment in which the organism is typically found, then evolution—without intending to—has caused it to function properly. But an organ 'functioning properly' cannot be understood to mean functioning the way its cause intended it to function if the notion is to have application (as Plantinga intends) even if there is no intentional creator of the world. I suggest that there is no reason to abandon our ordinary understanding of proper functioning.

Plantinga gives imagined examples of organs functioning in a way that contributes to the survival of their organisms, which he says would clearly not constitute cases of those organs functioning properly. They show, he claims, that we distinguish contribution to survival (and so, we may add, more widely, well-being) from proper functioning:

> Hitler and his thugs induce [a] visual mutation into selected non-Aryan victims; it results in near blindness and constant pain. He and his henchmen also begin a sys-

tematic and large-scale program of weeding out the non-Aryan nonmutants before they reach reproductive maturity. Then consider some unfortunate whose visual system works the new way. Its working that way will confer a 'sep' [survival enhancing propensity] upon its owner all right (in view of the intentions of the Nazis), but it surely won't be the case that her visual system is functioning properly, or that its function is to produce pain and a visual field displaying nothing but a uniform expanse of green.[18]

My aorta is riddled with tiny holes; therefore my heart's beating very gently and at a rate of only fifteen beats per minute would confer an enormous sep [for if it beats 'normally', that is at the rate it does in most of us today, there will be extensive haemorrhaging leading to debilitation and death]. But that is not sufficient for its being one of the functions of my heart to beat at that rate. If it *does* beat at that rate, it is malfunctioning, no matter what the state of the rest of my body.[19]

But suppose both of these unfortunate phenomena became normal to the species. In that case, my intuitions are that certainly the second, and probably the first, would count as cases of proper functioning. A heart that beats at 70 beats per minute would not be functioning properly; it would be beating too fast for the health of the organism. And, I am inclined to think, a visual system that worked so well as to lead to elimination would be just as much a case of not functioning properly, as would any organ functioning in such a way as to lead to the organism almost automatically being killed by predators. The function of the visual system would be to secure surivial; it would do so by producing pain and a green visual field. (And there are cases in which we would all argue that an organ is functioning properly, and yet its doing so involves the organism being in pain—as when the womb gives birth.) But to the extent to which my intuitions are held to be erroneous, I am at a loss to say what is meant by an organ functioning properly—except in the case where organisms have an intentional creator. But, to repeat, we cannot beg the question about whether they do (and Plantinga does not intend that we should), since atheists as well as theists use the term 'proper function' in apparently the same sense. So we need an account of the use of this expression, which gives it application even if there is no intentional creator of organisms, such as God.

Plantinga's definition of 'warrant' in terms of proper functioning is as follows. For Plantinga the 'central and paradigmatic case' of warrant is that a belief *B* has warrant if (and only if) (1) the cognitive faculties involved in the production of *B* are functioning properly, (2) the cognitive environment is sufficiently similar to the one for which those faculties were

[18] Alvin Plantinga, *Warrant and Proper Function* (Oxford University Press, 1993), 206.
[19] Ibid. 208.

designed, (3) the 'purpose or function' of the design plan governing the production of *B* is the production of true beliefs, and (4) there is a high 'statistical or objective probability' that a belief produced in accordance with the relevant segment of the design plan 'in that sort of environment' is true.[20] Thus, on looking at the desk in front of me, I acquire the belief that there is a desk in front of me. This belief results from my perceptual faculties functioning properly if—according to Plantinga—they are functioning the way God or Evolution intended them to work. They would have been intended to work only in a certain kind of environment. If I am put in some psychologist's trick-room, my perceptual faculties may function perfectly properly; but the unusual room may lead to me acquiring false beliefs about the furniture there. Or, if I am put in a society of liars, the beliefs I acquire from testimony will not be warranted, because my faculty of trusting-testimony will not be functioning in the environment for which it was designed. (2) requires that the environment be right. But the production of true beliefs is not the only function of our cognitive faculties. There is also the function of producing comforting beliefs or beliefs that will enable us to perform life-saving acts. We may sometimes need some belief—for example, that some child of ours is alive, even if it is false, to enable us to cope with living. Or we may need a belief that we can perform some act that will enable us to survive (for example, the belief that we can jump over some crevasse), a belief that—though probably false—will make it more likely that we shall succeed in the act (of jumping over the crevasse) than if we do not have it. So (3) requires that the process that produced my belief be one designed to produce true beliefs. But some designers may not design very well. If we were created not by God but by a low-grade inefficient deity (or evolutionary process), processes designed to produce true beliefs may frequently fail to do so. (4) requires that the process designed to produce true beliefs shall be largely successful (in the environment for which it was designed).

On the normal non-Plantingesque understanding of proper functioning, Plantinga's four conditions will need to be understood in a more down-to-earth way than by Plantinga. Condition (1) will be satisfied if *B* is produced by a mechanism that conduces to survival (or well-being) in the normal environment of members of the species. Condition (2) must be understood as saying simply that the environment is normal. (For, again, to insist that the environment be similar to that for which the faculties were 'designed' in a literal sense presupposes an intentional creator.) Condition

[20] Alvin Plantinga, *Warrant and Proper Function* (Oxford University Press, 1993), 194.

(3) must be understood in a sense in which it is not distinct from condition (4)—namely, as saying that the mechanism conduces to survival (or well-being) (in a normal environment) by producing mostly true beliefs. Barring an intentional creator—there is no distinction to be made between a properly functioning mechanism that does produce mostly true beliefs (in a normal environment) and one whose 'purpose or function' is to produce mostly true beliefs (in a normal environment). The function of the faculty just is what it does—where what it does conduces to survival or well-being in a normal environment. Only if there is an intentional creator can one distinguish between purposes or plans that are executed and those that are not.

So understood, Plantinga's theory becomes a slightly more sophisticated form of reliabilism. A belief is warranted if it is produced in a normal environment by a process that produces mostly true beliefs (in a normal environment), when that process conduces to the survival (or well-being) of the organism (or the species) by producing mostly true beliefs (in a normal environment). In so far as we suppose that almost any process of production of true beliefs contributes to the well-being of the organism or species, the last clause becomes otiose, and Plantinga's theory collapses into reliabilism. And it inherits all the advantages and disadvantages of that approach, including above all the problem of how precisely we are to construe the type. So I will in future confine the discussion to the largely internalist accounts of warrant (in which objective justification plays a central role), on the one hand, and to reliabilist theories, on the other, as alternative kinds of analysis.

Why the Different Accounts of Knowledge but not of Justification Largely Coincide

It has been the theme of the first seven chapters of this book that the intuitions of philosophers and more generally speakers of language about when a belief is 'justified' are very diverse, and that this is because there are many different concepts of 'justification' in play. With regard to knowledge, there is a lot more agreement on actual cases, but the rival kinds of analysis extrapolate from them in different directions, yielding different results with regard to various thought experiments as to whether someone knows or does not know something that is true. A major reason for the difference is that 'knowledge' (and its associated words and words so translated) is a word that has played a major role in ordinary language, and been a focus of philosophical interest for millennia. 'Justified belief' (and its associated words and words so translated) have not played nearly such a major role in ordinary language. Whether someone was justified in believing what they did is a question that arises only in the course of a careful examination of their conduct. By contrast, people are always claiming to 'know' things in order to assure others that they may take these things for granted; and investigating what other people 'know'. And, as we saw in the Introduction, philosophical investigation of what makes a belief 'justified' was a latecomer on the philosophical scene. In consequence there are a far larger number of paradigm cases of 'knowledge' than of 'justified' belief. Most of us 'know' where we live and work, who are our friends and relations, and a large number of items of general knowledge; and any philosophical theory that did not yield those results would not be giving an account of our ordinary concept. By paradigm cases, I mean not merely agreed cases but cases such that in virtue of their similarity to them other cases of true belief would count as knowledge, cases whose status as knowledge antedated any theory of what knowledge consisted in. They constrain any philosophical theory; if, for example, we adopt a reliabilist theory, they constrain the types to which we can refer the token process of belief-production to reliable ones.

There are other reasons, as well as the existence of far more paradigms of 'knowledge' than of 'justified' belief, why there is to be expected a lot more agreement on whether or not a belief amounts to knowledge than on whether or not it is justified. One is that the claim that a belief is 'justified' may, according to context, be a claim either of synchronic or of diachronic justification. And, since clearly a belief that is the justified response to evidence in some sense at a time may not be the result of adequate investigation and so not be justified in any diachronic sense, there is plenty of scope for disagreement about whether a belief is 'justified'. Then, in so far as justification is to be analysed in an internalist way, there is a further scope for disagreement according to whether justification is by correct criteria or by the subject's criteria. Neither of these two sources of disagreement operates with respect to knowledge. Whether you know something at some time depends on how you are situated at that time; it has nothing to do as such with whether you have devoted time to investigating it. Of course (contingently) if you have not devoted enough time to investigating it, you may not have enough evidence (or be well enough placed in other ways) for it to be the case that you know it. But, as long as you do have enough evidence at the time (or are well enough placed to satisfy externalist accounts of knowledge), you know it—even if you ought to have investigated it further because of its tremendous importance. And, if knowledge is determined in part by the internalist considerations of whether your belief was rendered probable by the evidence, then only an objective internalist account is plausible. Someone who has the true belief that he will win the lottery only because it is rendered probable by his own crazy standards does not know that he will win.

Further, as I noted in Chapter 3, what is logically probable on evidence may never happen. More generally beliefs that are sychronically objectively internally justified may never prove true. If our criteria of probability were the correct ones, we would, of course, need continued miracles to save us from the consequences of our false beliefs in a world in which in virtually no area did objectively justified beliefs prove true; but a world is certainly conceivable in which in some respects (for example, in respect of the results of horse races), objectively justified beliefs are never true. But, on reliabilist accounts of justification, by definition most justified beliefs will be true. Hence, again with respect to justification, there is a scope for divergence of kinds of justification and so for disagreement about whether a belief is 'justified'. But to amount to knowledge a belief has to be true; and so there is no comparable source for disagreement about whether a belief amounts to 'knowledge'.

I conclude that major sources of disagreement for whether or not a belief is 'justified' do not operate when we are considering whether a true belief amounts to 'knowledge'; and so—as well as for the reason that there are a large number of paradigm cases of 'knowledge'—we should expect a far wider range of disagreement about the former than about the latter. Even so, an adequate theory of knowledge needs to explain why the very different accounts of the nature of knowledge frequently coincide in their verdicts as to whether some new or possible case of (strong) true belief amounts to knowledge. For in general strong true beliefs that are justified (not via a false proposition or ignorance of a true one) also satisfy precise and more general reliabilist conditions for knowledge (on many natural ways of spelling these out); and conversely.

Some connection between a precise 'truth-tracking' theory of knowledge and more general reliabilist accounts is easy to explain. If it is the case *S* would not have believed *p* if *p* were false, and would have believed *p* even if circumstances were slightly different from the actual ones, that is because the token process that produces *p* belongs to a precise type (of processes very like this one in similar circumstances) that is reliable. Now our world is an integrated world in this sense—precise regularities are consequences of relatively simple more general laws of nature for particular circumstances. Thus

Galileo's law of fall (that all bodies, small relative to the earth, near the surface of the earth are accelerated towards the centre of the earth with an acceleration of 32 ft/sec^2) follows from Newton's three laws of motion and his law of gravitational attraction, given the mass, size, and shape of the earth. I stress the words 'relatively simple' above. All precise regularities will, of course, follow from a law constituted by their conjunction (that is, writing them all together); but what is characteristic of our world is that they are particular applications of simple generalizations. This holds also for human belief acquisition processes. If a precise type of belief acquisition process (defined by time and believer, as well as particular features of his sensory apparatus, location, lighting in the room, and so on) is reliable, that will hold in virtue of some more general simple regularity connecting variations in reliability with features of sensory apparatus, and so on. Hence, if there is a precise type that is reliable, its reliability will follow from that of some more general type. There are no doubt exceptions even in our world (my eyes may suddenly and unpredictably work well for ten seconds). And it is certainly only a contingent feature of our world that normally precise regularities are consequences of more general simple regularities for particular circumstances. And, of course, if a belief amounts to knowledge on some more general reliabilist account, it will also amount to knowledge on whatever more precise account applicable to the circumstances of its occurrence follows from the former. It does not follow from this connection that, if a true belief amounts to knowledge, given a precise truth-tracking account of knowledge, that it will amount to knowledge on all more general accounts in which the type to which the belief-forming process belongs is picked out in different ways; nor, if it amounts to knowledge on some more general account, does it follow that it will amount to knowledge on every more precise account. But in practice many of the ways of describing the token process in terms of a more general type may yield not too dissimilar results as to whether a process of that type is reliable. Yet the paradigm cases of knowledge constrain theorists to choose both precise truth-tracking accounts and more general reliabilist accounts in such a way that they choose types that yield the result that these paradigm cases are indeed produced by reliable processes, and so the precise and more general accounts will coincide in their claims about the paradigm cases, and so also about many similar cases.

The connection between largely internalist theories of knowledge and reliabilist theories is, however, initially more puzzling. Why, for example, is a true belief that is objectively internally justified (some Gettier condition also being satisfied) likely to be also a belief that we would hold in and only in the closest possible worlds to our own in which it is true (as these notions are spelled out by Nozick)? We saw in Chapter 2 that—in so far as we think about it—we regard our beliefs as subjectively probable on the evidence of our basic beliefs. We saw in Chapter 3 n.15 that we will, therefore, regard them as logically probable on that evidence. We must think of our basic beliefs as rightly basic. Hence, in the later terminology, we must regard our beliefs as objectively internally justified. Otherwise we would think them improbable and so would not believe them. That involves thinking that any belief on which any inference of ours depends is true—for, if we thought such a belief (for example, that Jones owns a Ford) false, we would not believe any other belief in virtue of its being made probable by the former. It also involves thinking that we are not ignorant of some belief we are expected to have that would make our belief improbable—for again, if we thought the former, we would not hold the latter belief. So we have to think of our own beliefs as warranted in the largely internalist sense; that is, involved in their being our beliefs.

To hold a belief involves thinking that it corresponds to how things are. Yet such correspondence would be, we have seen, immensely improbable unless there is some sort of process ensuring that our beliefs are largely sensitive to how things are. In the case of beliefs about contingent matters, that will be because there is a (direct or indirect) causal connection (if the process of belief production is traced back far enough) between our belief and the state of affairs believed, in consequence of which we hold the belief when things are that way and would not hold it otherwise. So—if we think about it—we will believe that the counterfactuals of precise reliabilism are satisfied. If we acquire evidence that they are not satisfied, that will greatly decrease the probability that a token belief produced by this process is true, and so we are likely to cease to believe it, and so not to believe that the total evidence (old evidence plus evidence about the process of belief acquisition) makes it probable that the belief is true. Suppose, for one example of how this could happen, that at stage one I have certain evidence and believe that that shows my friend innocent of the crime and so I believe. You then show me that I would have believed him innocent whether or not he did the crime, because the evidence with which I am being provided has been filtered—my informants provide me only with evidence favourable to my friend's innocence, and suppress any evidence that points in a contrary direction. But, if I now come to believe that the evidence I see comes from a collection, the rest of which suggests that my friend is guilty—this extra evidence (about the way in which the previous evidence was filtered) eliminates any justification I may have for believing my friend innocent. But, if I believe that, I will cease to hold the belief that he is innocent. For I cannot think a belief of mine to be improbable given my evidence. So it is probable that I will believe with respect to myself that justification goes with satisfaction of the precise reliabilist's (and so some more general reliabilist's) conditions for warrant. (This will not, however, always happen. I may regard some belief as made so very probable by my original evidence that new evidence that I would have believed it whether it was true or false may not be enough for the total evidence to render the original belief improbable.)

But what about other people? We saw in Chapter 2 that we have in the end no other grounds for attributing particular beliefs to other people except their public input (the stimuli that land on their sense organs) and the resulting brain states, and their public output (the way they behave—given their brain states—and in particular the actions they perform). Other humans are like ourselves in their bodily construction. Hence in the absence of counter-evidence we rightly suppose that they form beliefs on the basis of other beliefs and sensory experience in the same way as we do; that the stimuli that land on their sense organs cause in them (in combination with other beliefs of theirs) the same beliefs as they would cause in us; and that their public behaviour is caused by the purposes and beliefs that would cause that behaviour in us. In so far as their public behaviour can be explained more simply in other ways, we accept the simpler explanation. But the principle of simplicity leading to a qualified principle of charity (see Ch. 2 n.12) in interpreting others as like ourselves constrains the interpretation of the mental lives of others in a massive way. Now on the objective internalist conception of synchronic justification with which I am operating, a belief being justified is a matter of its relations to the subject's other beliefs. But since in general—except in special cases where public output counts against this for stretches of a particular individual's life—we must suppose that others are like ourselves in their processes of belief formation, we must suppose that the processes that produce beliefs in them produce beliefs with similar patterns of relation among them to those that they produce in us. And since we must suppose that our own beliefs are objectively internally justified, we must suppose that so too in general are the beliefs of others.

The connection, however, of the true beliefs of others that I must in general assume to be (objectively internally) justified, with the satisfaction of Gettier conditions, is a contingent matter that, we observe, normally holds. Most people who make justified inferences to a true conclusion do not do so by means of a false proposition, nor do they do so because of their ignorance of some true proposition of which they are socially expected to be aware—as we can check out by our inferences to their beliefs (especially by means of what they say about those beliefs). The same applies to the connection of the true beliefs of others that I assume to be objectively internally justified with the satisfaction of the counterfactual conditions of a precise reliabilist theory of warrant. This too is a contingent matter that, we observe, normally holds. Other people, like ourselves, are most of the time in situations where internally objectively justified beliefs are truth-tracking. Thus, when others are shown a desk and then—I infer—acquire the justified belief that there is a desk in front of them, the situation is normally such that (given what I justifiably believe to be their processes of belief acquisition), the belief is one that they would still have if the lighting and positions of other objects were changed a little but would not have if the desk were not there. But, of course, there will be cases where inferring by my normal procedures to which justified beliefs others have, I can see that the counterfactual conditions involved in a truth-tracking theory are not satisfied. Others can be subjected to all kinds of tricks. They can be shown a desk that they can see only if the lighting and positions of other objects are exactly such-and-such; but, if the desk is not there, they would be shown a hologram of a desk visible from all angles. They would then, because mentally in the same condition as myself when I have a justified belief that there is a desk in front of me, have a justified belief that there is a desk in front of them; but the counterfactual conditions would not hold. And it might have been the case that—we could have observed—many people were very often living under such conditions. In that case it would very often happen that satisfaction of the largely internalist theories' criteria for warrant would not coincide with those of precise (and so some form of more general) reliabilism.

I have been arguing in this section that often, when it is probable that the criteria of one account of knowledge are satisfied, it is also probable that the criteria of a different account of knowledge are satisfied, or at any rate the criteria of some versions of a different account are satisfied. This will mean that, when the subject having a true belief is not a matter of luck on the understanding of 'luck' involved in one account, it will often be the case that the subject having a true belief is not a matter of luck on the understanding of 'luck' involved in another account.

So knowledge is strong true warranted belief—where a belief about some matter being warranted is a matter of the subject having a true belief about that matter not being a matter of luck. But there are a variety of conceptions of 'luck', since there are a variety of conceptions of what are the proper procedures for belief acquisition, the non-following of which constitutes a belief being true being a matter of luck. Often these procedures will coincide, and we will all agree that when they do we have knowledge. But there will be a considerable penumbra of cases of strong true belief about which there will be disagreement as to whether they constitute knowledge. This will arise, not merely because there are borderline cases for the application of the concepts involved in the description of the proper procedures for belief acquisition—for example, what constitutes 'justification' or 'reliability'—but because on one account of the proper procedures the belief will count as knowledge but not on another account. Some of the difficult puzzle cases that philosophers devised over the last forty years of the twentieth century illustrate this, including ones described earlier in this chapter. It is certainly not obvious to every reliabilist that, if reports in the *National Enquirer* were extremely reliable, the belief that a statue of Elvis was found on Mars would be unwarranted. And some people would certainly hold that if my eyes work well for just ten seconds (and the counterfactuals hold), I know what is written on the page; while others would hold that the one-off character of my true belief disqualifies it from being knowledge. And consider a child who has, for once, added up correctly and is convinced that $256+17=273$. His calculations proceed through no false premisses and do not depend for their justification on his ignorance of some true proposition. The fact that he does not very often get his calculations correct, or even the fact that his doing so on this occasion depends on some very special circumstances (that is, the counterfactuals are not well satisfied), might not debar some of us from saying—'this time he knows the answer'. In all of these cases, luck is not involved if the proper procedures of belief acquisition are described in one way, but it is involved if they are described in another way.

I conclude that ordinary language contains different concepts of knowledge—largely internalist, precise reliabilist, and general reliabilist; and that both the latter can be applied in different ways according to the type to which we refer the token process of belief production. These concepts do, however, largely coincide in their verdicts on when some belief counts as knowledge—given that we must choose types in such a way that most of the large pool of paradigm cases of beliefs that are said to amount to 'knowledge' do constitute cases of knowledge.[21]

[21] See Additional Note Q for the account of knowledge very different from all the accounts discussed in this chapter, developed by Timothy Williamson.

Is Knowledge Worth Having?

I argued in Chapter 2 that strong true belief is good to have. In *Meno*,[22] Plato has Socrates make the suggestion that 'right opinion will be in no way inferior to knowledge, nor will it be less useful as regards our actions, nor will the man who has right opinion be inferior to him who has knowledge'. Is he right? Is it no better for me that I know something than that I merely have a strong true belief that it is so? Or does its resulting from luck make a strong belief less valuable than it would otherwise be? I argued in Chapter 6 that a true belief is no more worth having for being synchronically epistemically justified either in a subjective internalist sense or in an externalist sense. However, I suggested that objective internalist justification is as such a good thing in itself to have (and strong justification more than weak), whether or not the belief is true, and so that having it adds to the value of a true belief. This kind of internal rationality is an intrinsically valuable thing for humans to have in their beliefs.

On a largely internalist account of knowledge, (strong) objective (strong) justification can fail to yield warrant only if it proceeds via some false belief or in the absence of some true belief. But, since false beliefs are a bad thing to have, and true beliefs are a good thing to have, warrant is better than mere justification. Knowledge, in which warrant is construed in the largely internalist way, is therefore a better thing to have than (strong) true belief and even than (objectively internally strongly) justified strong true belief. This is because the sort of luck involved in having these without having knowledge means a lack of something valuable in the particular case—true beliefs *en route*. But in general luck is a good thing to have; and, I suggest, the absence of luck of externalist kinds in the process of its production does not make a particular belief more worth having. The child's true objectively internally justified belief that $256 + 17 = 273$ is no less worth having for being untypical in its correctness. So knowledge of externalist kinds is not intrinsically more worth having than true belief.

However, if it is not a matter of luck in some externalist sense that a given process of belief production produces a true belief on some occasion, then

[22] *Meno* 98c. Note that this comment is made about knowledge in a narrower sense than our ordinary sense. (See my Introduction.) Timothy Williamson ('Is Knowing a State of Mind', *Mind*, 104 (1995), 533–65, at 557) writes that 'factive mental states are important to us as states whose essence includes a matching between mind and world, and knowing is important to us as the most general factive static attitude'. But the necessary constituent of knowledge that involves such a matching is true belief; and it needs to be shown why anything else beyond that is important.

that fact makes it probable that other beliefs (of the believer and of others) produced by the same process will be true. If, for example, my true belief on a particular occasion that *p* is produced by a reliable process, that fact makes it probable that other beliefs of mine produced by that process on other occasions will be true. To the extent to which I have reason to believe that some belief is produced by a reliable process, I have reason to believe other beliefs produced in me by the same process. It will also be the case—if the belief being true is not a matter of luck—that the believer will continue to have a true belief on the matter in question if various circumstances change. As Timothy Williamson has put it,[23] knowledge is more stable than mere true belief. Edward Craig argued that the concept of knowledge evolved in society in order 'to flag approved sources of information'.[24] If someone's belief about some matter is not true by accident but results from some reliable process, then (assuming that they tell us their beliefs and do so honestly) they will be good sources of information about similar matters. So, if we have an objectively internally justified belief that their belief about some matter resulted from a reliable process, we have good reason to suppose that their beliefs on similar matters are probably true. Here the value of knowledge over true belief on one occasion is its value for the beliefs of others on other occasions. But in none of these ways does its amounting to knowledge add anything to the intrinsic value of the particular belief itself for the believer.

I conclude that a strong true belief is none the worse at the time at which it is held for being the result of luck—unless the luck involves the belief being (objectively internally) unjustified or it involves having also a false belief or not having some other true belief. Only some sorts of knowledge have greater intrinsic value than the strong true belief that is involved in them; but other sorts of knowledge have value as evidence of other things.

[23] See Timothy Williamson, 'The Broadness of the Mental: Some Logical Considerations' in J. Tomberlin (ed.), *Philosophical Perspectives 12* (Blackwell Publishers, 1998).

[24] Edward Craig, *Knowledge and the State of Nature* (Clarendon Press, 1990), 11.

APPENDIX. PREDICTIVISM

The Normal Irrelevance of Novelty Evidence

On the account that I have given in Chapter 4 of whether and how far evidence *e* makes logically probable a hypothesis *h*, it is irrelevant whether *e* was known before *h* was formulated and perhaps taken account of in the formulation of *h*, or whether *h* was formulated first and then *e* was discovered, perhaps in the process of testing *h*. The contrary view that the time or circumstances of the formulation of *h* (relative to when *e* was discovered or utilized) make a difference to whether and how far *e* 'confirms' h, I shall call predictivism; and I shall contrast it with the timeless view which I endorse that such considerations are irrelevant. The predictivist view has been defended by various writers, some of whom derive their ideas from Karl Popper. These writers have urged that it is always very easy to construct some hypothesis which fits the evidence obtained so far; but once we have constructed a hypothesis, then nature may very well turn up evidence which falsifies it (or at any rate, strongly disconfirms it) in a clear objective manner. Hence subsequent testing provides objective support in a way that mere fitting the data does not, Popper claimed. This appendix will investigate how far there is any truth in the predictivist view.

In order to consider predictivism in its most plausible form, we need to separate off from it two aspects of the way in which Popper himself expressed it. Popper claimed that a hypothesis *h* has a high degree of 'corroboration' only in so far as it has passed severe tests. And he claimed further that those tests had to be sincere attempts to show *h* false. ('Our $c(h|e)$ can be adequately interpreted as degree of corroboration of *h*—or of the rationality of our belief in *h* in the light of tests—only if *e* consists of reports of the outcome of sincere attempts to refute *h*, rather than attempts to verify *h*'[1]). It might look to the unwary as if Popper is suggesting that a hypothesis is confirmed—that is, has its probability increased—only if it is subjected to 'sincere attempts' to refute it. But Popper does not mean by 'corroborates' anything like 'confirms'. For he holds that corroboration is solely a measure of past performance and is no good guide to the future, that it in no way makes the predictions of the hypothesis more probably true. This is, of course, intuitively a highly unappealing view—surely scientific theories will more probably give true predictions in so far as they have passed severe tests. So let us regard the claim of the importance of testing as a claim about confirmation. Secondly,

[1] Karl Popper, *Logic of Scientific Discovery* (Hutchinson, 1959), 414.

Popper understood by severe tests 'sincere attempts to refute h, rather than attempts to verify h'. But it seems implausible that the scientist's private intention when performing his tests can have any relevance to whether his results confirm or disconfirm h. For their confirming effect is a public matter, measurable and equally accessible to other scientists who did not themselves perform the tests—whereas intentions are mental (the subject has privileged access to them), and may be quite unknown to others. Also, I think it unreasonable to require that the evidence be obtained in the course of a (publicly recognizable) 'test' of h; so many of the most important pieces of evidence for or against a hypothesis turn up by accident. What, I think, Popper and others are best represented as saying is that if you 'fit' a hypothesis to the evidence, that evidence does not give as much support to it as it would if it was discovered after the hypothesis was formulated.

What is at stake is, therefore, best phrased in terms of confirmation and of public evidence; and it is in these terms that most predictivists phrase their claims. The issue then is whether certain evidence would make a certain hypothesis more probable if it was in some way novel evidence instead of being already known. To put the issue more formally, suppose that we have some evidence e_1 (about the time of discovery of which we are ignorant), which is such that it gives to a hypothesis h on background evidence k a probability $P(h|e_1\&k)$. Then does the addition to e_1 of further evidence e_2 to the effect that e_1 was in some sense novel evidence ever affect the value of that probability—for example, by increasing it if it is greater than $P(h|k)$ or greater than $\frac{1}{2}$, or decreasing it if it is less than $P(h|k)$ or less than $\frac{1}{2}$? For simplicity's sake I shall concern myself mainly with the former (the possibility of an increase of $P(h|e_1\&k)$); if my arguments hold with respect to that, similar arguments will clearly hold with respect to the latter possibility. Is $P(h_1|e_1\&e_2\&k)$ ever greater than $P(h_1|e_1\&k)$?

There are different understandings in the literature of what the novelty of e_1 and so of the priority to it of h consists in. e_2 might report the temporal priority of the formulation of h to the discovery of e_1; e_1 is then temporally novel. Or e_2 might report that e_1 was not 'used' in the formulation of h; it was not taken account of in the (public) justification of h and so e_1 is 'use novel'. And finally there is the epistemic priority of the formulation of h; people at the time had no good reason provided by hypotheses then current for believing that e_1 would occur, before h was put forward. This I shall call the 'relative novelty' of e_1—e_1 is relatively novel if, while it is quite probable given h and k, it is very improbable given the actual hypotheses in vogue when h was formulated. This 'relative novelty' is a historical feature of the circumstances of the discovery of e_1 (in what climate h was formulated)—to be distinguished sharply from the low prior probability of e_1—$P(e_1|k)$ or its low probability if h is false—$P(e_1|{\sim}h\&k)$. The latter two values arise from the probability of e on all the various hypotheses that might hold (whether or not in vogue), weighted by their prior probabilities—whether or not they were recognized at the time of the formulation of h. It is certainly the case, as I stated on p. 104 in my exposition of the criteria of logical probability, that e confirms h

more, the less probable is *e* given not-*h*; more precisely, the lower is $P(e|{\sim}h\&k)$, the more $P(h|e\&k)$ exceeds $P(h|k)$. To the extent to which *e* is to be expected anyway, then, even if it is a prediction of *h*, it is not much evidence in favour of *h*. But that is not a controversial claim, and, as we have seen, follows straightforwardly from the probability calculus.

Of the three kinds of novelty, most predictivists discount temporal novelty as the relevant kind, preferring either use novelty[2] or relative novelty[3]. I shall call any such evidence of the novelty of e_1 novelty evidence. Novelty evidence e_2 is in effect historical evidence of when (relative to the evidence e_1 of what was observed) a hypothesis *h* was formulated, by whom or under what circumstances. I shall argue that, for normal *k*, novelty evidence is irrelevant to the confirmation of *h*, but that, for certain *k*, such e_2 is relevant.

I include within normal *k* not merely the evidence of how things behave in neighbouring fields of enquiry, but also the circumstances in which e_1 occurs. (We could include these within e_1, but it would make the account of some simple examples that I am about to discuss more complicated.) The crucial condition is that *k* is not to include any historical evidence about who formulates or advocates *h*, when and under what circumstances (and so any historical information about the success rate in prediction of the formulator, or of others before that time or in similar circumstances.)

Here is a trivial example in which *k* is normal and of which, I suggest, the timeless view gives a correct account. Let *h* be 'all metals expand (of physical necessity) when heated'. (The words 'of physical necessity' make the claim that all metals expand when heated a claim about a law of nature, not a mere accidental regularity.) Let *k* be '1,000 pieces of metal were heated', e_1 be 'those 1,000 pieces of metal expanded', e_2 be some novelty evidence such as that *h* was put forward before e_1 was known. *k* and *h* (if true) would explain e_1—the metals expanded because they were heated and all metals expand when heated. The timeless theory then claims that $P(h|e_1\&k) = P(h|e_1\&e_2\&k)$. I suggest that the simplicity of the theory *h* and its ability to explain (given *k*) a large amount of evidence e_1 is what makes it likely to be true, quite independently of when it was put forward. It is also quite independent of what led anyone to formulate *h*, and of whether e_1 was very probable or very improbable given the theories in vogue at the time of the formulation of *h*. Some very crazy astrologically based theories might have been in vogue then that (together with *k*) predicted and explained e_1. Yet that would not make e_1 any less good evidence for *h*.

In the above example *h* is a universal lawlike hypothesis. The timeless view also works for predictions—given normal *k*. Observational evidence is typically

[2] See John Worrall, 'Fresnel, Poisson, and the White Spot: The Role of Successful Predictions in the Acceptance of Scientific Theories', in D. Gooding, T. Pinch, and S. Schaffer (eds.), *The Uses of Experiment* (Cambridge University Press, 1989).

[3] See Alan Musgrave, 'Logical versus Historical Theories of Confirmation', *British Journal for the Philosophy of Science*, 25 (1974), 1–23.

evidence for predictions by being evidence confirmatory of universal (or statistical) lawlike hypotheses of which the prediction is a deductive (or inductive) consequence; and (although we noted on pp. 109–10 that there are exceptions) normally the most probable prediction is that yielded by the most probable hypothesis. Let e_1 and e_2 be as before, k be '1,001 pieces of metal were heated', and h be 'the 1,001th piece of metal expanded'. e_1 with k is evidence that confirms 'all metals expand when heated', and so that the 1,001th piece of metal will expand when heated. h derives its probability from being (with k) a consequence of a simple hypothesis able to explain a large amount of evidence, independently of whether or not e_1 was novel in any sense. $P(h|e_1\&k) = P(h|e_1\&e_2\&k)$.

My intuitions on this simple example are also my intuitions on more sophisticated real-life examples, where my condition on background knowledge holds. They are, for example, my intuitions with respect to Mendeleev's theory, recently discussed by Maher[4] on the predictivist side, and by Howson and Franklin[5] on the timeless side. Mendeleev's theory (h) entailed and (if true) explained the existence and many of the properties of the newly (1871–8) discovered elements scandium, gallium, and germanium (e_1). Mendeleev's was not just any old theory that had this consequence; it was not just e_1 plus some unrelated f. It was an integrated theory of groups of related elements having analogous properties recurring as atomic weight increased, from which the existence of the sixty or so elements already known (k) followed. In virtue of being a more integrated and so simpler theory than any other theory from which k followed and by which it could be explained, it was already more likely to be true than any other theory. The further information that other results (e_1) followed from it and could be explained by it was therefore plausibly further evidence for it independently of when and how they were discovered. Howson and Franklin compare the relation of Mendeleev's theory to chemical elements to the relation of the 'eightfold way' to elementary particles; and the prediction of the three elements by the former to the prediction of the Ω-particle by the latter. They cite a passage from Yuval Néeman, one of the proponents of the eightfold way in which he also makes the comparison and comments that 'the importance attached to a successful prediction is associated with human psychology rather than with scientific methodology. It would not have detracted at all from the effectiveness of the eightfold way if the Ω-had been discovered before the theory was proposed.'

That theories can acquire a very high degree of support simply in virtue of their ability to explain evidence already available is illustrated by the situation of Newton's theory of motion at the end of the seventeenth century. It was judged by very many—and surely correctly—to be very probable when it was first put forward. Yet it made no new immediately testable predictions, only the predictions

[4] Patrick Maher, 'Howson and Franklin on Prediction', *Philosophy of Science*, 60 (1993), 329–40.

[5] Colin Howson and Allan Franklin, 'Maher, Mendeleev and Bayesianism', *Philosophy of Science*, 58 (1991), 574–85.

that were already made by laws that were already known and that it explained (for example, Kepler' s laws of planetary motion and Galileo's law of fall). Its high probability arose solely from its being a very simple higher-level theory from which those diverse laws are deducible. My intuitions tell me that it would have been no more likely to be true, if it had been put forward before Kepler's laws were discovered and had been used to predict them.

So much for my intuitions. But my intuitions clash with those of the predictivist. So I need to show that my intuitions fit into a wider theory of confirmation for which other reasons can be adduced, and I need to explain why the predictivist has the inclination to give a wrong account of cases such as I have cited. My intuitions fit into the whole Bayesian picture, in favour of which there are the other good reasons that have been given in Chapters 3 and 4. Consider my first simple example in which h='all metals expand when heated', k='1,000 pieces of metal were heated', e_1='those 1,000 pieces of metal expanded', and e_2='h was put forward before e_1 was known'. On Bayes's theorem

$$P(h \mid e_1 \& k) = \frac{P(e_1 \mid h \& k)}{P(e_1 \mid k)} P(h \mid k)$$

and

$$P(h \mid e_1 \& e_2 \& k) = \frac{P(e_1 \& e_2 \mid h \& k)}{P(e_1 \& e_2 \mid k)} P(h \mid k)$$

Then $P(h|e_1\&e_2\&k)$ will be greater than $P(h|e_1\&k)$, as the predictivist typically claims that it is, only if the addition of e_2 to e_1 lowers $P(e_1|k)$ (and so $P(e_1|\sim h\&k)$) by a greater proportion than it lowers $P(e_1|h\&k)$. What this would mean is that, on the mere information that the 1,000 pieces of metal were heated, it would be more likely that the hypothesis that all metals expand when heated would have been proposed before it was known that the 1,000 pieces of metal expanded if the hypothesis was true, than if it was false. That seems to me, and I hope also to the average predictivist, massively implausible. The same applies if we take e_2 as 'e_1 was not used in formulating h'. Then a Bayesian predictivist is committed to: on the mere information that k, it would be more likely that h would have been proposed without taking e_1 into account if h were true than if it were not. And if e_2 is 'the hypotheses in vogue at the time of the formulation of h were such that e_1 is improbable given them', the Bayesian predictivist is committed to: it would be more likely that h would have been proposed when the theories then in vogue did not predict e_1, if h were true than if it were not. All of this is again massively implausible. Hence the predictivist can save his thesis only by abandoning Bayes's theorem; and there are, I suggest, good reasons for not doing so.

But what, if predictivism is false, is the source of the temptation to espouse it? I think that there are two sources. First, there is the consideration that moved Popper that any collection of evidence can always accommodate some hypothesis—that is, for any e_1 and k one can always devise a theory h, such that

$P(e_1|h\&k)=1$ or is high. (Indeed, one can always devise an infinite number of such hypotheses.) That has seemed to suggest, totally erroneously, to some that there are no objective criteria for when a hypothesis so constructed is supported by evidence. Whereas, the contrast is made, once we have a hypothesis that makes a prediction, we can look to see whether the prediction comes off, and whether it does or not is a clear objective matter. But, as I have urged throughout this book (and especially in Chapter 4), there are very clear objective criteria for when a hypothesis is supported by a collection of evidence already obtained. In the trivial metal example that I used earlier, equally accommodating to the evidence that 1,000 pieces of metal had been heated and expanded, are *h* 'all metals expand when heated', h_1 'metals 1–1,000 expand when heated, and other metals do not', and, supposing all the metals observed so far were observed by physicists in Britain, h_2 'all and only metals observed by physicists in Britain expand when heated.' Quite obviously, h_1 and h_2 are not supported by evidence, whereas *h* is. (Or rather, to put the point more carefully, all of these hypotheses are 'confirmed'—that is, have their probability increased by the evidence that they predict—since many rival hypotheses are incompatible with it; but only *h*, being far simpler than other hypotheses that predict the evidence, obtains any significant degree of probabilty.) The obvious reason for this is that *h* is a simple hypothesis, whereas h_1 and h_2 are not simple theories (by the criteria analysed in Chapter 4).

The second source of predictivism, as I see it, is this. A hypothesis *h* that entails (or renders very probable) for some circumstances *k* the occurrence of some event e_1 has, as we have noted, its probability raised by e_1, the less likely e_1 is to occur if *h* were not true—the lower $P(e_1|{\sim}h\&k)$ and so the lower $P(e_1|k)$. If we have already formulated h_1, we know which e_1 to look for that will have this characteristic of $P(e_1|h\&k)$ very high and $P(e_1|{\sim}h\&k)$ very low. We can bring about *k* and see whether ${\sim}e_1$ or e_1 occurs, and that will provide a 'severe test' of the hypothesis. If we formulate *h* after accumulating evidence, we may or may not have among that evidence an e_1 with that characteristic—but we are much more likely to get it if we are actually looking for it. Hence, producing hypotheses and then testing them may indeed be a better way of getting evidence that (if they are true) supports them strongly, than trying to fit them to evidence we already have. But that has no tendency to cast doubt on the fact that, for given evidence e_1, $P(h|e_1\&k)$ has a value that is unaffected by the addition of evidence about when e_1 was discovered.

Looking for Favourable Evidence

There is, it is true, always the temptation for the accommodator to use methods of looking for evidence that will make it fairly improbable that he will find evidence against his hypothesis. But the probability that ought to guide action is that relative to total available evidence. All relevant evidence should be taken into account, and that will include evidence about any methods used to obtain other evidence.

If the methods are such as to ensure that only evidence that the chosen hypothesis predicts will be observed, then intuitively that evidence will not give support to the hypothesis. But that gives no support to predictivism or any other non-Bayesian account of the relation of evidence to hypothesis, for that result follows straightforwardly from Bayes's theorem (without bringing in any evidence about when h was proposed relative to the discovery of e). For, if e and only e must be observed, and e is entailed by hypothesis h, not merely does $P(e|h\&k)=1$ but $P(e|k)=1$. And so, by Bayes's theorem $P(h|e\&k)=P(h|k)$, and e does not increase the probability of h. Thus, suppose you test your hypothesis that all fish in the sea are more than 10 cm in length by using a net with a 10 cm mesh, then the fact that you catch only fish longer than 10 cm is no evidence in favour of your hypothesis—whereas it would be substantial evidence if you had got the same result with a net of much smaller mesh. And this is because, using a 10 cm mesh net, you can get no other result from fishing, whether or not your hypothesis is true.

However, it does not follow from that that, if you secure certain evidence by a method designed to obtain that evidence, then necessarily that evidence is less supportive of your hypothesis than it would otherwise be. Everything depends on the relative probability of that evidence being obtained by that method or alternatively by a different method, on the favoured hypothesis and on its rivals. If using a certain method increases the probability that e will be found if h is true and also if its rivals are true by the same proportion, then the evidence is equally supportive whether it is obtained by that method or not. (The trouble with the fishing-net case is that using the 10 cm mesh net rather than a net with a smaller mesh increased the probability of the evidence being found by much more on the preferred hypothesis, on such rival hypotheses as that all the fish are larger than 5 cm.

Consider the example of 'optional stopping'. You look for evidence relevant to choosing between h_1 and some rival hypotheses, but—keen to prove h_1 as probable as possible—you go on looking until you have got evidence that (if we ignore the procedure used to obtain it) would make h_1 very much more probable than its rivals. Intuitively, one might suppose that the evidence would not be nearly as favourable to h_1 if it is obtained by optional stopping than if it were obtained by choosing in advance which areas to investigate.[6] But that will not be so if—as is often the case—the use of the method of optional stopping increases or decreases equally the probability that the evidence will be found both on the preferred hypothesis and on its rivals. In a description of an optional-stopping experiment, it is important to be precise about what is the evidence obtained by which method of optional stopping.

[6] See Deborah Mayo, *Error and the Growth of Experimental Knowledge* (University of Chicago Press, 1966), 341–59, for this claim.

The paradigm case of an optional-stopping experiment is where you have two hypotheses about the statistical probability of a coin landing heads (statistical probability in an infinite sequence under a distribution of initial conditions typical of that under which tosses are made). You go on tossing until you reach a proportion of heads to total throws that is that most probable on one of the hypotheses and stop there. The suggestion is made that the fact that this result was obtained by this means makes it less strong evidence in favour of the chosen hypothesis than if you had decided in advance to stop after exactly that number of tosses. It follows from Bayes's theorem that in this case optional stopping is irrelevant; and it is used as an objection to Bayes's theorem and so to the use of the probability calculus for calculating logical probability that this is so.

Assuming that the alternative hypotheses have equal prior probabilities, everything depends on the 'likelihood ratio', the relative probability on the two hypotheses of getting the given result. Let h_1 claim that the statistical probability is $\frac{1}{2}$, h_2 claim that it is $\frac{2}{3}$. You go on tossing until you get exactly 50 per cent heads and then you stop. The 50 per cent ratio can be obtained by many different sequences of heads and tails. For example, a 50 per cent ratio after 4 tosses could be obtained by HTTH or by HTHT or by TTHH and so on. The possibility of each different sequence of $2n$ tosses that would result in obtaining the required ratio (that is, n heads), given h_1, is $(\frac{1}{2})^{2n}$; given h_2 it is $(\frac{1}{3})^n (\frac{2}{3})^n$. Given that the only evidence is that the ratio was obtained after $2n$ tosses (that is, there is no evidence of optional stopping), then there are $\frac{2n!}{n!n!}$ distinct sequences by which the required ratio can be obtained. ($n!$ is $1 \times 2 \times 3 \ldots \times n$; $2n!$ is $1 \times 2 \times 3 \times \ldots \times n \ldots \times 2n$.) The probability of reaching it given h_1 is $(\frac{1}{2})^{2n} \frac{2n!}{n!n!}$; the probability of reaching it given h_2 is $(\frac{1}{3})^n (\frac{2}{3})^n \frac{2n!}{n!n!}$. The larger is $2n$, the larger is the difference between the two probabilities, since $(\frac{1}{2})^{2n}$ is greater than $(\frac{1}{3})^n (\frac{2}{3})^n$ for any n. But, if we have the further evidence e_3 that the result (e_1) was obtained by optional stopping, this amounts to evidence that it was *not* reached after 2 tosses or 4 tosses or 6 tosses . . . up to $(2n-2)$ tosses. So, for fixed n, the number of ways in which the required ratio can be obtained by optional stopping will be less—indeed very much less—than the number of ways it could otherwise be obtained. For example, while the 50 per cent ratio can be reached in 6 different ways after 4 tosses, 4 of these involve reaching it after 2 tosses as well; and it can be reached only after 4 tosses but not after 2 tosses in only 2 ways (HHTT or TTHH). So the result being obtained after 4 tosses by 'optional stopping' is *less* probable than it being obtained after having tossed the coin the exact number of times decided in advance. So, while the probability of each of these ways remains $(\frac{1}{2})^{2n}$ on h_1 and $(\frac{1}{3})^n (\frac{2}{3})^n$ on h_2, the number of ways in which the 50 per cent ratio could have been obtained is much less if optional stopping has been used. But that will make no difference to the ratio of the probabilities of getting the evidence on the two hypotheses, which will remain $(\frac{1}{2})^{2n} : (\frac{1}{3})^n (\frac{2}{3})^n$. In consequence, while optional stopping makes it in this case less probable that you will find your required ratio after $2n$ tosses, given either h_1 or h_2, that makes no difference to the probability that the total evidence gives to the respective hypotheses. For, while $P(e_1\&e_3|h_1\&k)$ is less than $P(e_1|h_1\&k)$, so is $P(e_1\&e_3|h_2\&k)$ less than $P(e_1|h_2\&k)$ in the same proportion. Hence $P(h_1|e_1\&e_3\&k) = P(h_1|e_1\&k)$. Optional stopping has made no difference. And once we see that in this kind of case optional stopping increases or decreases by the same proportion the probability that the required ratio will be obtained both on the preferred hypothesis *and* on rival hypotheses, we recognize that the fact that the result was obtained by optional stopping is irrelevant to its evidential force. Bayesianism yields this initially surprising but on reflection intuitively plausible result.

There are, however, other kinds of optional-stopping experiment in which the optional stopping does make a difference to the likelihood ratio and so to the probabilities of the hypotheses being tested. Suppose our hypotheses as before. But suppose that all we learn at the end of the experiment is that the 50 per cent ratio was obtained at some stage *within* 2N tosses, but we are not told at what stage. That is, *either* after 2 tosses, there was $\frac{1}{2}$ heads; *or* after 4 tosses, there were $\frac{2}{4}$ heads; *or* after 6 tosses there were $\frac{3}{6}$ tosses, and so on. It does, of course, become very likely indeed, if we take a large 2N, that at some stage we will get the 50 per cent result if h_1 is true. It also becomes quite likely that we will get that result if h_2 is true. But, the larger is 2N, the greater the likelihood of getting the 50 per cent result if h_1 is true exceeds the likelihood of getting it if h_2 is true. The ratio of the two likelihoods, for 2N=2 is 1.125; for 2N=4 is 1.151; for 2N=6 is 1.171. But compare that sequence with the likelihoods of getting the 50 per cent ratio at an exact number of tosses. The 'likelihood ratio' of the likelihood of getting the 50 per cent result if h_1 is true divided by the likelihood of getting it if h_2 is true at exactly 2N tosses, for 2N=2 is 1.125, for 2N=4 is 1.266, for 2N=6 is 1.423. So, if we compare two different sorts of evidence—evidence that the 50 per cent ratio was obtained at some stage within 2N tosses, with evidence that the ratio was obtained at exactly 2N tosses—then clearly the latter evidence is much better evidence in favour of the hypothesis on which it is the most probable outcome; it renders that hypothesis more probable than does the former evidence.[7] That follows straighforwardly from the probability calculus. It was perhaps the unexplicit assumption that this was the kind of comparison involved in an optional-stopping experiment—a comparison between a result having been obtained at some stage or other before a number of tosses fixed in advance had been made, and that result having been obtained at exactly that fixed number of tosses—which led to over-general claims

[7] As we make more and more tosses and N and so 2N $\rightarrow \infty$, the latter ratio—the ratio of the likelihood of getting the 50% result at 2N throws on h_1 divided by its likelihood on h_2— being $3^{2n}/2^{3n}$ gets larger without limit. However, the former ratio of the likelihood of getting the 50% result at some stage within 2N tosses on h_1 divided by the likelihood of getting it on h_2, approaches a maximum of 1.5 as 2N $\rightarrow \infty$. For p as the probability of heads and q as the probability of tails on one throw, the probability that 'no return to equilibrium ever occurs', i.e. that the 50% ratio is never reached is $|p-q|$, that is 0 on h_1 and and $\frac{1}{3}$ on h_2. (See W. Feller, *An Introduction to Probability Theory and its Applications*, i (3rd edn., John Wiley & Sons, 1968), 274.) So the ratio of the likelihood of getting the 50% ratio within 2N throws, as N $\rightarrow \infty$, is $\frac{3}{2} = 1.5$.

that any evidence obtained by optional stopping was weaker evidence than that evidence would be if it had not been obtained by optional stopping. The general point is that *if* using a certain method to obtain evidence *e* has the consequence that obtaining *e* is more probable on h_1 than h_2 by a smaller amount than it would be if you used a different method, then the use of that method diminishes the evidential force of *e*; that is, *e* increases the probability of h_1 less than it would do if the other method had been used. But optional stopping as such need not have that consequence.

The Occasional Relevance of Novelty Evidence

So, reverting to the main theme of this appendix, we have seen no reason to suppose that, for normal background evidence *k*, novelty evidence about when and by whom the hypothesis was formulated has any tendency to affect the probability of that hypothesis on any other evidence; and I have given some explanation of why people have, wrongly, sometimes thought otherwise. But it would be mistaken to suppose that my claim holds for every *k*, since, for any evidence and any hypothesis, there is always some background evidence that makes the former relevant to the latter. In particular, my claim does not hold in many cases where *k* reports evidence of a historical kind, the force of which (together with e_1 and e_2) is to indicate that someone has access to evidence relevant to *h* that is not publicly available. (e_1 is the evidence of what was observed; e_2 is novelty evidence about e_1 of the kind described in the earlier section.)

Here is an example where *k* is evidence of this historical kind. Let *h* be Grand Unified Field Theory, and e_1 be some observed consequence thereof. Let *k* be that *h* was formulated by Hawks, who always puts forward his theories after assembling many pieces of observational evidence that he does not reveal to the public, and that—so long as, subsequent to being formulated, they make one true new prediction—are always subsequently confirmed and never falsified. Then of course the evidence that a consequence of the theory (e_1) was observed subsequent to its formulation (e_2) increases its probability above that given by the mere evidence that a consequence of the theory was observed—$P(h|e_1\&k) < P(h|e_1\&e_2\&k)$.

Now let us consider in more detail an example recently brought forward by Maher in defence of the predictivist thesis that observation of a consequence of a theory subsequent to the formulation of the theory is more evidence in favour of the theory than the mere occurrence of the consequence:

> We imagine an experiment in which a coin is tossed 99 times, and a subject records whether the coin landed heads or tails on each toss. The coin seems normal, and the sequence of tosses appears random. The subject is now asked to state the outcome of the first 100 tosses of the coin. The subject responds by reading back the outcome of the first 99 tosses, and adds that the 100th toss will be heads. Assuming that no mistakes have been made in recording the observed tosses, the probability that the subject is right about these 100 tosses

is equal to the probability that the last toss will be heads. Everyone seems to agree that they would give this a probability of about $\frac{1}{2}$.

Now we modify the situation slightly. Here a subject is asked to predict the results of 100 tosses of the coin. The subject responds with an apparently random sequence of heads and tails. The coin is tossed 99 times, and these tosses are exactly as the subject predicted. The coin is now to be tossed for the 100th time, and the subject has predicted that this toss will land heads. At this point, the probability that the subject is right about all 100 tosses is equal to the probability that the 100th toss will land heads. But in this case, everyone seems to agree that they would give it a probability close to 1.

The difference between the two situations is that in the first the subject has accommodated the data about the first 99 tosses, while in the second that data has been predicted. Clearly the reason for our different attitude in the two situations is that the successful prediction is strong evidence that the subject has a reliable method of predicting coin tosses, while the successful accommodation provides no reason to think that the subject has a reliable method of predicting coin tosses.[8]

Let e_1 be the outcomes of the first 99 tosses, h be e_1 plus the proposition that heads will occur on the 100th toss, e_2 be that h was formulated before e_1 was observed, and k be a description of the set-up 'where the coin seems normal and the sequence of tosses appears random'. k will also have to include the information that h was the only (or almost the only) hypothesis formulated, for, as Howson and Franklin[9] point out, if all possible hypotheses have been formulated, the example will not work. h would be no more likely to be true than the hypothesis consisting of e_1 plus the proposition that tails will occur on the 100th toss, if that had been formulated. The fact that someone guessed the lottery numbers correctly is no reason for supposing that he will guess the numbers correctly next time, when on the successful occasion all possible numbers had been guessed by someone or other.

However, given k above, claims Maher, 'everyone seems to agree that' $P(h|e_1\&e_2\&k)$ is close to 1. Everyone is surely correct on this. Yet, Maher also claims, 'everyone seems to agree' that $P(h/e_1\&{\sim}e_2\&k)$ is about $\frac{1}{2}$. Hence it will follow that $P(h|e_1\&e_2\&k) > P(h|e_1\&k)$, and so historical evidence increases confirmation. Now, even if 'everyone agrees' that $P(h|e_1\&{\sim}e_2\&k)$ is about $\frac{1}{2}$, it is possible that they are mistaken. That apparently random sequence may not be really random. It may be that there is a pattern of regularity in the first 99 tosses from which it follows that the 100th toss will very probably be heads, which the subject who put forward h has alone spotted. Then $P(h|e_1\&k)$ will also be close to 1 (even though most of us are too stupid to realize that), and the historical information e_2 is irrelevant.

But suppose there is no observable pattern in the tosses. In that case, what 'everyone agrees' about the probabilities is correct. So we ask why is $P(h|e_1\&e_2\&k)$ close to 1. The answer is that k includes historical information that h was the only

[8] Maher, 'Howson and Franklin on Prediction', 330.

[9] Howson and Franklin, 'Maher, Mendeleev and Bayesianism', 577.

hypothesis put forward. That together with e_1 and e_2—the fact that his predictions were so accurate—is very strong evidence that the hypothesizer has access to information about bias in the set-up that we do not (either via some publicly observable evidence other than that of the results of the 99 tosses, or via some internal intuitions—maybe he has powers of telekinesis). This is for the reason[10] that (e_1&e_2&k) would be very improbable if the hypothesizer did not have this information. That is, we trust the prediction because of who made it, not because of when it was made. That that is the correct account of what is going on here can be seen by the fact that, if we add to k irrefutable evidence that the hypothesizer had no private information, then we must conclude that his correct prediction of the first 99 tosses was a mere lucky guess and provides no reason for supposing that he will be right next time.

So Maher's example gives no reason to suppose that in general mere evidence of the novelty of other evidence adds to the confirming force of that other evidence. I know of no plausible example to show that it does so, except in cases where the background evidence k includes historical evidence; typically evidence about who formulated or advocated the hypothesis, when the force of the novelty evidence e_2 is to indicate that that person knows more about the subject matter than the public evidence e_1 shows. In this case alone, I suggest, where the historical evidence shows private information, is the 'method' by which the hypothesis is generated of any importance for its probability. In general, the method by which the hypothesis was generated is irrelevant to its probability on evidence. Whether or not Mendeleev's theory was generated 'by the method of looking for patterns in the elements', its probability depends on whether it *does* correctly entail patterns, not how it was arrived at. Kekule's theory of the benzene ring is neither more or less probable on its evidence because it was suggested to Kekule in a dream. Only if the evidence suggests that someone has private information does it become important whether the hypothesis was generated in the light of consideration of that information. If it was, then evidence that the hypothesis has been generated by a method that has had success so far is (indirect) evidence in favour of its truth. But if we have the private evidence for ourselves we can ignore all that, and assess its force directly.

[10] Given by Colin Howson in 'Accommodation, Prediction, and Bayesian Confirmation Theory', *Philosophy of Science Association Proceedings, 1988* (Philosophy of Science Association, 1989), 381–92; see pp. 383–4.

ADDITIONAL NOTES

A. *Alston on Individuating Types of Process* (see Ch. 1 n. 10)

In 'How to Think about Reliability' (*Philosophical Topics*, 23 (1995), 1–29), William Alston urges (p. 5) that psychological facts (probably) 'pick out a unique type as the one of which a particular process is a token'. We must, he holds, confine ourselves to causal factors within the subject's skin affecting whether or not he will hold the relevant belief. The process is defined by the function from input to belief-output, which (p. 16) 'reflects or embodies the actual dynamism of the process, what is responsible for this belief with this content being formed on this basis'. That settles the issue of what should be the depth of the type, though it is unclear why the issue should be settled in this way, except that, as Alston writes, 'reliabilist epistemology' does assume this. But there is no reason intrinsic to its reliabilist nature why it should make this assumption. What, however, about the width of the type? Alston advocates a psychological hypothesis 'that each case of belief formation involves the activation of a certain disposition (habit, mechanism . . .) that "embodies" or "realizes" a certain function that determines a belief with a certain content (and perhaps certain strength) on the basis of certain features of input. This function endows the (token) process with a certain generality, and it is this that marks out the unique type that is, as I say, "actually operative in the process"'. (Alston, private letter to the author, 21 December 1999; I quote this letter because he was concerned in this to make especially clear his claim in the cited article). Then we consider whether (p. 10), 'over a wide range of situations of the sort we typically encounter', that process usually yields true beliefs. If so, it is reliable, and—the reliabilist can use Alston's theory to claim—all those beliefs (whether true or not) are justified.

However, I remain unpersuaded that Alston has solved the generality problem. The problems to which I drew attention in the text of Chapter 1 remain. For surely—even confining ourselves to processes 'within the skin'—there will be *a* function from input of all kinds to output (of beliefs) of all kinds. Even if Alston were correct (and this is only a psychological hypothesis) in supposing that this general function subdivides readily into a small number of different functions describing different dispositions of belief production, it seems in no way obvious why for epistemological purposes one should refer the token to the type of one of these functions, rather than to some narrower type or to the type of belief production in general. And, even if Alston is right about the psychology and right in supposing that we should use the dispositions discussed by psychology for assessing the epistemological adequacy of the grounds of a token belief, there remains the problem of just how wide should be the environment in which we measure the reliability of processes of the type. That phrase 'a wide range of situations of the sort we typically encounter' can be cashed out in many ways, yielding different results—varying with who are the believers, and in which places and times we study them. Alston acknowledges that the notion of 'a wide range' is 'far from precise', but I do not think he appreciates just how far it is—as illustrated by the different possibilities in the Oblonsky example. And the issue next discussed in the text remains—are we concerned with reliability in the actual world or over which range of possible worlds?

B. *Decision Theory* (see Ch. 2 n. 10)

Decision theory formalizes the consequences for actions of people's purposes and beliefs in a way that allows the ascription of more precise values to their beliefs about the probable consequences of their actions and the strengths of their purposes. The normal version of Decision Theory is known as 'Bayesian' decision theory and uses the principle of 'maximum expected utility'. The name 'Bayesian' can be misleading in suggesting that it is the natural form of decision theory for someone committed to the traditional axioms of the probability calculus and so to Bayes's theorem (on which see Chapters 3 and 4). Alternative principles for which action is the action to be done are perfectly compatible with ascriptions of probability conforming to the traditional axioms, as we shall see below.

Decision theory can be put to two rather different uses: to calculating the strengths of people's beliefs and purposes manifested in their actions; and to calculating the actions that a 'rational' agent would do, if he had beliefs and purposes of certain strengths (or perhaps—instead of purposes—beliefs, including beliefs about the worth—'utilities'—of certain goals). Decision Theory was developed as a theory of rational behaviour by J. Von Neumann and O. Morgenstern, in *Theory of Games and Economic Behaviour* (Princeton University Press, 1944). But F. P. Ramsey had adumbrated earlier the main idea of how this kind of apparatus could enable us to infer an agent's beliefs and purposes from his actual behaviour. (See his 1926 paper 'Truth and Probability', in D. H. Mellor (ed.), *Foundations* (Routledge and Kegan Paul, 1978).)

In its first (and perhaps less usual) use in analysing actual behaviour, Bayesian decision theory can be used so as to entail the very few precise relations between what I have called a subject's ultimate purposes (and shall here just call 'purposes'), his means–end beliefs, and his more basic purposes—that is, which more basic action the subject will attempt to perform, which I analysed in Chapter 2, so as to give strengths of purposes and beliefs more precise values. In effect it gives precise form to the relation stated in the text that whether a subject will so some action 'will depend on whether her strongest purposes . . . are ones which, she believes, will more probably be attained' by doing that action than by doing any incompatible action. Strength of purpose is to be measured by the utility for the subject of the goal he has the purpose of achieving. This goal has 4 units of utility, that one 8. (If the pay-off of some action is monetary, these units may or may not be proportional to the money units involved. For example, the utility of winning £1 million may not be 100,000 times as great as the utility of winning £10.) We suppose that subjects have precise beliefs about the probability of some action of theirs bringing about some outcome (a means–end belief). Then the expected utility of some action is defined as the sum of the utilities of the various possible outcomes of the action, each multiplied by the probability (the subject believes) of that action achieving that outcome. Suppose that there are n possible actions—A_1, A_2, . . . A_n—open to the subject, one and only one of which he must do; and there are m possible outcomes—X_1, X_2, . . . X_m; and that they have respectively (for the subject) the utilities U_1, U_2, . . . U_m. Positive utilities represent goals the agent is seeking; and greater values thereof represent stronger purposes to attain those goals. Negative utilities represent states of affairs that the agent has the goal of avoiding; greater negative values represent stronger purposes of avoiding. Let us represent by $P(X_j|A_i)$ the probability (in *S*'s belief) that some action A_i will attain X_j. This is often called *S*'s 'subjective probability' that A_i will attain goal X_j. Then the expected utility of action A_i is defined as

$$\sum_{j=1}^{j=m} P(X_j \mid A_i)U_j$$

Each action open to the agent will have an expected utility—higher in so far as it is more probable that the action will bring about goals with higher utilities. In this model, *S* will then attempt to do, and—on the assumption that he has normal bodily powers—will do the action with the highest ('maximum') expected utility (or one of the actions with maximum expected utility, if there is more than one).

A study of a subject's behaviour in certain artificial situations will then constrain within limits the strengths of his purposes and the (subjective) probabilities he ascribes to the effects of his actions. For example, suppose that the subject is offered a variety of bets on the outcome of a particular horse race; by which (if any) of these bets he accepts, we can reach conclusions about the comparative values he places on various possible winnings, and the probabilities he ascribes to each of the horses winning. Suppose there are just two horses—Eclipse and another. Jones is willing to bet £10 at 2–1 on Eclipse winning, after having refused to bet £10 at evens on this. Let A_0 be the action of not betting at all, A_1 be the action of betting £10 at evens, A_2 the action of betting £10 at 2–1; X_1 the outcome of gaining £10, X_2 the outcome of gaining £20, X_3 the outcome of losing £10, and X_0 the outcome of neither winning nor losing; U_1 the utility of X_1, U_2 the utility of X_2, U_3 the utility of X_3, and U_0 the utility of X_0. Then the expected utility of A_1 will be $P(X_1|A_1)U_1 + P(X_3|A_1)U_3$; the expected utility of A_2 will be $P(X_2|A_2)U_2 + P(X_3|A_2)U_3$; and the expected utility of A_0 will be X_0. Then the expected utility of A_2 will exceed that of

A_0, which will exceed that of A_1. That result is, of course, compatible with ascribing many different values to the probabilities and utilities involved. If we assume that Jones ascribes probabilities in accordance with the axioms of the calculus, so that the probabilities of exclusive and exhaustive outcomes sum to 1, that will narrow the probabilities and utilities that can be ascribed. If we assume that Jones values winning more money more than winning less money, and winning more than losing, and also that he believes that the outcome of the race is unaffected by whether and how he bets on it, all that will narrow the values we can ascribe a bit further. And if we assume that he values winning £20 twice as much as winning £10, and gives to losing £10 the value of minus the value of winning £10, then we can reach some definite conclusions about his beliefs about the comparative probabilities (i.e. the relative strengths of his beliefs). From his willingness to bet at 2–1 and unwillingness to bet at evens, we can conclude that he believes the probability of Eclipse winning lies between $\frac{1}{2}$ and $\frac{1}{3}$. Further study of Jones's betting behaviour will mean that we need to make less initial assumptions—e.g. that he values winning more than losing—because we can test these. But we can get such results out of subsequent tests only if we assume that Jones's beliefs and the strengths of his purposes remain the same—the simplest and so the most probable supposition, but not necessarily a correct one. We may assume that Jones is like most of us in some of the ways in which he ascribes probabilities and in putting a higher value on winning rather than losing money. These assumptions are themselves assumptions of simplicity to the effect that Jones and other people have similar purposes and similar ways of ascribing probabilities, and so, I shall be arguing in Chapter 4, for a priori reasons probably true. Note that the point made in the text remains that to infer any more theoretical beliefs from a person's means–end beliefs involves a further inductive step. Note too here that the notion of the 'utility' of some goal for a subject just is a measure of the strength of his purpose to achieve it. It is not a measure of the subject's belief about how valuable the goal really is. For subjects may evince weakness of will. A subject may believe that giving up smoking is more valuable than smoking and yet smoke all the same. His purpose to smoke is then stronger than any purpose to give up; and so, in terms of this model, the utility of smoking for him is greater than the utility of giving up.

This use of decision theory seeks merely to formalize our procedures of inference from people's public behaviour to the purposes and beliefs that direct that behaviour; and to give content to precise measurements of the strengths of those purposes and beliefs. It does that by analysing the behaviour of people in an artificial setting such as (in a literal sense) betting. It is typically used by advocates of the 'subjective theory of probability' to show how we can measure people's 'subjective probabilities', i.e. the strengths of their beliefs (see pp. 70–1). The more usual use of decision theory is to show which actions are rational in the sense of best conducive to achieving certain goals. For this purpose the utility of a goal is a measure, not of a subject's actual strength of purpose but of how valuable she considers the goal to be; and the probabilities are supposed (in effect) to be logical probabilities on the evidence available to the subject, and not the subject's beliefs about what these are. Bayesian decision theory then commends the action that maximizes expected utility as the rational one, 'rational' in the sense that it will probably do better than any other one in forwarding what the subject considers valuable. If the subject does not do the action with maximum expected utility, then this will be the result either of logical incompetence (not being able to work out which action that is) or of weakness of will.

The trouble with this application of 'Bayesian' decision theory is, however, that, for given assumptions of probabilities to actions achieving their goals, it is normally so much more obvious to someone committed to the principle of maximizing expected utility which action is the rational one than what are the utilities of different states of affairs, that their ascription of utilities is determined by their view on which action is the rational one rather than vice versa. So the principle is not helpful. Thus, if we assume an assessment of the logical probability (on the evidence) of Eclipse winning the race at $\frac{2}{5}$ to be correct, will a rational person bet £10 on Eclipse at 2:1? Obviously he should if (and only if) he values being in a situation with {a probability of $\frac{2}{5}$ of winning £20, with a probability of $\frac{3}{5}$ of losing £10}, more than he values (neither winning nor losing). Decision theory says that this is to be determined by the utility he ascribes to the different states—winning £20, losing £10, neither winning nor losing. But intuitively it is more obvious to the subject whether he values being in a situation with {a probability of $\frac{2}{5}$ of winning £20 with a probability of $\frac{3}{5}$ of losing £10}, rather than {neither winning nor losing}, than which utilities he ascribes to the different states. It may, however, sometimes seem obvious to someone what are the utilities of various states of affairs (e.g. because those are the utilities that, given that his conduct on a previous occasion is rational in maximizing expected utility, those are the utilities that the states must have). But it then becomes open to question whether it is rational to follow the principle of maximizing expected utility rather than some other principle, e.g. the maximim principle suggested by Wald: do the action that has the consequence that the maximum disutility (loss) is smaller than if you do any other action. (See Abraham Wald, *Statistical Decision Functions* (Wiley, 1950). Bayesian decision theory is not often a very useful theory for determining rational action.

C. *Randomness* (see Ch. 3 n. 4)

Some writers on probability insist that one should talk about there being a probability of an *A* being a *B* in a class of *A*s only if the process that determines which of them are *B* is a random one. One kind of definition of such a process being random is that it is random iff any process of selecting a sub-class from the class of *A*s would yield a sub-class with the same proportion of *B*s as the main class. Richard von Mises put on this the restriction that the process must not pick out the members of the sub-class to any extent in virtue of whether or not they are *B*s. (See his

Probability, Statistics and Truth (George Allen & Unwin, 1957), ch. 1.) But a stronger restriction is required if any process is to turn out to be random. Alonzo Church, for example, added the restriction that any sub-class must be selected by an effectively computable function generating the numerical indices of the *A*s (numbered by the order in which they occur in the class). (See his 'On the Concept of a Random Sequence', *Bulletin of the American Mathematical Society*, 46 (1940), 130–5.) And more refined suggestions have been made subsequently—see Jan von Plato, *Creating Modern Probability* (Cambridge University Press, 1994), 233–7. Any definition of this kind is liable to rule out all talk about probability in a finite class—for there will be always be some process of selecting from any class of *A*s all the *B*s. (For example, we could simply give each of the *A*s a number and then select the 3rd, 5th, 10th etc., when as a matter of fact the 3rd, 5th, 10th, etc. were all *B*s.) And it is also liable to rule out much talk about probability in infinite classes. There would, for example, be no probability of a natural number being even, because there is a process (describable by an effectively computable function) of selecting from natural numbers a sub-class in which all the numbers are even (the process of selecting alternate numbers, beginning with 2); and so the proportion of even numbers in the sub-class is different from that in the class of natural numbers as a whole. But, since a lot both of useful ordinary talk and sophisticated reasoning about probability concerns the probability of an *A* being *B* where the process of selection is not random, it seems an unnecessary restriction to insist on randomness in this way.

D. *Laws of Nature* (see Ch. 3 n. 6 and Ch. 4 n. 2)

Given the logical equivalence claimed in the text of Chapter 3 between claims about laws of nature and claims about physical probabilities, there remain two metaphysical issues to which I need to draw attention but with respect to which I do not need to defend a particular view. The first issue is whether the fundamental causally influential elements are physical probabilities or laws of nature.

On one account the fundamental causally influential elements are physical probabilities; talk about laws of nature is just talk about the physical probabilities of individual events belonging to some event-kind *A*, when all events (actual and physically possible) of that kind have the same physical probabilities. That allows for the logical possibility that there may be some particular event α which belongs to some event-kind *A*, which has some physical probability *p* of being *B*, when events similar to α in all respects do not have that physical probability (in which case there would not be a universal law about all *A*s having one certain physical probability of being *B*). On the second account the fundamental causally influential elements are the laws of nature. Physical probabilities exist only in so far as they are consequences of laws of nature. A particular event α can have a physical probability of *p* of being *B*, only if all events of some kind to which α belongs (for example, all *As*) have the same physical probability of being B. Since causation is a matter of some event α making another event β physically probable, when β does actually then occur, the issue as to whether there can be 'singular causation' (α causing β, without α-like events causing β-like events under circumstances the same in some respect), turns in part on which of the above views is correct.

Those who adopt the first account may naturally develop it so as to hold that it is not really events, but the substances involved in those events, that do the causing. The cause or causes are not events, but the substances of which the events are states—not the ignition of the gunpowder, but the gunpowder itself. The substances have causal powers, including a power to bring about an effect of the kind of the event being explained; and liabilities to exercise those powers (a liability to exercise them of physical necessity or with some particular degree of physical probability) under circumstances such as those in which the event being explained occurred. The gunpowder has the power to produce an explosion, and the liability to exercise that power when ignited under certain conditions of temperature and pressure in the presence of oxygen, conditions that were manifested at the relevant time; and so in virtue of its powers and liabilities the gunpowder caused the explosion. Substances of the same kind have similar powers and liabilities, and then statements of the 'laws of nature' are simply statements to the effect that all substances of certain kinds have certain powers and liabilities to exercise them under certain conditions. These liabilities are physical probabilities. So the 'law of nature' that all copper expands when heated is just the regularity that all pieces of copper have the power to expand and the liability to exercise it when heated. Laws of nature are not then themselves causally efficacious factors; they are just contingent regularities in the causal powers and liabilities of substances. We may call the second account, used in the text of Chapter 4, the laws and initial conditions (LIC) account; and the first account, developed in the above way, the substances, powers, and liabilities account (SPL).

SPL was perhaps the normal way in which scientific explanation was couched until talk about 'laws of nature' became fashionable in the seventeenth century. SPL was brought back into modern discussion in R. Harré and E. H. Madden, *Causal Powers* (Basil Blackwell, 1975). For my own reasons for preferring an SPL account to an LIC one, see my 'The Irreducibility of Causation', *Dialectica*, 51 (1997), 79–92. One of those reasons is that it makes the pattern of inanimate explanation much more similar to the pattern of personal explanation. Personal explanation explains by substances (persons), their powers to act, and their liabilities to do so. The differences from inanimate explanation on the SPL model are that in personal explanation liabilities to act, to use powers, arise from beliefs and desires; and that the powers of persons are powers to bring about effects intentionally, i.e. because they have the purpose of doing so.

If we adopt the SPL account, the upward inference from data to law has a more complicated form than I have represented it in the text. We infer from many particular phenomena to the simplest account of the powers and liabilities of substances that cause the phenomena, and we often find that this involves attributing the same powers and liabilities to all observed objects of some kind, whose behaviour we have studied. We find, for example, that many separate pieces of copper expand when heated; and infer that (it is logically probable that) each such piece of copper has the power to expand and the liability to exercise that power when heated. This explanation is the simplest explanation of the particular expansion, because the expansion occurs when, and only when, the only observed change in the situation is that heat is applied to the copper. We then infer that there must be some common cause (in the Big Bang, or whoever caused the Big Bang) of all the observed objects of the same kind, e.g. all observed pieces of copper having the same powers and liabilities. This leads us to expect (makes it logically probable) that all other pieces of copper will have the same powers and liabilities, and so that it is a law of nature that all copper expands when heated. This is clearly a less direct route of inference to laws than that described in the text of Chapter 4. For the sake of simplicity of exposition, I assume in the text the LIC account; nothing else in this book is affected by whether we adopt the LIC account or the SPL account.

What, however, is incompatible with the text is the extreme version of the second account advocated by David Lewis, who holds that not merely do 'chances' (which are the nearest equivalent in his system to physical probabilities) supervene on laws of nature, but that laws of nature supervene on the actual history of the world, past and future, i.e. on statistical probabilities. (See his 'Humean Supervenience Debugged', *Mind*, 103 (1994), 473–90, esp. pp. 473–82). I have suggested in the text that our ordinary understanding distinguishes between what does happen and what has to happen (or has a physical propensity to happen); and I have sought to analyse the logical relations between these notions. Lewis's claim, in effect, is that there is no such thing as physical probability in my sense. To accept this is to accept a revised system of metaphysical categories, which I see no reason to adopt, and whose epistemology I do not discuss.

E. *Epistemic Probability in the writings of Garber and Jeffrey* (see Ch. 3 n. 12)

Epistemic probability, in my sense, is a very general form of the system put forward by Daniel Garber under the name of 'local Bayesianism'. (See Daniel Garber, 'Old Evidence and Logical Omniscience', in J. Earman (ed.), *Testing Scientific Theories, Minnesota Studies in the Philosophy of Science vol 10* (University of Minnesota Press, 1983)). Garber expounded a calculus modified from the Bayesian and confined to a particular language L^*, consisting of a countably infinite number of atomic sentences. Not all the logical truths of L^* are built into the rules of the calculus for calculating probabilities, but as they are acquired as evidence, so that affects the probabilities of hypotheses. (Garber did require the investigator to know all the tautologies of L^*. That is, however, quite a lot of logical knowledge, rather too much perhaps to expect of simple people in their assessments of what is likely to happen.) A somewhat similar approach is that of Richard Jeffrey (see his *Probability and the Art of Judgment* (Cambridge University Press, 1992), 103–7). Jeffrey's account is also in effect confined to a particular language, where the investigator ascribes prior probabilities to conjunctions of propositions in ignorance of any logical relations between them; then discovering new logical relations leads to automatic adjustment of those prior probabilities. Discovering, for example, that p entails q, leads to (p & not-q) having a prior probability of zero. But both of these writers in effect assume that investigators are right to ascribe prior probabilities in the way they do before acquiring new evidence. But, in any normal use of inductive probability, we can criticize an investigator for not having calculated the probability correctly in a respect that amounts to ascribing wrong values to prior probabilities. And neither of their systems has any application to the more interesting cases where a new hypothesis may be discovered not formulatable in the limited language. They do not answer the question of how probabilities should be adjusted when a new hypothesis is suggested, as opposed to when new logical relations are discovered between already available propositions. My sketch of an account for indexing different kinds of epistemic probability does not suffer from either of these deficiencies—for example, h might include quite new predicates, so long as the 'criteria of logical probability' include general enough rules for ascribing prior probabilities to hypotheses including new predicates. But any particular way of axiomatizing these criteria and measuring deductive steps would prove very arbitrary.

F. *The Computational Account of Simplicity* (see Ch. 4 n. 12)

There is an interesting and superficially much more precise and unified account of the simplicity of a formula in terms of the reciprocal of the minimum number of computational symbols (in 'bits', 0's or 1's, that is) needed to express that formula, called its 'string length'. To give an example of string length—a random string of 10^8 bits would have a string length of about 10^8, whereas a string of 10^8 1's or a string of alternating 1's and 0's could be expressed by formulae using far less bits. R. J. Solomonoff ('A Formal Theory of Inductive Inference', *Information and Control*, 7 (1964), 1–22) first proposed giving formulae intrinsic Bayesian probabilities by this method. His account gives a weighting to mathematical formulae of much the same kind as that given by my fourth and subsequent 'facets' of simplicity. But Solomonoff gives no rules for comparing formulae relating different physical variables. Thus the formulae $F = \frac{Gmm'}{r^2}$ for the gravitational force and $F = \frac{\alpha ee'}{r^2}$ for the electrostatic force have the same mathematical form but relate different physical variables. And so do 'all emeralds are green' and 'all emeralds are grue'. We need to give preference to formulae relating to the more readily observable variables. A formula $x=y$ could hide a very complicated relationship if it needs a great number of observations and complicated extrapolation therefrom to detect the value of x. This is the point of my third facet. We can, however, deal with this in the spirit of the computational approach by assuming a common langugage of predicates designating variables equally easy to observe (as analysed in my third facet), and weight other predicates by the number of bits needed to introduce them via the former predicates into the language.

The major divergence of my account from a computational formula of this kind arises from its clash with my first two facets. It can often require far fewer bits to postulate a large number of entities or properties or kinds thereof than to postulate a small number. Suppose that for some theoretical reason deriving from some simple theory overwhelmingly supported by our data that there can only be 10 kinds of quarks. We look for signs of a randomly chosen 5 of these in experiments where they might 'show up', i.e. when if they exist the observed data would be different; but we find signs of only 3 of them. Consider now the following hypotheses of equal scope fitting equally well with our background evidence (our quark theory) and yielding the data equally well: h_1—all kinds of quark exist except the two that did not show up; h_2—only three kinds of quark exist (those that have shown up); h_3—all kinds of quark exist except the two that did not show up and a third named one (which is not one of the ones that did show up). The computational account yields the result that h_1 is the simplest hypothesis (because to state it, given the background theory, we need only to describe the two quarks that do not exist), and then h_2 and h_3 are equally simple each requiring the description of three quarks—either ones that do or ones that do not exist. Given that all hypotheses satisfy the three other criteria for a probable explanation equally well, it would follow that h_1 is the most probable hypothesis, and then h_2 and h_3 are less probable than h_1 but equally probable with each other. This seems to me counterintuitive. Of course, much vaguer hypotheses (that is, ones of less scope) than these will be more probable than any of them, e.g. h_4 'the three kinds of quark that have shown up exist and one or two others (we do not know which) as well' or h_5 'the three kinds of quark that have shown up exist' (h_5 not being committed to whether or not other quarks exist). But if we have to opt for one of the more precise hypotheses, it seems clear to me that we would not judge that h_1 is more probable than both h_2 and h_3. My second facet of simplicity yields the result that h_2 is simpler than h_3, and h_3 than h_1. I suggest that intuition favours my account in the sense that in the situation described above where all three hypotheses satisfy the other criteria of a probable explanation equally well, we would judge that h_2 is more probable than h_3, h_3 than h_1. But, as I emphasize in the text, nothing very much for the purposes of this book turns on exactly how simplicity is spelled out.

G. *Countable Additivity* (see Ch. 4 n. 24)

Axiom 4 is called the Axiom of Finite Additivity. There follows from it a more general principle of finite additivity, that for any finite number n of exclusive alternatives $p_1, p_2, p_3 \ldots p_n$, the probability that one or other of them is true is equal to the sum of the probabilities of each of them.

$$P(p_1 v p_2 v \ldots p_n | r) = \sum_{i=1}^{i=n} P(p_i | r)$$

It would seem a natural addition to this principle to suggest that a similar principle holds where the number of alternatives are infinite, and in that form it is called the Principle of Countable Additivity.

Designating by $\cup p_i$ the disjunction of i exclusive alternatives p_i the principle reads:

$$\underset{i=1}{\overset{\infty}{P}} (\cup p_i | r) = \sum_{i=1}^{\infty} (p_i | r)$$

This principle does not, however, follow from the Axiom of Finite Additivity, but would constitute an additional axiom. Theorists are, however, reluctant to adopt it, since it seems to lead to contradiction. For consider a situation where there are an infinite number of exclusive and exhaustive alternatives, each with equal prior probability. For reasons given earlier in the chapter, I do not think that it holds generally that each of an infinite number of exclusive and exhaustive alternatives has equal prior probability. Lawlike statements of the form $F = \frac{mm'}{r^2}$ have, for example, greater prior probability than statements of the form $F = \frac{mm'}{r^{2.001}}$ and these have greater prior probability than statements of the form $F = \frac{mm'}{r^{2.00001}}$ and so on. But let us suppose—plausibly—that for some infinite set of exclusive and exhaustive alternatives—not lawlike statements, but statements reporting values of intrinsic properties of particular objects such as the length (between 1 metre and 2 metres) of my desk—each one has an equal prior probability. Let us suppose that there is an equal prior probability that my desk is exactly 1.006 or 1.007 or 1.00065 and so on metres long. There are an infinite number of such possible values; and let us suppose that our background evidence entails that the desk does have a length between 1 metre and 2 metres. In that case, if we say that the prior probability of each such length has some finite value greater than zero, however small, it will follow that the sum of an infinite number of such values will be infinite; and so it would follow from the Principle of Countable Additivity that the probability that the desk has a length between 1 and 2 metres is infinite. Yet there cannot be probabilities greater than 1. But, if we attribute a value of 0 to the prior probability of each possible value of the length, the probability that the length will lie between 1 and 2 metres will (by the Principle of Countable Additivity) be 0—contrary to what is stated by the background evidence. For this reason, most theorists are unwilling to adopt the Principle of Countable Additivity.

No contradiction is generated, however, if we adopt a mathematics of infinitesimal numbers, in which there are an infinite number of such numbers greater than 0 but less than any finite number. Such a mathematics, called non-standard analysis, was developed by Abraham Robinson (see his *Non-Standard Analysis* (North-Holland Publishing Co., 1966)). This allows us to attribute the same infinitesimal value to each of an infinite number of prior probabilities, which sum conjointly to 1. If we do not adopt non-standard analysis, not merely will we be unable to calculate the probability of an infinite disjunction from the probabilities of each of its disjuncts and conversely; but we shall still have a problem about what to say about the probability of each of an infinite number of equiprobable disjuncts, one only of which is true. If we attribute a finite value to it, then, however small that value is, the more general Principle of Finite Additivity will have the consequence that the probability of the disjunction of some very large finite number of disjuncts will be greater than 1—which would mean that the disjunction was more probably true than a tautology (since it follows from Axiom 3 that a tautology has a probability of 1 on any evidence). So we would have to attribute to each disjunct the probability 0. But that would involve saying that such a disjunct was just as certainly false as a self-contradiction. That seems implausible. There is *some* chance of winning in a fair lottery with an infinite number of tickets! However, if we attribute the value 0 to the probability of each of an infinite number of equiprobable disjuncts, we need to understand probabilities of '1' and '0' in a wider way than the way in which I first introduced them: '$P(h|e)=0$' will need to be read as, 'given e, h is as or less probable than the probability of some particular member of a (denumerably) infinite set of equiprobable (exclusive and exhaustive) alternatives'. '$P(h|e)=1$' will need to be read as, 'given e, h is as or more probable than the probability of the disjunction of all the members (other than one particular member) of a (denumerably) infinite set of equiprobable (exclusive and exhaustive) alternatives'. But clearly, all this is far more complex and less readily applicable than my original definition of probabilities of 1 and 0, and assimilates probabilities that ought to be kept distinct. So we should adopt the Principle of Countable Additivity as an axiom additional to the Axiom of Finite Additivity, and, if necessary, use infinitesimal numbers in our calculations. However, for the sake of simplicity of exposition and because nothing further in this book turns on it, I have not made this addition to the text.

H. *Neyman-Pearson Statistics* (Ch. 4 n. 25)

Those many statisticians who deny that we can measure the probability of a hypothesis on evidence, because in their view we cannot measure prior probabilities, normally still hold that satisfactory rules can be constructed for how evidence should influence our conduct by way of leading us to 'accept' or 'reject' hypotheses. Such statisticians develop some variant of the Neyman–Pearson Theory of significance tests, or some variant thereof. (See J. Neyman and E. S. Pearson, *Joint Statistical Papers* (Cambridge Unversity Press, 1967).) This tells us to 'reject' some hypothesis h if the data (e) are such that (on background evidence k) $P(e|h\&k)$ is very low—that is, it is very improbable that you would find these data if the hypothesis were true; and it tells us to 'accept' the hypothesis if $P(e|\sim h\&k)$ is very low—that is, if it is very improbable that you would find the data if the hypothesis was false. These statisticians provide a precise way of measuring 'very low' in terms of the 'significance level' of a test (that is, the method by which e was obtained). They tell us to use tests of low 'significance levels'. A test to decide whether to reject h has a significance level of 0.05 if it tells us to reject h if the data are such that $P(e|h\&k) \leq 0.05$. A test to decide whether to accept h has a significance level of 0.05 if it tells us to accept h if $P(e|\sim h\&\text{k}) \leq 0.05$.

There are, however, two problems with such theories, one resolvable, the other in no way resolvable. The first problem is that talk of 'accepting' or 'rejecting' a hypothesis suggests treating the hypothesis as true or false (as the case may be) always in future and for all purposes. But, as Chapter 2 and Additional Note B should have made clear, whether we are or ought to be guided by some hypothesis does and ought to vary with the action that we are considering doing. So, in Neyman–Pearson terminology, a hypothesis 'rejected' in one context should not be 'rejected' in another one; and a hypothesis 'accepted' in one context should not be 'accepted' in another one. Consider, for example, the hypothesis h that eating beef taken from a herd exposed to BSE will cause the fatal disease CJD many years later. When considering whether to serve exposed beef at a party where all the guests are under 20 years old and in these circumstances to 'reject' the hypothesis, we would need the relevant data e to be such that $P(e|h\&k)$ was very low indeed. But if we are considering whether to serve beef at a party where all the guests are over 70 years old, we would not need $P(e|h\&k)$ to be quite so low—since, even if the hypothesis is true, all the guests would probably be dead anyway before they contracted CJD.

Now, Neyman and Pearson provide no general guidance as to what the 'significance levels' of tests should be. But clearly, as statisticians in practice recognize, you need tests of smaller significance levels, the worse the consequences if the test leads us to reject a true hypothesis or accept a false one, and the better the consequences if the test leads us to reject a false hypothesis or accept a true one. So, such a theory must lay down levels of rejection and acceptance varying with the uses to which the theory is to be put (including, I suggest, the intrinsic value of having a true belief on the matter in question). And rejection and acceptance can only be provisional, for new data may turn up accidentally (that is, not as a result of a test designed to obtain them), which are such that, when added to the previous data, they have the consequence that a hypothesis previously rejected should no longer be rejected, or a hypothesis previously accepted should no longer be accepted. A Neyman–Pearson-type theory could in principle take account of this point by providing rules for acceptance and rejection that vary with the uses to which a hypothesis is to be put. Such a system of rules would play the same role as Decision Theory (spelled out in Additional Note B) which relies on the notion of the probability on evidence of a hypothesis being true, a notion avoided by Neyman– Pearson Theory.

The irresolvable problem with any Newman–Pearson-type theory is, however, this: how are we to calculate $P(e|{\sim}h\&k)$, the probability that we would obtain the data if h were false. There are, as we saw on pp. 83–99, always an infinite number of different theories that give a probability of 1 to e, and an infinite number that give a probability of 0 to e (as well as infinite numbers of theories that give intermediate values to the probability of e). We can work out whether to expect e if h were false, only if we can rank these theories in advance of observing whether or not e and say that some are immensely improbable and a few of these, perhaps only one, are the ones that would probably be true if h were not true. Only then can we begin to work out what is the probability of e if not-h. It will be the probability of e if one of these theories was true. But which theory or theories would probably be true if h were false depends on their prior probabilities—and, if we include all the relevant contingent evidence in e, that means their intrinsic probabilities. No theory that does not allow prior probabilities can give a value to probability of certain data occurring if some hypothesis h were false. And to allow our 'acceptance' in some sense of a hypothesis to depend solely on the probability of the data given that hypothesis ($P(e|h\&k)$) still leaves us open to the difficulty that innumerable crazy hypotheses give a probability of 1 to any collection of data you like to name.

For somewhat more extensive discussions of the deficiencies of Neyman–Pearson statistics, see C. Howson and P. Urbach, *Scientific Reasoning* (2nd edn., Open Court, 1993), ch. 9. For a modern defence of a theory centred on Neyman–Pearson statistics, see Deborah Mayo, *Error and the Growth of Experimental Knowledge* (University of Chicago Press, 1996).

J. *Conditionalization* (Ch. 4 n. 32)

The objection is rightly made against subjective Bayesianism that the kind of arguments given in support of it, and in particular Dutch-book style arguments, do not give any good reason to hold that we should learn from experience by 'conditionalizing'. Suppose that, knowing that k but not having observed whether or not e, I judge that $P(h|k)=0.4$ and that $P(h|e\&k)=0.8$ (and these allocations together with my other allocations at the time conform to the axioms of the calculus). So I ought to judge that the probability of h on my total available evidence (k) is 0.4 and to be guided by that probability in my conduct and belief. I then observe that e is true. Intuitively we may suppose that in that case I ought now to judge that the probability of h on my total available evidence is 0.8, and to be guided by that probability in my conduct and belief. The Dutch-book style arguments that justify subjective Bayesianism, however, require only that my allocation of probabilities at a given time should conform to the calculus; they do not prohibit my changing my allocations entirely at some subsequent time in accord with a rule not determined in advance. So why should I not refuse to learn from experience (the observation that e is true), and judge that $P(h|e\&k)=0.4$ and so hold that the observation of e should make no difference to my conduct—so long as my allocations of probability at the later time conjointly conform to the calculus? The 'subjective Bayesian' finds it very difficult to justify conditionalizing (that is, moving from the probability of h on total evidence k being 0.4 and $P(h|e\&k)=0.8$, to the probability of h on the new total evidence that now includes e being 0.8).

But an 'objective Bayesian' who holds that there are correct a priori principles for allocating values to ascriptions of probability has no problem here. For he holds that these principles should be used at all times. If the correct values are $P(h|k)=0.4$ and $P(h|e\&k)=0.8$, then, if I move from knowing only k to learning also e, it follows that I ought to be guided in my conduct and belief by supposing that the probability of h is 0.8. But if $P(h|e\&k)=0.4$, then I am right to consider e irrelevant. Conditionalizing is right if (and only if) I am operating with correct probability values.

While this argument is correct, I draw attention to the fact that, when we acquire new (contingent) evidence, we must conditionalize on all the new evidence and not just some of it. Since the new evidence will be acquired by experience (e.g. by perception and by some particular mode of perception), the new evidence will never be just that some state of affairs occurred but that, for example, the subject perceived it occurring. I point out on p. 137 that I normally gloss over the distinction between a basic belief that e and a basic belief that the subject perceived that e. But occasionally this distinction is all important, and it is all important when we are considering conditionalizing. For while e may give h a certain probability, the perception (or more widely, experience) of e may give h quite a different probability. This will arise for those odd hypotheses that make it more probable that e than that e will be perceived. Consider the hypothesis 'Jones burgles houses every week but no one ever perceives him doing so'. The fact of his burgling a certain house last week (e) increases the probability of this hypothesis, but my perceiving his burgling the house last week decreases, indeed falsifies, the hypothesis. The conditionalizing that it would be right to do in this case is not conditionalizing on e but conditionalizing on f = 'I perceived e'. $P(h|f\&k)=0$; when I learn f, I must ascribe a probability to h on the total new evidence of 0. The mode of experience of e will also be part of the new evidence f, and in other cases a hypothesis might have the consequence that it is improbable that e would be detected in this particular way. And finally, where k is background evidence other than mere tautological evidence, it (rather than h) may make it improbable that the experience of e (at all or by a certain mode of perception) will raise the probability of some other h (for example 'Jones burgles houses every week') as much as does *e* unexperienced. We may have background evidence that the only burglars ever seen burgling never burgle as often as once a week.

For discussion of the difficulty of justifying conditionalization by a Dutch-book style argument, and the application of such arguments to the similar principle of Reflection, see Howson and Urbach, *Scientific Reasoning*, ch. 6, and David Christensen, 'Clever Bookies and Coherent Beliefs', *Philosophical Review*, 100 (1991), 229–47.

K. *Audi on Believing for a Reason* (see Ch. 5 n. 1)

In 'Belief, Reason and Inference' (in his *The Structure of Justification* (Cambridge University Press, 1993)) Robert Audi has developed an account of believing *q* for a reason *r*, which—he holds (p. 270)—'can, with at most minor qualifications, at least explicate [the relation of a belief that *q* being based on a belief that *r*]'.

> S believes that *q*, for a reason, *r*, at time *t*, if and only if, at *t*, there is a support relation, C, such that (1) S believes that *q* and that *r*; (2) S believes C to hold between *r* and *q* (or believes something to the effect that *r* bears C to *q*); (3) S's basis belief, that *r*, and at least one connecting belief, i.e., his believing C to hold between *r* and *q*, or his believing something to the effect that *r* bears C to *q*, are part of what explains why S believes *q*, and, together, fully explain this; (4) S is non-inferentially disposed, independently of seeking reasons he has, had, or might have had, at or before *t*, for believing *q*, to attribute his belief that *q* to the explaining beliefs specified in (3); (5) those explaining beliefs do not (singly or together) accidentally sustain or produce S's belief that *q*; and (6) those beliefs do not (singly or together) sustain or produce it via an alien intermediary. (p. 262; I have replaced his '*p*' by '*q*' to secure conformity with my notation)

C is a relation of 'giving support to'—that is, in my terms a relation of inductive probability. (2) requires that *S* believes that such a relation holds between *r* and *q*; and, since what is required is that an objective relation holds, one that is independent of his own capacities, the belief must concern logical probability. The phrase in parentheses ('or believes something to the effect that *r* bears C to *q*') is meant to deal with those cases where *S* is epistemically naive, e.g. a young child, and so does not have the concepts of belief or support; it is designed to do the same job as my phrase 'in so far as he thinks about it'. What clause (2) seems to demand is that *S* has a belief with respect to his belief that *r* (though he may not think of it as a belief) that it bears *C* (though he may not think of this as a relation, let alone the relation of probability) to his belief that *q*. (3) is the causal requirement that it is because of his belief that *r and* his belief ('to the effect that') that *C* holds, that *r* supports *q*, that he believes *q*. (4) seems equivalent to the requirement that (in so far as he thinks about it) *S* believes that his belief that *q* is caused by his belief that *r* and that *r* makes *q* probable. (6) lays down that the causal process must not proceed through an 'alien intermediary', which is the condition that the causal chain should not be deviant. Some of Audi's examples of deviance are examples of deviance in my sense, i.e. of a causal process of some very narrow type. For example, *S*'s belief that *r* and that *C* holds might cause some brain scientist to produce in *S* the belief that *q*. Such a scientist would be an 'alien' intermediary if the process causing the intervention only did so under certain very special conditions or at a certain time, making *S* form a belief that he would not otherwise have formed. (5) then seems redundant in that it also seeks to rule out this kind of case by its use of the adverb 'accidentally'. But other of Audi's examples are cases where a belief that *r* and that *C* holds cause the belief that *q* to be held subsequently without then being sustained by their original causes. Such examples seem irrelevant to the synchronic justification of a belief, which involves what causes it to be held at the time in question. If some cause does not constitute grounds for the belief at that time, then the belief is not at that time based on those grounds; and its justification (if any) at that time cannot consist in any part in its being based on that cause, even if such basing formed part of its justification at an earlier stage. But, given a satisfactory spelling-out of the 'no-alien-intermediary' condition in terms of non-deviance in my sense, and a satisfactory spelling-out of the latter, Audi's account of believing for a reason seems to coincide with the full mixed causal and doxastic theory of basing, which I have developed in the text.

L. *Swain on Pseudo-over-Determination* (see Ch. 5 n. 5)

Given the results of my Chapter 2, *S* believes that *q* if (and only) if he believes that his total evidence makes it probable that *q*. The gypsy lawyer does believe that his total evidence renders it probable that his client is innocent; for his evidence includes the evidence of the cards. He also believes that the evidence of the cards alone renders it probable that his client is innocent (which belief—we assume—is false). He also believes that the other public evidence alone renders it probable that his client is innocent (which belief—we assume—is true). It therefore follows that, if he had not read the cards *and everything* else was the same, he would still believe his client innocent (because of the complicated line of argument). The trouble is that there are (as Lehrer expounds his example) 'emotional factors surrounding the crime' which—but for the influence of the cards—would prevent him from being guided by the complicated line of reasoning. But that suggests to me that his belief in the complicated line of reasoning is playing some kind of causal role in sustaining his belief in his client's innocence, even if the deliverances of the cards are in fact necessary and sufficient for his holding the belief. For, while sufficient, they are necessary only because of the emotional factors. This point leads to a broader yet essentially causally related sense of basing, developed by Marshall Swain, which might account for Lehrer's intuition that the gypsy lawyer is justified in his belief in his client's innocence, without denying that this requires that his belief be based on the public evidence (*r*, which he correctly believes to hold), which probabilifies it (in the way captured in the complicated line of reasoning).

(See Marshall Swain, 'Justification and the Basis of Belief', in G. S. Pappas (ed.), *Justification and Knowledge* (D. Reidel, 1979).) Swain requires that, for a belief to be based on a reason (a further belief in my terms), the reason must be either a cause or a pseudo-over-determinant of the belief.

Swain's definition of an event *C* being a pseudo-over-determinant of an event *E* is—to state it in the simplest possible terms relevant to basing—that *C* and *E* both occur, but *C* does not cause *E*, because some other event *D* does; but, if *D* had not occurred, but *C* and *E* had both occurred, *C* would have caused *E*. So the lawyer's belief in the complicated argument (*C*) (that is, his belief that *r* and that *r* makes *q* very probable) does not cause the belief in the client's innocence (*E*). That is because his belief in the cards (*D*) does. But suppose *D* had been absent, and yet *C* and *E* had both occurred, would *C* have caused *E*? If so, the belief in the complicated argument is a pseudo-over-determinant of the belief in the client's innocence. The answer to the question is plausibly yes. For, if we suppose that both *C* (the belief in the complicated argument) and *E* (the belief in the innocence) do occur, that the actual cause of the later (*D*) does not occur *and* no other changes are made in the situation (e.g. a new complicated argument is discovered) then it would have been the case that *C* caused *E*. So, Swain concludes, on his account of basing the gypsy lawyer's belief is based on the complicated line of reasoning; and it is this (together with the fact that the line of reasoning is a good one) that makes the gypsy lawyer's belief a justified one.

In asking what would have happened if such-and-such had not happened, we must implicitly or explicitly make it clear what other alterations we may suppose in the world if we suppose such-and-such not to have happened—e.g. which of its causes or effects may we also suppose to have occurred or not to have occurred. Swain implies and later makes clear (see his *Reason and Knowledge* (Cornell University Press, 1981), 70) that we may not suppose new events that are not actual and could cause the belief to occur. Thus it might be (in a natural sense) that, if the gypsy had not read the cards, he would have gone to a fortune teller instead and the fortune teller would have told him that his client was innocent, and it is this that would have caused his belief. And in that circumstance his belief in the complicated argument would not have caused his belief in his client's innocence. However, we are not allowed to add such events, when we ask what would have happened if the actual cause had been absent.

The connected problem that surely requires an amendment to Swain's definition arises when there is another actual event (or several actual events) that would have caused the belief if the actual cause (the reading of the cards) had been eliminated. (This amendment is suggested by Jonathan Kvanvig, 'Swain on the Basing Relation', *Analysis*, 45 (1985), 153–8.) Suppose that the gypsy lawyer in fact consulted a fortune teller but the fortune teller's pronouncement that his client was innocent, though strong enough to overcome the force of emotional factors, had a weaker influence on the lawyer's belief system than did his belief in the cards. Then, if the reading of the cards had not caused his belief, the pronouncement of the fortune teller would have done so. Only if both the reading of the cards and the fortune teller's pronouncement (and any further such factors) had been eliminated and the belief remained (and so the emotional factors had ceased to have as much influence) would the complicated line of argument have caused the belief in the client's innocence. So, in the spirit of Swain's approach, we need to define a pseudo-over-determinant as any actual event that would have caused the effect in question if any other actual events that would have had this effect instead of it had been eliminated. Then the complicated line of argument remains a pseudo-over-determinant in the new postulated situation.

With this clarification and amendment, the force of Swain's definition of pseudo-over-determination for the basing of belief is now clear. But intuitions may still differ about whether a belief being based on its evidence, even in Swain's wider sense, is sufficient (together with the latter being adequate grounds for the former) for the belief to be justified. My intuitions are that to allow pseudo-over-determination does not adequately capture the causal element in our ordinary understanding of basing—whatever would have been the case if the gypsy lawyer had not read the cards, he did read the cards; that caused his belief in his client's innocence and his belief in the complicated line of argument played no causal role that would make his belief in his client's innocence based upon it. So, in so far as a belief being 'justified' requires it to be 'based' on another belief (in so far as ordinary use of these words determines what we should say), the latter has to cause the former belief.

M. *Uncertain evidence in the Probability Calculus* (see Ch. 5 n. 19)

Before the work of Richard Jeffrey, the use of the probability calculus to analyse the probability of hypotheses on evidence assumed that evidence consists of a categorical proposition stating (e.g.) that something physical had a certain property (that the cloth was green, or that the car number plate contained a five). But, as I have noted in Chapter 5, such basic beliefs come to us with varying strengths—our evidence is rather that there is a certain probability resulting from experience that something physical has a certain property. Richard Jeffrey (*The Logic of Decision* (McGraw-Hill, 1965), ch. 11) classically began the work of showing how the probability calculus could take account of uncertain evidence.

To put his account in my notation—suppose that we have some contingent proposition *e*, which, if it were true, would give a certain probability (say 0.6) to some hypothesis *h* given total evidence *k* ($P(h|e\&k)=0.6$), and which, if it were false, would give to *h* a probability of 0.3 ($P(h|{\sim}e\&k)=0.3$). Suppose that the prior probability on *k* of *e* is 0.4 and so the prior probability of ${\sim}e$ is 0.6. $P(e|k)=0.4$, $P({\sim}e|k)=0.6$. Then the probability of *h* on the total evidence *k* $P(h|k)$ is $P(h|e\&k)$ $P(e|k)+P(h|{\sim}e\&k)$ $P({\sim}e|k)=(0.6\times 0.4)+(0.3\times 0.6)=0.42$. We then make an observation in which we believe that we have observed that *e* is true, but we are not fully confident of this. Jeffrey represents this as moving to a situation of new total evidence k_1 instead of k, since, he claims, it is difficult to put the new evidence in the form of a separate proposition added to k. Rather we are in a situation where, as a result of our apparent perceptual experience, e is more probable than it was previously. Then maybe $P(e|k_1) = 0.7$ and so $P(\sim e|k_1) = 0.3$. On the assumption that having apparently observed that e is true makes no difference to how probable e if it were true would make h–$P(h|e\&k) = P(h|e\&k_1)$ and $P(h|\sim e\&k) = P(h|\sim e\&k_1)$. So the new probability of h on the total evidence k_1 is $P(h|e\&k)\ P(e|k_1) + P(h|\sim e\&k)\ P(\sim e|k_1)$, that is $(0.6 \times 0.7) + (0.3 \times 0.3) = 0.51$. Jeffrey shows how a change in the prior probability of e as a result of observation brings changes to the probabilities of other propositions. The ordinary process of 'conditionalization' (considered in Additional Note J) is the process whereby acquiring evidence that e is certainly true affects the probability of other propositions. This process whereby acquiring uncertain evidence affects the probability of other propositions is known as 'Jeffrey conditionalization'. Like ordinary conditionalization, it requires for its justification that the subject be operating with correct probabilities.

The assumption mentioned above is not, however, universally true, for the reason that I give in Additional Note J. There are cases where e and having observed that e have different effects on the probability of h; and analagously there are cases where probably e and probably having observed that e will have different effects on the probability of h. So we must use a more complicated formula for the new probability of h: $P(h|k) = P(h|e\&k_1)\ P(e|k_1) + P(h|\sim e\&k_1)\ P(\sim e|k_1)$, while allowing that normally $P(h|e\&k_1) = P(h|e\&k)$, and $P(h|\sim e\&k_1) = P(h|\sim e\&k)$.

Can any rules be given for how an apparent experience of e should lead us to ascribe a particular value to $P(e|k_1)$? My concern in the text was with the probability to be ascribed to rightly basic propositions (that is, to propositions in so far as the subject believes them not because—in his view—he believes other propositions). In terms of the calculus, this is the issue of how the addition of the apparent experience to mere tautological background evidence (k), represented by the move from k to k_1, affects the probability of e. The answer given there is that the apparent experience of e must raise its prior probability above its intrinsic probability in a way proportional to the subject's degree of conviction that he has experienced e. I do not think that any more rules can be given for what is the right degree of conviction. How things seem to be is our starting point. If more substantial background evidence is now introduced, the effect of the apparent experience may be very different. The effect of an apparent experience of the cloth looking green on the proposition that it is green will be very different if one has background evidence that the lighting is deceptive. (For this point, and for the history of the discussion of how the calculus can take account of uncertain evidence, see David Christensen, 'Confirmational Holism and Bayesian Epistemology', *Philosophy of Science*, 59 (1992), 540–57). My account in the text allows for the Bayesian to claim that, if our evidence consists of the apparent experience (k_1) and some more substantial background evidence m, then $P(e|k_1\&m)$ may differ from $P(e|k_1)$. Among the more substantial evidence may have been a previous experience of e. To the extent to which a second experience has just the same quality as the first (e.g. it is made by the same subject via the same sense-modality from the same position relative to the object, and produces the same very uncertain conviction), to that extent it must raise the probability of e very little if at all.

N. *Naturalized Epistemology* (see Ch. 6 n. 2)

In his famous essay 'Epistemology Naturalized', W. V. O. Quine argued that, since no scientific theory could be deduced from incorrigible reports of observations, there was no worthwhile work for philosophers to do in the investigation of knowledge. The argument seems to be that claims to know or justifiably believe the truth of a scientific theory or a prediction about the future go beyond the observations we (seem to) make and—as Hume showed—philosophers cannot justify our taking a step in favour of one theory or prediction rather than another: 'The Humean predicament is the human predicament.' The most that can be done is to describe the steps that humans do in fact take:

> Epistemology, or something like it, simply falls into place as a chapter of psychology and hence of natural science. It studies a natural phenomenon, viz., a physical human subject. This human subject is accorded a certain experimentally controlled input—certain patterns of irradiation in assorted frequencies, for instance—and in the fullness of time the subject delivers as output a description of the three-dimensional external world and its history. The relation between the meager input and the torrential output is a relation that we are prompted to study for somewhat the same reasons that always prompted epistemology; namely, in order to see how evidence relates to theory, and in what ways one's theory of nature transcends any available evidence. (W. V. O. Quine, 'Epistemology Naturalized', in his *Ontological Relativity and other essays* (Colombia University Press, 1969), 82–3)

'Naturalizing' epistemology involves not merely describing only actual processes (instead of 'justified' processes) of input leading to output, but confining input to the physical—not the subject's 'awarenesses', but patterns of stimulation of sensory receptors. But, if input is to be so described, output should in consistency also be so described, as noises coming out of mouths. To get from those to 'description[s] of the three-dimensional external world and its history' needs inference, along the lines described in my Chapter 2 (whereby we infer from people's behaviour etc. to their beliefs), using the criteria of logical probability analysed in my Chapter 4. (This kind of point is argued by Jaegwon Kim 'What is Naturalized Epistemology?', in James E. Tomberlin (ed.), *Philosophical Perspectives 2.* Epistemology (Ridgeview Publishing Company, 1988), where he argues that to attribute beliefs to subjects requires interpreting their utterances on the assumption that they are 'rational and coherent'.) Even to get this process started, we have to rely on memory and testimony about which 'patterns of irradiation in assorted frequencies' occurred. Now Quine can say *either* that we just do use evidence and construct theory in these ways *or* further that we are right to do so. If he claims only the first, that description of past performance will in no way legitimize any future inference—even inference to how people will react to stimuli in the future. So why bother to do the 'psychology' at all? If Quine claims the second, then he is claiming that there are correct criteria of what is evidence for what—the ones that (on the whole) we actually use. But that claim is an a priori claim, I believe a basically correct one. There is no avoiding the a priori in epistemology. And to my mind it is definitely more obvious that our criteria of probability are roughly correct than that we had various particular inputs (of stimulation of sense organs) and outputs (of noises) in the past. Any construction of a world view has to begin from what seems most evident.

'Naturalized epistemology' is often understood today not as a claim that we can do without the a priori, but rather as a claim that our a priori standards are such that, given what we know about the natural world, it is the ways in which human beliefs are formed by 'natural' processes (i.e. publicly observable processes conforming to scientific laws) that make it the case that beliefs are justified or unjustified as the case may be. This is externalism *plus* the requirement that the external factors that determine justification are public and lawlike. Now we can lay down a sense of 'justified' for which this holds. But the issue then surfaces as to what advantage beliefs having this kind of justification have over other beliefs. There arise all the old difficulties of externalism—of how widely or deeply the lawlike process is to be specified, and of what use is an externalist justified belief if the subject has no awareness of the external processes. And there is the further difficulty that it needs quite a bit of inference from things even more obvious (particular straightforward observations in the laboratory) to discover what the lawlike processes of generation of a belief are. Any believer can begin only from where he finds himself (the beliefs that he already has—whatever they are about); and the only kind of justification to which he has access concerns the a priori steps from evidence to hypothesis. To the extent to which there is any useful justification for a naturalist position of any kind, it will be in part an a priori one.

P. *Chisholm's Theory of Knowledge* (see Ch. 8 n. 10)

Roderick Chisholm (*Theory of Knowledge* (3rd edn., Prentice Hall, 1989), 97–9) has given an account of knowledge within the fundamental 'justified true belief' model that seeks to deal with Gettier examples in a complicated way. In his terminology, an 'evident' proposition is a justified one. One proposition is 'made evident by' another one if it is made (in my terminology) logically very probable by it. 'Accepts' is 'believes'. He begins his detailed account of knowledge by introducing the notion of a proposition that is 'defectively evident': '*h* is defectively evident for *S*=*Df.* (1) There is an *e* such that *e* makes *h* evident for *S*:

and (2) everything that makes *h* evident for *S* makes something that is false evident for *S*.' He then continues:

> The proposition 'Jones owns a Ford or Brown is in Barcelona' [*h*] is defectively evident for Smith. It is made evident for *S* by the proposition *e* ('Jones has at all times kept a Ford in his garage . . . etc.') and *everything* that makes *e* evident for Smith also makes a false proposition evident for Smith—namely, the proposition that Jones owns a Ford . . . Shall we, then, add '*h* is not defectively evident' as the fourth condition of our definition of knowledge? This would not be quite enough. For, if we were to do this, then we would have to say, incorrectly, that Gettier's Smith does *not* know that *e* ('Jones has at all time in the past . . . etc.') is true. For *e*, like *h*, is defectively evident by our definition. So we must make the definition slightly more complicated. The conjuncts of *e* (e.g. 'Jones keeps a Ford in his garage'), unlike *e* itself, are not defectively evident. Although in conjunction they make a false proposition evident, none of them by itself makes a false proposition evident. This fact suggests the following definition:
>
> *h* is known by *S*=*Df.* (1) *h* is true: (2) *S* accepts *h*: (3) *h* is evident for *S*: and (4) if *h* is defectively evident for *S*, then *h* is implied by a conjunction of propositions each of which is evident for *S* but not defectively evident for *S*.

This definition needs tidying up in two respects. First I take it that 'is implied by' in the second line of the definition is to be read as 'is made evident by'. (*S*'s evidence need not (formally) imply *h*.) And secondly there seems to be a discrepancy between Chisholm's fourth condition and the way in which he illustrates it by example. According to the definition of 'defectively evident', *h* is defectively evident when everything that makes it evident (let us say a conjunction e of propositions e_1, e_2 . . .) makes something that is false evident for *S*. So the requirement of the fourth condition is, for each of these propositions—for example, e_1—that, if it is made evident by some *other* proposition, say f_1, f_1 does not make something false evident for *S*. But the example to illustrate the fourth condition is one where—the point is—the conjuncts such as e_1 do not by themselves make a false proposition evident. So there seem to be two different understandings of Chisholm's definition in play: either what makes the conjuncts (e_1, e_2 . . .) evident does not make something false evident, or the conjuncts themselves do not make something false evident.

However, neither of them are going to be very satisfactory. For, as I wrote above, 'makes evident' is to be read as 'makes very probable'—Chisholm claims explicitly that the relation is an 'inductive' one. Let us give 'very probable' a numerical value and say that it amounts to 'more than 0.999 probable'. In that case, all propositions will make some false proposition evident, in the sense that for every proposition *e* there is some false proposition *h* that is evident, given *e*. Suppose that there are a million tickets in this week's lottery, each with an equal (statistical) probability of winning, and that ticket *n* in fact will win. Let h_n be the proposition 'In this week's fair lottery with a million tickets, ticket *n* will not win'. Almost all propositions will make h_n evident (in the sense that the probability of h_n given almost any proposition is very high); certainly e_1 'Jones keeps a Ford in his garage' will make h_n evident. True, e_1 is not very relevant (in some sense) to h_n. In that case conjoin h_n to some evidently relavent proposition f that is entailed by e_1. Then e_1 will make the conjunction (h_n&f) probable to more than the 0.999 level—that is, it will make it evident. Its evidence will be just as relevant to it, as was its evidence to the original disjunction, 'Jones owns a Ford or Brown is in Barcelona', which caused all the trouble in the first place. So, since all propositions make some false proposition evident, the second understanding of Chisholm's definition is useless. The first understanding will also be open to this problem if any of the conjuncts (e_1, e_2 . . .) are allowed to derive their status as evidence from another proposition (say f_1). But, as we could add the stipulation that they be evident, without deriving their status as evident from elsewhere, I cannot think that Chisholm intended his condition (4) to be understood in this way for—if so—he could have said so very easily. And anyway Chisholm's account cannot deal with cases such as the assassination attempt, where the trouble lies not with any false belief of the subject, either actual or derivable from his actual beliefs, but with a true belief that he does not have.

Q. *Williamson on Knowledge* (see Ch. 8 n. 21)

Timothy Williamson has given an account of knowledge very different from all the accounts analysed in Chapter 8. (See his 'Is Knowing a State of Mind?', *Mind*, 104 (1995), 533–65). While he agrees with the other accounts that true belief is necessary for knowledge, he seems to claim that the remaining element—which I am calling 'warrant'—is not capable of analysis, but can be recognized straight off by trained language-users. But there are two alternatives under this unanalysability alternative. Is the 'extra' beyond true belief a further constituent of the world, such that what it amounts to in each case of knowledge cannot be described in other terms? Or can the 'extra' in each case be described fully in other terms, although what all these 'extras' have in common cannot be defined? Williamson's comparison (p. 562) of the relation of knowing to believing (and in effect to true believing) with that of red to crimson (although the comparison is made for a slightly different purpose) suggests an interest in the first alternative. But this alternative is not plausible. If you describe with respect to any true belief of mine that amounts to knowledge how it is related to my other beliefs, how it is caused, how reliable are the processes by which it is caused, etc., we reach the stage where there is nothing left over in which its being a case of knowledge could consist.

What the second alternative suggests is that the situation with 'knowledge' is like the situation that Wittgenstein described with respect to 'game'.

> Consider . . . the proceedings that we call 'games'. I mean board-games, card-games, ball-games, Olympic games, and so on. What is common to them all? . . . If you look at them you will not see something that is common to *all* . . . We see a complicated network of similar-

ities overlapping and criss-crossing: sometimes overall similarities, sometimes similarities of detail. (L. Wittgenstein, Philosophical Investigations, trans. G. E. M. Anscombe (Basil Blackwell, 1953), i. 66)

That, once we have separated off the (strong) true belief component common to all cases of knowledge, this is the situation is in effect what I have argued in Chapter 8. Michael Ayers (*Locke*, i (Routledge, 1991), ch. 15) also claims that knowledge is a family resemblance concept, the unity of which is provided by central cases of 'primary knowledge'. The large number of cases where we agree that someone knows that *p* provide the paradigms for knowledge. Other cases count as cases of knowledge in virtue of their similarity to these. The different philosophical accounts of knowledge draw out major strands of similarity that bind many, but not all, the other cases to the paradigm cases.

Williamson, however, seems to want to say more than that—that cases of knowledge have a greater unity to them than this, which we cannot bring out by a further definition. One reason that he gives for this is that knowledge 'matters' (p. 541) in a way that could not be explained by some complicated analysis. By contrast, I have suggested (above pp 219–20) that knowing does not always matter more than having (strong) true belief, and I have sought to analyse when and why it does matter more.

Another reason that Williamson seems to give for the unanalysability of knowledge is that a subject's knowledge can sometimes provide a better explanation of his behaviour than his belief (or even his true belief)—which suggests that it is a central concept for our account of the world in terms of which other concepts should be analysed, rather than the other way around. Thus:

A burglar spends all night ransacking a house, risking discovery by staying so long. We ask what features of the situation when he entered the house led to that result. A reasonable answer is that he knew that there was a diamond in the house. To say that he believed truly that there was a diamond in the house would be to give a worse explanation, one whose explanans and explanandum are less closely connected. For one possibility consistent with the new explanans is that he entered the house with a true belief that there was a diamond in it derived from false premises. For example, his only reason for believing that there was a diamond in the house might have been that someone told him that there was a diamond under the bed, when in fact the only diamond was in a drawer. He would then probably have given up his true belief that there was a diamond in the house on discovering the falsity of his belief that there was a diamond under the bed, and abandoned the search. In contrast, if he *knew* that there was a diamond in the house, his knowledge was not essentially based on a false premise. (pp. 548–9)

Yet while the burglar's 'knowledge' might provide a better explanation than his true belief, a more precise description of his epistemic situation that did not involve the concept of knowledge would provide an even better explanation. For the truth of his strong belief (involved in its amounting to knowledge) plays no role in explaining his behaviour. What explains it more fully is the particular nature of his belief (e.g. that someone whom he trusted totally told him that there was a diamond in the house, but that it was well hidden). 'Knowledge' is here only a loose placeholder for a more precise explanation. Even if there were some particular cases in which the full explanation of a subject's behaviour includes all of what made his beliefs knowledge, that would not show that knowledge is a concept of wide use for the explanation of behaviour. Innumerable scientifically and epistemologically unimportant concepts can function occasionally in explaining particular bits of behaviour, because on that occasion everything that is involved in them plays a causal role. I see no reason to suppose that knowledge is an important, let alone a fundamental, concept in the explanation of very much.

INDEX